Pentecostal and Postmodern Hermeneutics

Pentecostal and Postmodern Hermeneutics

Comparisons and Contemporary Impact

BRADLEY TRUMAN NOEL

WIPF & STOCK · Eugene, Oregon

PENTECOSTAL AND POSTMODERN HERMENEUTICS
Comparisons and Contemporary Impact

Wipf & Stock
An Imprint of Wipf and Stock Publishers
199 W. 8th Ave., Suite 3
Eugene, OR 97401
www.wipfandstock.com

ISBN 13: 978-1-60608-905-7

Manufactured in the U.S.A.

This work is dedicated to my nieces and nephews:

Jordan Noel
Christian, Joey, James, and Katelyn Morgan
Ryan and Drew Whalen
Maria and Claire Roberts

It is for you and your generation that I write.

Contents

Acknowledgments

THIS WORK IS THE partial fulfillment of my calling by God to be a student of his Word first, a student of culture second, and then a teacher of theology and praxis to Pentecostals. I thank God for his great plan of salvation, the study of which is inexhaustible. This study is taken in his service and for his glory alone.

Special love and thanks to my wife Melinda, who has endured many hours of conversation about Pentecostal hermeneutics and Postmodernity, and my mental absences while writing. She has become something of a theologian in her own right! Many thanks are given to the rest of my family for their encouragement and support during this process.

The material herein is an adaptation of that which was submitted to the University of South Africa for the Doctor of Theology degree. Deep appreciation is extended to my promoter, Dr. Jacques P.J. Theron. His encouragement and expertise have been significant, and the kindnesses shown to me during this project are forever appreciated. In addition, several others read through this manuscript and offered helpful comments, including my mother, Gail Noel, Julia Budgell, one of my students, for carefully proofreading the footnotes, and my always diligent and professional copyeditor, (and friend), Burton K. Janes. I appreciate greatly the help received.

Warm thanks are extended to my former students at International Biblical Online Leadership Training (IBOLT), (Edmonton, AB), and Master's College & Seminary (Toronto, ON). Appreciation is also extended to current students at Acadia Divinity College (Wolfville, NS), and Tyndale University College (Toronto, ON). One learns far more by teaching than by studying, and I appreciate the insights and depth of knowledge I have gained from so many of you since I began teaching. I trust you will continue to walk faithfully in the calling God has given to each of you.

My theological education has been strengthened through my ministry with the Pentecostal Assemblies of Newfoundland and Labrador, Canada. Warm thanks are extended to E.R. Rideout, B.D. Brenton, C. Buckle, H.P. Foster, D.L. Newman and other friends in the PAONL. These colleagues have supported and encouraged me during these last few years, and have been conversation partners for many of the ideas contained herein. During my years of youth ministry with this denomination, I have been privileged to witness firsthand the wonderful, creative, and talented human beings that are teenagers. I have had opportunity to observe these youth in ministry and in recreation, and have learned a great deal about God, and the acceptance of his love, from these Postmodern youth.

Preface

MY ROOTS IN PENTECOSTALISM run deep. In 1910, a petite, single, American woman named Alice Belle Garrigus (1858–1949) left New England on a vessel bound for Newfoundland. Having come into contact with the Azusa Street Revival via meetings held by Frank Bartleman (1871–1936), Garrigus had been seeking God for her own place of mission. When the word "Newfoundland" came via a message in tongues and interpretation, she had to secure a map to learn where this Island east of Canada was located. Through the efforts of "Miss Garrigus," as she was affectionately known, the Pentecostal message eventually spread across the Island. Garrigus eventually came into contact with Muriel Greta Noel (1912–96), my paternal grandmother, in about 1931. Garrigus and my grandmother became well acquainted, and, as Garrigus advanced in years, my grandparents opened their home to her, for a time providing a place to live.

I have childhood memories of sleeping in "Miss Garrigus' room," though not with much comprehension about the life of this early Pentecostal pioneer. As I grew older, I became increasingly aware of the prominence of Pentecostalism in our home and in my life. My maternal grandparents were Pentecostals, as well. Gertrude Maude Penney (1919–93) raised my mother in a Pentecostal home in small-town Badger, Newfoundland, at a time when scorn for converts to Pentecostalism was in full force. My parents were both Pentecostal teachers, for in those days Newfoundland had a Government-funded denominational school system. My father eventually became an Assistant Superintendent with the Pentecostal Assemblies Board of Education. Thus I grew up in a home where I was made aware that I was a Pentecostal, as well, even if a full theological understanding of what that meant escaped me in my younger years. Through my childhood years, our home assembly, Springdale Pentecostal Church, was vibrant, for a period ministering to over 400 Sunday school children, for example, from a community with a population of just 3,000. As a child and teenager, I enjoyed solid Sunday school teaching, and a robust mid-week Pentecostal youth program, first in Pentecostal Crusaders, and then in Christ's Ambassadors.

By the end of my high school years, I was the President of our youth group, and, by all accounts, my friends and I were a passionate lot! We searched the Scriptures for examples of God's supernatural power, and excitedly prayed for the same miracles and wonders we read of in the Bible. The arrival of Pastor Truman L. Robinson as our senior pastor in 1987 was significant for me as a senior high student, for this old-time Pentecostal preacher taught us what it meant to be Pentecostal, and increased our faith to unheard of heights. We started to believe God for salvations, healings, and deliverances, and we began to see them right in our small youth group. My life was forever changed.

As I progressed through my undergraduate and graduate training, I became more fully aware of the Pentecostal world around me. With this awareness came pause for concern. Many of the friends that had come out of our youth group over the years no longer professed faith in Christ. The expectancy in which we had learned to live as late teenagers was difficult to find in many of the Pentecostal assemblies I visited. It was present, to be sure, in the independent Charismatic world, with which I had some familiarity during those years, but the lack of depth of Scriptural teaching I witnessed among the Charismatics assured me that this was not the Pentecostal pattern I wished to follow.

During my graduate studies, I met my wife-to-be, Melinda Roberts, who was also a Pentecostal. She and I began the process of building a home together, with an outlook on life informed by our shared roots in the Pentecostal faith. She sharpened my focus on the challenges ahead by asking questions and posing issues from a layperson's viewpoint. Though trained in the sciences, Melinda is very curious about the workings of Pentecostalism, and we have spent many hours discussing both the past and future of the movement.

My graduate training brought renewed focus to the issues I observed in the Church. When my thesis supervisor suggested that I focus on Gordon D. Fee and his discussions with Pentecostals concerning their hermeneutics and subsequent distinctive doctrines, something within rang very true, and I readily agreed. From this thesis grew an even stronger interest in Pentecostal theology, and this began to intersect with another strong interest of mine—youth ministry. My involvement with youth continued through my postsecondary education, and I was privileged to serve as a youth pastor in Calgary, Alberta, and, despite Jesus' warnings in Matthew 13:57, my home church in Springdale, Newfoundland! Armed with graduate degrees in theology, I was now able to observe how theology, Pentecostalism, and youth ministry coexisted in this microcosm of the larger Pentecostal world. Again what I discovered was troubling. Reciting the Pentecostal worldview was within the grasp of many of the church youth I came in contact with, but their ability to handle the Scriptures in that regard was dismal. More encouraging, however, was the openness of youth in the community to the Pentecostal message of a God who saves, heals, and works miracles today—just as in the Scriptures. These Postmodern youth did not hesitate to believe in a God who manifests his presence supernaturally.

The years following the end of that pastorate in 2001 brought further teaching opportunities, and increased youth ministry involvement, but this time via our denomination, the Pentecostal Assemblies of Newfoundland and Labrador. As I volunteered with our youth department, eventually becoming the Provincial Youth Director, I was able to observe firsthand our efforts to disciple youth from among our Pentecostal assemblies. I was encouraged to note that many of our teens believe in a God of miracles, both in Bible times and today. Sadly, however, many are unable to satisfactorily articulate their faith or defend their innate beliefs from Scripture. They inhabit a world where traditional "proofs" are increasingly unnecessary. Yet they carry with them a strong desire to understand the Scriptures, and to be able to articulate the Pentecostal worldview scripturally. Further, theirs is a generation given to evangelism, though in the most relational of approaches, and they desire to handle God's Word of Truth properly as they face the questions of their peers.

This book arises, therefore, from my twin passions: Pentecostal hermeneutics/theology and youth ministry. When the time came for me to choose a topic for my D.Th. dissertation, the mix of my ministerial and academic interests came to the fore. I am intrigued by how the hermeneutics of contemporary Pentecostals impact the generations just spreading their wings on the world scene. The success of Pentecostalism in the Western World in the coming decades will depend in large part on its ability to come to terms with its own identity vis-à-vis Evangelicalism, and then translate this identity into the worldview of Pentecostal youth and their peers. Hermeneutics will play a key role in this endeavor.

My intended audience is varied, to be sure. I pray that my Pentecostal colleagues in higher education will be encouraged to carefully consider the role of hermeneutics in our efforts to evangelize the youngest Western youth. As academics, we may write the most magnificent tomes on the most important theological questions, but I pray that the Church, including youth, will never be far from our minds.[1] Far from writing for academics alone, however, my goal here is to speak to the Pentecostal Church, for it is on the front lines of the battle for the souls of youth and young adults. I trust that I have kept the style and language of this work appropriate to that end. Finally, I hope this book speaks a word of caution to the students of Pentecostalism, who may be in the beginning stages of their own exploration of Pentecostal hermeneutics and theology. May all of your theological efforts edify Christ's Church!

Bradley Truman Noel
Springdale, Newfoundland, Canada
Thanksgiving, 2009

1. Clayton has just released an important book, *Transforming Christian Theology For Church and Society*, in which he argues that theologians must cease writing for the academy alone, and begin to consider the Church in all they do and write. See also Cobb, *Reclaiming the Church*.

1

Defining the Issues

As a postmodern paradigm increasingly dominates the thinking of our culture in general, any hermeneutic which cannot account for its loci of meanings within that postmodern paradigm will become nonsensical and irrelevant. If for no other reason than that, we must move beyond the Fundamentalist-Modernist Controversy to explore the possibilities of a Pentecostal hermeneutic in a postmodern age.[1]

TIMOTHY B. CARGAL

A strict adherence to traditional evangelical/fundamentalist hermeneutical principles leads to a position which, in its most positive forms, suggests the distinctives of the twentieth century Pentecostal movement are perhaps nice, but not necessary; important but not vital to the life of the Church in the twentieth century. In its more negative forms, it leads to a total rejection of Pentecostal phenomena.[2]

MARK D. MCLEAN

Get your learning but keep your burning.[3]

J. O. PATTERSON

---

1. Cargal, "Beyond the Fundamentalist-Modernist Controversy," 187.
2. McLean, "Toward a Pentecostal Hermeneutic," 37.
3. Cited in Vinson Synan's endorsement of Nañez, *Full Gospel, Fractured Minds.*

PROBLEM STATED

THE PRECEDING QUOTATION BY Timothy Cargal clearly expounds the importance of recognizing the prominence of Postmodernism/ Postmodernity[4] in today's culture.[5] As is suggested, Postmodern[6] values are becoming increasingly tied to the values and attitudes of the Western World. The ultimate arbiter of truth for increasing numbers of people is no longer scientific thinking and reason, as was the case during the centuries following the Enlightenment.[7]

The focus of this work is Pentecostalism, and in particular the relationship between Postmodernity, the hermeneutics of Pentecostalism, and the youngest generations of Western youth. Changes to culture directly impact Pentecostalism, for it has been a spiritual movement of the people. Indeed, Pentecostalism's tremendous growth[8] can be attributed in no small part to its common touch, for the Pentecostal message has spoken a word of truth sorely needed among the outcast and oppressed. The many histories of Pentecostalism testify that from its beginning, it has thrived where other representations of Christianity have struggled,

---

4. Some scholars clearly differentiate between Postmodernism and Postmodernity. As Postmodernity is a peripheral and supporting concept to the main purposes of the present work, the terms will be used interchangeably. On those who differ, see Adams, "Toward a Theological Understanding of Postmodernism."

5. For an excellent summary of Postmodernism, particularly as it intersects Christianity, see Grenz, *A Primer on Postmodernism*; Veith, *Postmodern Times*; Middleton and Walsh, *Truth is Stranger Than it Used to Be*; and Dockery, *The Challenge of Postmodernism*.

6. As this work refers to the term "Modern" in two senses—one current, the other the thinking resulting from Modernism—it is necessary to distinguish between the two. Thus, Modern, Modernity, and Modernism are capitalized when referring to the philosophical approach known as "Modernity." To be consistent, Postmodern, Postmodernism, and Postmodernity are also capitalized.

7. The Enlightenment was a period of great intellectual growth following the rediscovery of classical thought and art in the late seventeenth century. Human thought and intellect were elevated in many ways to the place of the divine, and science widely replaced religion as the determiner of truth. See Grenz and Franke, *Beyond Foundationalism*; Himmelfarb, *The Roads to Modernity*; and Livingston, *Modern Christian Thought*.

8. Barrett and Johnston count the total number of Pentecostals/Charismatics in 2000 as just over 523 million, some ninety-four years after the beginning of the modern Pentecostal movement in 1906. Their projection for 2025 is 811 million Pentecostal/ Charismatic believers worldwide. See Barrett and Johnston, "Statistics, Global," 284–302.

simply by meeting the everyday spiritual needs of the world's most ordinary people.[9]

Postmodernism is an important topic for Pentecostals, for it represents a significant shift in the presuppositions of Western society.[10] The Modern era,[11] ushered in with the Enlightenment, promoted scientific rationalism, humanism, and, in the first part of the twentieth century, logical positivism.[12] Modern thinking believed in human reason coupled with science as the final arbiter of truth, and with humanity elevated to the apex of the universe, felt unbridled optimism in the abilities of human reason and science to bring positive change to a world marked by decay and destruction. The children of Modernism often challenged the truth of Christianity based on those cherished presuppositions.[13]

As the twentieth century drew to a close, these assumptions of Modernism were increasingly abandoned. Postmodernism is taking its place. It will be demonstrated that many scholars view as very sobering the basic presuppositions of Postmodern thought, although it is somewhat varied in scope and interpretation. For individuals soaked in the Modern mode of thought, the interpreted values of Postmodernism may be considered shocking; truth, meaning, and individual identity may not exist. These may simply be concepts created by humanity and celebrated in the Modern era. Human life may have no special significance; no more value than plant or animal life. In many Postmodern minds, Relativism[14] reigns supreme. For Pentecostals, who uphold the revelation of God in Scripture as absolute truth, complete with the Gospel message of the

---

9. See, for example, Anderson, *An Introduction to Pentecostalism*; Dempster et al., *The Globalization of Pentecostalism*; Anderson, *Vision of the Disinherited*; and Wacker, *Heaven Below*.

10. Veith suggests that "postmodernism pervades everything, and none of us can escape it." *Postmodern Times*, 177.

11. The Modern era may be defined as the period beginning with the Enlightenment and continuing in part until the present time.

12. Logical Positivism is a "contemporary philosophical movement associated with the Vienna Circle (1920s), which sought to rid philosophy of all metaphysical statements and to restrict it to only those statements which can be verified by empirical evidence." McKim, "Logical Positivism," 163. See also Madison, *The Hermeneutics of Postmodernity*, x.

13. See Ramm, *Protestant Biblical Interpretation*, 63–69.

14. "Most generally, a philosophical term for the belief that no absolutes exist. It is also used for the view that all knowledge is relative to the knower." McKim, "Relativism," 235.

worth of humanity and the divine plan of salvation, the challenges associated with Postmodernity are many.

Essential aspects of Christianity are again being challenged, but on a different front. The Modern era may be said to have rejected the more supernatural[15] claims of Christianity (such as the doctrine of the Virgin Birth, miracle stories, and the bodily resurrection of Jesus Christ) because of the difficulty in validating these claims empirically. In many of its forms, Postmodernism rejects the Christian claim to have *the* truth. Both historical Christianity and Modernism believe in absolute truth. From all indications, many Postmodern thinkers do not.[16]

DEFINITIONS AND LIMITATIONS

Although I will define each term as it is used, a framework for understanding the core concepts used in this work is beneficial.

By *Pentecostals*, I am referring to *Classical* Pentecostals, who trace their roots to the turn of the twentieth century and the Azusa Street Revival. Essentially, Pentecostals believe that the outpouring of the Holy Spirit on the 120 believers at Pentecost, as recorded in Acts 2, should be normative for all Christians. Further, the key sign associated with this Spirit Baptism is *glossolalia*, as it was in Acts.[17] "Classical" was added in about 1970 to distinguish Classical Pentecostals from Charismatics.

Charismatics are those believers who have received the Pentecostal experience of Spirit Baptism, usually with *glossolalia*, but have remained in one of the mainline Protestant denominations or Roman Catholicism.[18] *Charismatic* refers to "all manifestations of pentecostal-type Christianity

---

15. Some authors believe the term "supernatural" to be relatively recent in usage, entering theological discussion only in the ninth century. "One could well argue that the construal of religion as supernatural is a result of a specific rationalizing theology, which was later adopted and inverted by rationalists who wanted to confine religion to the area of the extra-ordinary, while handing over the ordinary world to secular reasoning." Gredersen, "What Theology Might Learn (and Not Learn)," 318.

16. See Veith, *Postmodern Times*, 21.

17. For more on the history and impact of the Azusa Street Revival and the subsequent Pentecostal movement, see Robeck, *The Azusa Street Mission and Revival*; Hunter and Robeck, *The Azusa Street Revival and Its Legacy*; Owens, *The Azusa Street Revival*; Hyatt, *Fire on the Earth*; Valdez, *Fire on Azusa Street*; Dayton, *The Theological Roots of Pentecostalism*; and Synan, "Pentecostalism," 836.

18. See Hocken, "Charismatic Movement," 477–519.

that in some way differ from classical pentecostalism in affiliation and/ or doctrine."[19]

Richard V. Pierard defines *Evangelicalism* as "[t]he movement in modern Christianity, transcending denominational and confessional boundaries, that emphasizes conformity to the basic tenets of the faith and a missionary outreach of compassion and urgency. A person who identifies with it is an 'evangelical,' one who believes and proclaims the gospel of Jesus Christ."[20] As such, it is important to note that while Pentecostals are themselves Evangelicals, most Evangelicals would not consider themselves Pentecostal.

The principles used to interpret Scripture properly are one's *herme-neutics*. All those who seek to interpret Scripture have some manner of hermeneutical principles, though they vary in presuppositions. This work focuses in particular on *Evangelical* Hermeneutics. In general,[21] Evangelicals interpret Scripture from the assumption that authorial intent is significant when determining the original meaning of the text. Substantial study of both the grammatical content of the text itself, and the historical background of the text, author, and original audience, may in part determine this intent. This process is termed the grammatico-historical approach to hermeneutics or the historical-critical method of interpretation. Only when this process has been followed, and authorial intent determined, might one begin to offer an exposition of the text from the pulpit, seeking modern application for the people of God.[22]

Postmodernism is at best a broad term. As such, this work focuses on the facets of the movement which most directly impact Pentecostalism. Although coined in the 1930s to denote the beginning of a major cultural shift, the word did not gain prominence until the 1970s, when it was first

19. Ibid., 477.

20. Pierard, "Evangelicalism," 379.

21. As with any movement of this size, most statements concerning Evangelicalism run the risk of generalization. So too does the assumption that Evangelicals are beholden to the historical-critical method of hermeneutics. Indeed, Evangelicals employ other methods, such as the text-immanent approach, speech act theory, and socio-rhetorical criticism. Notwithstanding the variety of hermeneutical methods employed by Evangelicalism at large, one may safely state that the historical-critical method plays a key role in the majority of Evangelical hermeneutical efforts.

22. So convinced are many Evangelicals that theirs is the correct method of interpretation, one writer equates the term "hermeneutics" with the historical-critical method plus exposition. See Bruce, "Interpretation of the Bible," 565.

used to describe changes in architecture and English language theories. Today it is used to describe a broader cultural phenomenon that is essentially a rejection of the key tenets of *Modernism*. The Enlightenment brought the quest for absolute truth into the scientific laboratory. Believing that knowledge is always good, and attainable through proper scientific method coupled with reason, the Enlightenment thinkers strove to unlock the secrets of the universe through *Rationalism*. All knowledge gained elevated human freedom, and promoted the individual as the autonomous self, separate from any tradition or community.[23]

Postmoderns no longer believe in the supremacy of reason as the arbiter of truth. Other valid paths to knowledge include experience, emotions, and even intuition. Contra the Modern view that knowledge is inherently good and progress is inevitable, some trends within Postmodernism are pessimistic. Today's generations are no longer confident that humanity will be able to solve each problem that faces the human race. Individuality is dethroned in favor of the shared stories of communities and traditions, within which the truth may be found.[24]

For the purposes of this work, description will need to be given for the youngest generations of North American youth. Taken from Douglas Coupland's best-selling novel of the same name, "Generation X"[25] is a moniker applied to the children of the Baby Boomers, born between approximately 1965 and 1984. This generation has commonly been viewed as having reacted to the financial and career success of their parents, in light of the devastating levels of divorce and family instability of the Boomer generation. Those born since 1985 are often referred to as the Millennials.[26] They have grown up in an era of unprecedented peace and prosperity, coupled with dramatic advances in technology. Unlike those of Generation X who resist change and seek stability, the Millennials seem to thrive where change occurs.[27]

---

23. See Grenz, *A Primer on Postmodernism*, 2–5.

24. See ibid., 7.

25. Coupland, *Generation X*.

26. See Howe and Strauss, *Millennials Rising*.

27. See Bibby, *Canada's Teens*, 165–67. While there are other accepted generational descriptors, I follow Bibby in employing Generation X and Millennials.

PENTECOSTALISM AND POSTMODERNITY:
A DESIRABLE PARTNERSHIP?

With the Pentecostal penchant for abandoning rationalistic Modern principles, some Pentecostal scholars debate whether Pentecostalism should develop a distinctive hermeneutic in line with those Postmodern values.[28] The Postmodern way of liberating readers to see for themselves the meaning within a text has a certain ring of truth with Pentecostals who have often been viewed as allowing their experience to help interpret the biblical text. While those who follow a more Modern/Evangelical approach shun the role of experience within biblical hermeneutics, many Postmodern thinkers have argued for increased recognition of the role presuppositions and life experiences of the individual play in textual interpretation.

Pentecostalism began primarily as a missionary movement, and therefore must keep in touch with the values and philosophy of current culture. With the increased focus upon relationality within key segments of Postmodernity, Pentecostalism must realize that it cannot evangelize a culture it does not understand. As contemporary culture increasingly embraces Postmodernity in all its various forms, some may wonder if Pentecostalism should not follow suit. Yet, there remains much about Postmodernity that directly contradicts Christian values and teachings. The Postmodern tendency to downplay the notion of absolute truth and reject overarching metanarratives such as the biblical account of human history is more than simply problematic for orthodox Christianity; it challenges the very core of the Christian faith.

Is it possible to harmonize such a philosophical mindset as Postmodernism with Pentecostal hermeneutical principles? There appear to be four responses to this question.[29]

The first response is in the affirmative: We ought to build a distinctive Pentecostal hermeneutic based on Postmodern viewpoints, free from rationalistic Evangelicalism. Supporters of this view argue that Postmodernism is fast becoming the standard philosophical mindset of the Western World, and the Church cannot afford to remain entrapped within Modern hermeneutical principles.

---

28. For the connection between Postmodernism and hermeneutics, see Madison, *The Hermeneutics of Postmodernity*; Aichele et al., *The Postmodern Bible*; and Wilkinson, "Hermeneutics and the Postmodern Reaction Against 'Truth.'"

29. The following categories are from Brubaker, "Postmodernism and Pentecostals," 39–44.

The second response is in the negative: We should reject Postmodern influence and build upon the foundation of an Evangelical hermeneutic. Some Pentecostal scholars reject the assumption that Postmodern thought will replace the system of Modern thinking that has prevailed for over three hundred years. As such, joining Pentecostal concerns to this trend will not serve the movement well in the long run.

The third response suggests that we should join Pentecostalism's concerns with traditional Evangelical hermeneutics. Supporters of this view believe that Pentecostalism has generally been well served by its affiliation with Evangelicalism, but should be cognizant of the essential differences between the two, and thus should fine-tune Evangelical hermeneutics to support traditional Pentecostal theology.

The fourth response concludes that we should cautiously develop a Postmodern Pentecostal hermeneutic. Some Pentecostal scholars believe that while Pentecostalism cannot afford to embrace many of the more troubling aspects of Postmodern thought, there is the significant need for a distinctive Pentecostal hermeneutic, separate from the prevailing Evangelical hermeneutic, but still availing of what is best from Modern scholarship.

The question of whether there can ever be a union of Pentecostal hermeneutics and the Postmodern mindset is of utmost importance, and will be given significant treatment throughout this work. Postmodern thought is here to stay. Pentecostalism must both acknowledge this and evaluate whether current approaches to evangelism are relevant on a going forward basis.

THESIS DEFINED

As Pentecostalism seeks to continue its expansion into the hearts and minds of the masses with the Gospel, it must acknowledge and contemplate the impact of Postmodern thought, which occupies increasing ground in the cultural mindset. Further, it must ask what influence Postmodernity should have upon the Pentecostal approach to Scripture.

The aim of this work is to seek to do just that. I will first explore Postmodern thought, particularly as it relates to Pentecostalism, including hermeneutics, and contemplate which of the four approaches to Postmodernism given above is the most advantageous to Pentecostalism.

I will then seek to determine in what manner Postmodernity can—and should—be allowed to contribute to Pentecostal hermeneutics.

To accomplish this task, I will attempt to determine in what sense Pentecostal hermeneutics shared several key Postmodern values. In terms of methodology, this work employs a literary search, examining the early Pentecostal approach to Scripture, and noting the many points of congruency between the hermeneutics of early Pentecostals and the key tenets of today's Postmodernism. In terms of their rejection of the "hegemony of reason,"[30] openness to narratives, the role of community, and the essential function of experience in epistemology, Classical Pentecostal writers and theologians shared much with today's Postmodern thinkers.

The goal of this work is to show that in the earliest days, the hermeneutics employed by Pentecostals shared many characteristics of today's Postmodern thought.[31] Pentecostals were thus roundly criticized by those dedicated to a more Modern approach to Scripture. Indeed, it is my belief that the lack of academic recognition of early Pentecostal theology stems directly from this fact. Modernism had been well entrenched in the thought patterns of theologians at the beginning of the twentieth century. The notion that theology could be determined from the narratives of Luke, as Pentecostals celebrated, was derided as theological immaturity by theologians who proclaimed that doctrine could be ascertained from Scripture's didactic portions alone. Almost sixty years after the genesis of modern-day Pentecostalism, John R.W. Stott wrote: "[T]his revelation of the purpose of God in Scripture should be sought in its *didactic*, rather than its *historical* parts. More precisely, we should look for it in the teaching of Jesus, and in the sermons and writings of the apostles, and not in the purely narrative portions of the Acts."[32] Worse still was the Pentecostal claim that experience, and not reason alone, was an essential component in formulating a vibrant, living theology of the Holy Spirit and his work. To the mind soaked in the precepts of Modernism, here was theology at its worst. For many theologians, experience was seemingly irrelevant in

---

30. This phrase is borrowed from Taylor, *Sources of the Self*, 147.

31. Writing about the traditional interpretive methods of Pentecostal pastors, Ahn notes, "[T]hese traditional forms of pre-critical biblical interpretation such as 'pragmatic' or 'pattern' hermeneutics have more in common with postmodern modes of interpretation than do the 'critical' interpretation of Pentecostal scholars. . . ." Ahn, "Various Debates in the Contemporary Pentecostal Hermeneutics," 31.

32. Stott, *The Baptism and Fullness of the Holy Spirit*, 8.

determining true Christian theology. Reason, coupled with the proper study of Scripture, would yield the nuggets of truth deposited within.

The biases of the early twentieth century are largely behind us, and Pentecostal academics are now enjoying unprecedented acceptance in the larger theological world. In part, the aim of this work is to determine why this has occurred. Have Pentecostal scholars, in a desire to gain greater recognition from their Evangelical counterparts, become increasingly Modern in their approach to biblical interpretation? A major personal concern is to determine whether, at a time when increasing numbers of Western youth and young adults are beginning to view truth in Postmodern terms, Pentecostals have begun to approach Scripture with a growing dependence on the Modern way of thinking. If so, a tremendous evangelistic opportunity may be hampered or lost.

This work demonstrates that Pentecostals must continue in the hermeneutical traditions of their early leaders if they are to remain relevant in the future. It is possible to adhere to the best of early Pentecostal hermeneutics, without ignoring the tremendous hermeneutical advances of the twentieth century. With the Holy Spirit's help as the starting point, and speaking the language of today's Postmodern generations, Pentecostals are in an excellent position to contribute to the Christian world a hermeneutic that will bring the masses of Postmoderns into contact with the one true God.

SUMMARY

The following chapter summary provides the reader with the objectives I pursue in this work and the path my research will take as we explore critical issues within Pentecostalism and Postmodernism.

Chapter 2 introduces the basic tenets of Postmodernism. For the purposes of this work, I will examine in particular the philosophical underpinnings of Postmodernity, note the Postmodern rejection of rationalism and metanarrative, and focus upon the role of experience and community. With their strong emphasis on the place of experience and the rejection of individualism, Postmoderns greatly appreciate the narrative aspects of life and history. The Modern mind was encouraged to learn through academics and scientific method; the Postmodern person learns through the stories and life experiences of others, as well.

As Postmodern thinking moves through the various disciplines of the academic world, and works its way through popular culture, observers are often amazed and sometimes incensed at the speed and propensity with which it impacts society at large. Should Pentecostalism in its earliest, Classical form, be found to have much in common with this movement, the ramifications for this growing missionary revival are substantial.

Chapter 3 begins to examine Pentecostal hermeneutics—past, present, and future—leading to the heart of the discussion: Did Pentecostal hermeneutics from the beginning share several Postmodern characteristics? Was the Pentecostal reliance upon experience and narratives, along with the rejection of hermeneutical rationalism, actually a forerunner of the current Postmodern movement? If it can be determined that Pentecostals began with a hermeneutic reflective of current Postmodern thought, we may conclude that should Pentecostals continue in the hermeneutical traditions of their forbearers, they are in an excellent position to communicate the Gospel to the Postmodern thinkers of this generation. It is my conclusion that, while early Pentecostalism was surely not Postmodern, however one may define that term today, Pentecostal hermeneutics bore many of the traits of current Postmodernity.

Chapter 3 shows that Pentecostals understood their very existence in terms of the narrative of "the former rain, and the latter rain" (Joel 2:23, KJV), found often in the Old Testament. Further, early Pentecostals were strongly attracted to a simple reading of the narratives of the book of Acts, where they found their distinctive doctrines clearly taught and supported. For much of their early history, Pentecostals were derided by most New Testament scholars and theologians for their heavy reliance on the Acts narratives. Indeed, the Pentecostal doctrines of subsequence and initial evidence are supported from five narratives (Acts 2, 8, 9, 10, and 19). Traditionally, biblical scholars have refrained from deriving too much theology from narratives, preferring instead to scour the didactic portions of Scripture. For the hermeneutically literal Pentecostals, however, anything put in Scripture by the Holy Spirit, including stories, was intended for learning and instruction.

The first leaders of the fledgling Pentecostal movement acknowledged the important role of doctrine in their lives and faith, but clearly preferred their actual experience as teacher and guide. Rationalism was not warmly welcomed. In both Postmodernity and Pentecostalism, the hegemony of reason has been toppled by a strong appeal to the senses, the emotions, and dare we say, faith? As Postmodernists are no longer content to allow reason to be the final arbiter of truth in their lives, so early Pentecostals were unwilling to allow only that which seemed reasonable to the cerebral cortex of the brain to pass for proper Scriptural interpretation. Pentecostals were open to the "plain reading" of Scripture, no matter how "unreasonable" the intellect might perceive what was discovered. Thus, we observe the convergent viewpoints of Pentecostalism with Postmodernity, in terms of Rationalism, narratives, and the place of experience in life and theology.

Chapter 4 continues with hermeneutical issues, the goal being to explore recent trends in Pentecostal hermeneutics. One question remains to be answered: Have current Pentecostal hermeneutics stayed true to the Postmodern tendencies of their forbearers? By highlighting the hermeneutical debate between Gordon D. Fee and his Pentecostal responders, it will be seen that some Pentecostals, in responding to Evangelical concerns over hermeneutical practices, have become more Modern in their approach to the Scriptures. While it cannot be denied that Pentecostals have gained remarkable acceptance in the larger Evangelical world, we must question whether it has come partially at the expense of their approach to Scripture. At a time when increasing numbers in the Western World are speaking the language of Pentecostal hermeneutics, an uncritical acceptance of Modern hermeneutics may prove detrimental to Pentecostal evangelistic efforts.

Chapter 5 seeks to interact with a theological giant seldom engaged by Pentecostals—Rudolf Bultmann (1884–1976). With his insistence upon the demythologization of the Gospel, though not so categorized in his time, Bultmann now represents the extreme of Modern thinking, rationalism gone awry. In the years since his considerable theological contributions, scholars have further applied Modern principles to the Scriptural accounts, culminating in the contemporary work of *The Jesus Seminar*. By engaging Bultmann's thought, as it pertains to the newest generation of truth-seekers, I show that at its core, a fully Modern hermeneutical approach inevitably leads to conclusions that are antithetical to Pentecostalism and detrimental to Pentecostal evangelism in this Postmodern age. It will be demonstrated that Bultmann's approach, the ultimate application of Modern hermeneutical principles, could hardly be more poorly suited as a platform upon which to present the Gospel of Christ to the youngest Western generations.

Having demonstrated the importance of a distinctively Pentecostal hermeneutic, I focus in chapter 6 on the future of Pentecostal hermeneutics by exploring the work of Kenneth J. Archer. While much has been written on Pentecostal hermeneutics in the last thirty years, few authors dared to put forth a proposal for a specific Pentecostal hermeneutic. Archer has done so, and thus his work is worthy of closer examination.

Archer begins by defining Pentecostalism in its many varieties, tracing the social and theological influences on this revivalist movement. He characterizes early Pentecostalism as *Paramodern*, a movement that emerged out of, though always existing on the fringes of, Modernity. Pentecostals rejected Modernity in terms of epistemology and sociology, but employed Modern technology, language, and inductive reasoning to advance their cause. Archer argues that in the hermeneutical debate between Fundamentalism and Liberalism, Pentecostals chose a third path, using the same pre-critical Bible Reading Method as other Holiness believers. What made the Pentecostal approach to Scripture different, however, was the unique understanding of the Pentecostal story—the place of this new movement in God's economy. The Pentecostal tendency to view everything through an eschatological lens provided the urgency and immediacy needed to view all interpretation of Scripture in terms of the experience of God through his Word.

Archer presents the contemporary Pentecostal debate. Must Pentecostals continue to use a modified version of traditional Evangelical historical-critical methods of interpretation,[33] or is it an authentic movement, whose identity cannot be "submerged" into Evangelicalism? If so, should not Pentecostalism have its own hermeneutical approach? Archer chooses the latter position, as will the present author. Finally, we present for Pentecostals a contemporary hermeneutical strategy, which embraces the Pentecostal story and derives meaning from a "dialectical process based upon an interdependent dialogical relationship between Scripture, Spirit and community."[34]

Chapter 7 contains practical suggestions for Pentecostals. I begin by exploring the role of the Holy Spirit in hermeneutics. To be sure, the

33. As observed in footnote 21 above, Evangelicalism as a whole has employed several hermeneutical approaches. Pentecostalism, however, when following the hermeneutical approaches of Evangelicals, tends to follow most closely their use of the historical-critical method.

34. Archer, *A Pentecostal Hermeneutic*, 5.

Spirit's role in the inspiration and preservation of Scripture is widely accepted. Apart from a few words in theological texts about illumination, however, there remains no firm understanding in the wider Christian world of the Spirit's role in hermeneutics. Pentecostals are in a key position to develop a proper pneumatological approach to hermeneutics. This work shows that the Spirit's guidance in hermeneutics is essential to the proper interpretation of the Word of God. Without the Holy Spirit working in the hearts and minds of the reader, one cannot hope to gain a truly spiritual understanding of Scripture.

I will strive towards a more concrete understanding of how the Holy Spirit assists us in understanding Scripture, through a survey of various proposals put forward by scholars. Further, I will examine four responses to the possibility of joining Pentecostal hermeneutical concerns with Postmodern trends. While the purveyors of Modernism often criticized Pentecostalism for its dependence upon experience, it is an important tool both for Pentecostals, and for those subscribing to Postmodernity. Indeed, some have argued that Pentecostal hermeneutics have benefited from the use of experience as a hermeneutical tool, and that for certain portions of Scripture in particular Pentecostals have a sharper focus than their Evangelical or Mainline Protestant counterparts.[35] I will ask whether it is possible that Pentecostals, by virtue of their experiences in the Spirit, may have a hermeneutical edge regarding passages of Scripture that speak to the very experiences Pentecostals have enjoyed. Debate surrounds this concept, and some consideration will be given to both viewpoints.

Chapter 8 summarizes the findings of this work. The retired typically do not win young adults to Christ; each generation wins their own peers. As Christians who believe strongly in the present-day working and moving of the Holy Spirit, Pentecostals are in an excellent position to reach Generation X, the Millennials, and others with the Gospel, should they not abandon what was best in early Pentecostal hermeneutics. As the newest generations are increasingly influenced by Postmodernity, these young men and women will also be more open to the supernatural and spiritual than the generations since the Enlightenment. If Pentecostals wish to fulfill their missional mandate, however, they must first reach those in their own homes—Pentecostal youth and young adults. As his-

---

35. See, for example, Pinnock, "The Role of the Spirit in Interpretation," 491–97; idem, "The Work of the Holy Spirit in Hermeneutics," 3–23; May, "The Role of the Holy Spirit in Biblical Hermeneutics"; and Stronstad, "Pentecostal Experience and Hermeneutics," 15.

tory has demonstrated, each generation of believers ultimately succeeds or fails in the relevance of its Gospel presentation to its peers.

It is my contention that Pentecostals must preserve their hermeneutical emphasis upon the three tenets of Postmodernity discussed above, if they wish to continue to interpret Scripture in a manner that connects most readily with the newest generations. The evangelistic benefits of maintaining a Postmodern approach to hermeneutics by Pentecostals are many. We now turn to the introduction of Postmodern thought, and areas of similarity and incongruence with conservative Christianity.

2

Postmodernity: A Summary

A massive intellectual revolution is taking place that is perhaps as great as that which marked off the modern world from the Middle Ages.[1]

DIOGENES ALLEN

There is now a consensus that consensus is impossible, that we are having authoritative announcements of the disappearance of authority, that scholars are writing comprehensive narratives on how comprehensive narratives are unthinkable.[2]

REBECCA JAICHANDRAN AND B.C. MADHAV

Pentecostalism is more an impetus for than a consequence of an emerging dominant worldview. Pentecostalism should then be viewed as a part of the mainstream that is forging the postmodern era.[3]

JACKIE DAVID JOHNS

THE VERY WORD POSTMODERNISM suggests a myriad of possible definitions. Even those writers considered Postmodern intone: "I have the impression that [the term Postmodernism] is applied today to anything the users of the term happen to like."[4] This should perhaps not be surprising, as it is a trend in philosophy and culture defined largely by what it is not and what it has moved past. Postmodernity first appeared in the arts

1. Allen, *Christian Belief in a Postmodern World*, 2.
2. Stephenson, "Christian Mission in a Postmodern World."
3. Johns, "Pentecostalism and the Postmodern Worldview," 85.
4. Eco, *Postscript to the Name of the Rose*, 65.

and architecture, and has now spread to almost every sector of society, its impact growing more substantial by the day. In perhaps no area will the impact of Postmodern thinking be more substantial than in Christian life and thought, particularly as it applies to the theology and methods of evangelism. This chapter limits itself to a discussion of Postmodernity as it interacts with Christian theology in particular.

At its core, Postmodern thinking contains a vast array of thoughts, ideas, and concepts. Several of these are antithetical to traditional Christian thought, particularly among Western Christian groups profoundly impacted by the Enlightenment. In particular, the Postmodern rejection of rationalism as the arbiter of truth, openness to the role of experience in determining truth, and recognition of the importance of narratives in communication, stand in stark contrast to many of the cherished values of Evangelicalism. At the same time, however, the student of Postmodernity is struck by some of the more intense similarities between the Postmodern way of thought and the thought patterns of the earliest Pentecostals. In this chapter, I explore various facets of Postmodern thought, noting the themes of community and narratives, importance of experience, and rejection of rationalism as they intersect early Pentecostal thought and hermeneutics. We now turn to these congruencies and contradictions.

POSTMODERNISM: AN OVERVIEW

At its essence, Postmodernism[5] is a worldview consisting of anti-foundationalism,[6] disbelief in pure objectivity, and deconstruction of "certain" knowledge, primarily characterized by a reaction to the prevailing worldview of Modernism. It is therefore beneficial to briefly examine the chief tenets of Premodernity, then Modernity, and the current reaction to the same. Although Postmodernity does encapsulate some thinking of the early Greek philosophers, it is not a return to the Premodern mindset. Rather, it seeks to modify the best from the Premodern mind

---

5. For a sample of attempts to define Postmodernity, see Finger, "Modernity, Postmodernity—What in the World Are They?," 353–68; Gitlin, "The Postmodern Predicament," 67–76; Percesepe, "The Unbearable Lightness of Being Postmodern," 118–35; and Van Gelder, "Postmodernism as an Emerging Worldview," 412–17.

6. McKim defines Foundationalism as: "Philosophical or theological approaches affirming specific truths as bases and criteria for all other truths" ("Foundationalism," 108). For the Christian, belief in the God who created humanity and the universe, and who revealed himself in Jesus Christ and through his Word, is foundational.

without falling prey to the dry rationalism and restrictive epistemological foundationalism of Modernity.[7]

Premodernity

In many ways, though certainly not all,[8] the Premodern era resembles the current sphere of thinking. The ancient Greeks struggled with a variety of worldviews, from the spiritual overtones of their pagan religions, to the rational philosophy of some of the greatest intellectual giants the world has seen—Plato (c. 428–c. 348 B.C.), Aristotle (384–322 B.C.), and Socrates (469–399 B.C.). Although surrounded by a culture bred in mythological paganism, inherited from the animistic religions of nature, these ancient Greek philosophers had begun to reject the world of myth, arguing instead that all causes must have a First Cause, which itself is uncaused. This First Cause could be compared with the transcendent God of Judaism, of whom there was only one, and was like no other. As God had put into place the key absolute principles, which guide every aspect of creation and human life, the world could be better understood and controlled. Through sheer force of will and reasoning, these ancient philosophers pushed the value and contribution of human reason to new heights.[9]

As has been well established, the Greek world was ready for the Christian Gospel. As Gene Edward Veith, Jr., observes,

> Already those nourished by Greek culture had an inkling of the immortality of the soul, the reality of a spiritual realm, and the existence of only one transcendent God. Paul discovered in Athens an altar "to an unknown God." The Greeks had come to realize that there is a God, but they did not know Him. Their reason, highly developed as it was, had to give way to revelation. "Now what you worship as something unknown I am going to proclaim to you" (Acts 17:23).[10]

7. "The Enlightenment project . . . took it as axiomatic that there was only one possible answer to any question. From this it followed that the world could be controlled and rationally ordered if we could only picture and represent it rightly. But this presumed that there existed a single correct mode of representation which, if we could uncover it (and this was what scientific and mathematical endeavors were all about), would provide the means to Enlightenment ends." Harvey, *The Condition of Postmodernity*, 27.

8. For example, the Postmodern approach would not accept the foundationalism inherent within the Premodern belief in "absolute principles" guiding every aspect of creation.

9. Veith, *Postmodern Times*, 30. The following section owes much to Veith's succinct, yet thorough, appraisal of the periods in question.

10. Ibid.

With the introduction of the Christian message, the ancient world now had three competing worldviews—pagan mythology, philosophical rationalism, and biblical revelation. While the biblical and classical worldviews did not agree, there were points of commonality in their belief systems, particularly in their acceptance of a transcendent reality to which this world owed its meaning. From various points of contact, Augustine (354–430) drew upon Plato as he formulated his version of Western theology,[11] much of which would guide the Church into the Modern era.

> For over a thousand years, Western civilization was dominated by an uneasy mingling of worldviews. . . . During the Middles Ages (A.D. 1000–1500), Christian piety, classical rationalism, and the folk-paganism of European culture achieved something of a synthesis. Although medieval civilization was impressive in its own terms, scholastic theology subordinated the Bible to Aristotelian logic and human institutions, sacrificing the purity of the Biblical revelation. Medieval popular culture further obscured the gospel message, often keeping much of the old paganism under a veneer of Christianity, retaining the old gods but renaming them after Christian saints.[12]

The Renaissance period of the 1500s and 1600s sought a return to the classical roots of both Greek philosophers and biblical revelation. Renaissance scholars such as Niccolò de' Niccoli (1363–1437) and Poggio Bracciolini (1380–1459) sought a return to the ancient texts of Greek philosophy in much the same manner as the leaders of the Protestant Reformation, such as Martin Luther (1483–1546), John Calvin (1509–64), and Ulrich Zwingli (1484–1531), sought a return to biblical authority. Pagan mythology was now viewed as outdated and unworthy of the Renaissance thinker. This return meant the end of the uneasy partnership between the three dominant worldviews that had managed to coexist thus far in a muddled tension. The 1600s brought the Enlightenment and the beginning of the Modern world.[13]

11. Just as Thomas Aquinas (1225–74) synthesized the Bible with Aristotle some 800 years later.

12. Veith, *Postmodern Times*, 31.

13. In a sense, the choice of dates for the beginning of the Modern era is an arbitrary one. A thorough analysis of the historical significance of particular dates is beyond the scope of this work. Therefore, I will align the end of the pre-Modern era and the beginnings of Modernity with the early stages of the Enlightenment and Age of Reason. In

Modernity

The foundations of the Modern era may be witnessed as early as the late 1500s. Renaissance thinker Francis Bacon (1561–1626) had begun to extol the virtues of human knowledge gained through scientific experimentation. He believed that expanded scientific knowledge would give humans the power they needed over the circumstances of life, altering them to their benefit.[14]

Often considered the father of modern philosophy, René Descartes (1596–1650) attempted to devise a scientific method of investigation, by which one could determine which truths were veracious. Though a sceptic in many areas, he allowed that one could doubt everything except one's own existence. Borrowing from Augustine, Descartes made popular the phrase *Cogito ergo sum*—"I think, therefore I am." His definition of the human person as a thinking substance and rational subject established the centrality of human mind in epistemology, and thus set the agenda for the next three hundred years of scientific and philosophical inquiry. Stanley J. Grenz notes:

> Descartes exercised immense influence on all subsequent thinking. Throughout the modern era, intellectuals in many disciplines have turned to the reasoning subject rather than divine revelation as the starting point for knowledge and reflection. Even modern theologians felt constrained to build on the foundation of rationalistic philosophy.[15]

Immanuel Kant (1724–1804), responding to widespread scepticism that the empirical model could ever lead to certain truth, published his *Critique of Pure Reason* in 1781.[16] His elevation of the active human mind in the process of knowing encouraged subsequent philosophers to focus on the centrality of the autonomous self. Moving beyond Descartes' self

---

many ways, the elevation of human reason by thinkers such as Francis Bacon and René Descartes heralded the arrival of the Modern age. Though scholars have not reached a consensus on the dating of the Enlightenment and the early years of the Modern era, many historians associate the beginning of the Enlightenment with the Peace of Westphalia in 1648, and its ending with the publication of Immanuel Kant's *Critique of Pure Reason* in 1781. As Grenz suggests, "The Age of Reason inaugurated the Modern era, which only now seems to be in its twilight state." *A Primer on Postmodernism*, 60.

14. See Wolterstorff, *Reason Within the Bounds of Religion*, 123–24.

15. Grenz, *A Primer on Postmodernism*, 65.

16. Kant, *Critique of Pure Reason*.

as the focus of philosophical attention, Kant raised the subjective self to become the entire subject matter in philosophy. This focus on the subjective self has become one of the chief identifying characteristics—and lingering problems—of the Modern era.[17]

Building upon the work of these and other individuals, later generations led a swift and impressive expansion of the scientific realm in the eighteenth century. Never before had scientific discovery achieved such startling levels, with such alacrity. This age of scientific prowess, exaltation of human reason, and greater human autonomy is variously termed the Enlightenment and the Age of Reason. Classical rationalism was now raised to such levels that biblical revelation was viewed with the same lens of suspicion and critique as had given place to the demise of pagan mythology. For many Enlightenment thinkers such as John Locke (1632–1704) and David Hume (1711–76), the stories of the Bible and of ancient Greek gods were of the one sort—mythological superstitions, beneath the dignity of the Modern mind.[18]

Enlightenment thinkers such as Locke and Hume did not discard belief in God entirely, however. Rather, they developed a rational religion, which essentially worshipped human reason. Based on the inherent order of the universe, Deism is one aberration which proclaimed the existence of a rational deity, albeit one that had little to do with creation; all was set running in the beginning, then left to function precisely as a machine. This by necessity excluded miracles and other supernatural aspects of biblical revelation such as the Incarnation and redemption. Eventually, an "uninvolved" Creator was not needed, and thus some came to see the universe as a closed system of cause and effect, all from within, based on principles accessible by human reason. Charles Darwin's (1809–82) removal of God from the category of First Cause completed the transformation of a society now sustained by scientific explanations and the manner of proof achieved in laboratories.

Moral absolutes, once the purview of the deity in Christian theology, were preserved only as they served utilitarian purposes. That which served the functioning of society was considered good and, conversely, that which hindered the growth and development of humanity was considered evil. Humanity and in particular human individualism became sovereign;

17. Ibid., 79.
18. For further reading, see Hampshire, *The Age of Reason.*

the value of the collective was sacrificed on the altar of the individual. As Millard J. Erickson notes, "In the premodern period the church's traditional authorities, the philosopher and the Bible, had prevailed, but in the modern period, the flight from these external authorities led to a focus on the individual as the basis for authority. . . . [T]he individual has priority over the collective."[19] As rationalism peaked, optimism soared in Modern thinkers, who felt they could remake society into a veritable utopia, with the assumption that, were reason applied properly and the principles of the universe discovered, human planning could solve all problems. Hence, Francis Bacon's famous dictum, "Knowledge is power."[20]

As Modernity moved from victory to victory, several smaller movements arose in reaction and formed the basis for Postmodernism. Early nineteenth-century Romanticism reversed the cold rationalism of the Enlightenment and instead saw the universe as a living organism, with feeling at the pinnacle of our humanity. With God close at hand and intimately involved in the physical world, some taught a new pantheism, as God became as close as the self, one with humanity and the universe, no longer transcendent. Thus, Romanticism cultivated irrationalism, encouraged introspection, and raised subjectivity and personal experience to new levels of influence.[21]

Existentialism arose in the early twentieth century as thinkers pondered the increasing failure of both Enlightenment rationalism and romantic emotionalism to offer meaning for the individual. For the existentialist, meaning is a purely human phenomenon, discovered quite apart from the objective world. As Veith astutely observes, "While there is no ready-made meaning in life, individuals can create meaning for themselves. . . . This meaning, however, has no validity for anyone else. No one can provide a meaning for someone else. Everyone must determine his or her own meaning. . . ."[22] Existentialism thereby provides the rationale for contemporary relativism; religion is a personal affair, as is morality. No one can decide religious affiliation or moral belief for another—what is right for one may not be right for another. By the mid-twentieth cen-

---

19. Erickson, *Truth or Consequences*, 28.

20. Grenz, *A Primer on Postmodernism*, 58–59. See also Wolterstorff, *Reason Within the Bounds of Religion*, esp. 123–35.

21. Veith, *Postmodern Times*, 35–37.

22. Ibid., 37.

tury, the foundation was well in place for Postmodern thought. Rebecca Jaichandran and B.C. Madhav conclude:

> Modernity is characterized by the triumph of Enlightenment, exaltation of rights of humans and the supremacy of reason. Modernism assumed that human reason was the only reliable way of making sense of the universe. Anything that could not be understood in scientific terms was either not true or not worth knowing. Human beings, by means of scientific reason, could make sense of the world and even manipulate it for their own benefit with or without reference to God (who or whatever he/she/it might be) .... [T]his ability to understand and manipulate the natural world . . . held out the promise of unlimited progress.

> As the twentieth century progressed, some of the first cracks began to appear in the modernist worldview and the myth of progress. Two world wars showed that the same scientific technological progress that promised great hope to humankind could also be used to inflict untold suffering on men, women and children and could even destroy the entire world. . . . Hope was shattered. . . . Thus, modernism and the myth of scientific progress is dead or at least in its final stages, but there is nothing to take its place. We do not know what is coming, only that it will be the worldview that replaces modernism. Until we know exactly what form it will take, we might as well call it postmodernism for the time being.[23]

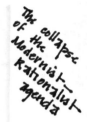

The collapse of the Modernist Rationalist agenda

POSTMODERN PHILOSOPHERS

Before one delves into the philosophical underpinnings of Postmodern thought, it is beneficial to briefly examine the writings of the key philosophers behind this new worldview.[24] New modes of thinking do not develop in a vacuum; those before and after the scholars of each generation are influential also. Several significant personalities have emerged in the development of Postmodern thought; a fuller understanding of Postmodernism will be obtained through passing familiarity with their thought and writings.

23. Jaichandran and Madhav, "Pentecostal Spirituality in a Postmodern World," 44–45. See also Stephenson, "Christian Mission in a Postmodern World."

24. Grenz (*A Primer on Postmodernism*, chapter 6) gives an excellent and readable overview of the work of Foucault, Derrida, and Rorty. See also Erickson, *Truth or Consequences*, chapters 4–5, for the major intellectual voices immediately preceding Postmodernity, and chapters 6–9, for an overview of Foucault, Derrida, and Rorty.

Jean-François Lyotard

According to Albert Mohler, Jr., Jean-François Lyotard (1924–98), profes-sor of philosophy at the University of Paris III, Vincennes, "emerged as the most formative defining force in the postmodern movement."[25] Lyotard's defining work, *The Postmodern Condition: A Report on Knowledge*,[26] was commissioned in 1979 by the government of Québec (Canada), as a re-port on knowledge in highly developed societies. According to Grenz:

> The publication of The Postmodern Condition put postmodern-ism on the intellectual map. The book did not so much initiate the discussion as describe in an accessible manner the revolution in outlook that lay beneath the cultural phenomenon occurring throughout the Western world and the theoretical and philosophi-cal basis of the postmodern view.[27]

Lyotard sets the context of Postmodernism within the cultural and ideological crisis of Western civilization, involving all cognitive issues, from ontology to epistemology. This crisis is foundationally a "crisis of narratives" which, of necessity, is a religious crisis, as well. The Modern age is marked by grand metanarratives, which have sought to explain the most significant questions of life, such as the nature of the universe and the origin of meaning.[28] Responding to the question, "What is modern-ism?," Lyotard replies:

> I will use the term *modern* to designate any science that legitimates itself with reference to a metadiscourse of this kind, making an explicit appeal to some grand narrative, such as the dialectic of the Spirit, the hermeneutics of meaning, the emancipation of the rational or working subject, or the creation of wealth.[29]

From this viewpoint, all grand narratives, from the unified field theory to the Christian Gospel, are considered Modern, and are therefore dead, as Postmodern thought views such metanarratives as untenable. More to the point, Lyotard suggests, "Simplifying to the extreme, I define *postmodern* as incredulity towards metanarratives."[30] For those who won-

25. Mohler, "The Integrity of the Evangelical Tradition," 56.

26. Lyotard, *The Postmodern Condition*.

27. Grenz, *A Primer on Postmodernism*, 39.

28. Lyotard, *The Postmodern Condition*, xxiii.

29. Ibid. Emphasis in original.

30. Ibid., xxiv. Emphasis in original. That is, metanarratives justified by modernistic

der just how society found itself in a place of such incredulity, Lyotard gives a classic defining statement of Postmodernism:

> The narrative function is losing its great functors, its great hero, its great dangers, its great voyages, its great goal. It is being disbursed in clouds of narrative language elements—narrative, but also denotative, prescriptive, and so on. Conveyed within each cloud are pragmatic valencies specific to each kind. Each of us lives at the intersection of many of these. However, we do not necessarily establish stable language combinations, and the properties of the ones we do establish are not necessarily communicable.[31]

As Albert Mohler notes, Lyotard asks the right question: "Where, after the demise of the meta-narratives, does legitimacy reside?" Following Lyotard's lead, the grand narratives of Modernity, along with those that precede it, such as Christianity, are fragmented into truncated mini-narratives, which function as "language games" for local communities and interest groups.[32] For the Christian, whose faith is based upon the grand narrative of God's dealing with humanity as represented in the Scriptures, the supposed demise of all metanarratives leads to a faith without foundation, and should be considered one of the more troubling aspects of Postmodern thought.

Michel Foucault

For many, Michel Foucault (1926–84)[33] is the epitome of the Postmodern scholar. Often classified as a cultural historian, Foucault referred to himself as an "archaeologist of knowledge,"[34] and at times, a philosopher. No truer disciple of Friedrich Nietzsche (1844–1900)[35] has emerged in the

---

universal rationalism.

31. Ibid.

32. Mohler, "The Integrity of the Evangelical Tradition," 57–58.

33. For a sample of Foucault's work, see "The Minimalist Self"; *The Use of Pleasure*; *The Archaeology of Knowledge and Language*; *The Order of Things*; and "Truth and Power."

34. See Foucault, *The Archaeology of Knowledge and Language*. Also cited in Phillips, *Lawyer's Language*, 70.

35. Often mischaracterized by his followers for exclusively promoting "God is dead" theology, Nietzsche is widely regarded as one of the earlier philosophical forerunners of Postmodernism. Through his often-complex writings, Nietzsche argued against morality as commonly understood, believing it to be infected by the controlling influence of the Christian Church. He mounted sustained attacks on Christianity as he promoted his idea of the value of power in a man; the Christian faith, he felt, taught men to submit in weakness. To his credit, however, Nietzsche differentiated between Christ and Christianity:

twentieth century; Foucault has been called the "greatest of Nietzsche's modern disciples."[36] In 1969 Foucault obtained the chair at the College de France, the pinnacle of the French academic system, thus finding the platform he needed to write, as well as lecture abroad. His rejection of the Enlightenment worldview was thorough, and his rejection of long-cherished moral absolutes was displayed both in his work and through his homosexual lifestyle.[37]

Rejecting the Modern focus on the autonomous self, he focused on the subjective self, arguing that our subjective experience is shaped entirely by external factors that we unconsciously internalize. Total objectivity in terms of discovering truth is impossible. Grenz notes:

> According to Foucault, Western society has for three centuries made a number of fundamental errors. He argues that scholars have erroneously believed (1) that an objective body of knowledge exists and is waiting to be discovered, (2) that they actually possess such knowledge and that it is neutral or value-free, and (3) that the pursuit of knowledge benefits all humankind rather than just a specific class.
>
> Foucault rejects these Enlightenment assumptions. He denies the modern ideal of the disinterested knower. He denies that we can ever stand beyond history and human society, that there is any vantage point that offers certain and universal knowledge. And hence, he denies the older understanding of truth as theoretical and objective, the belief that truth is a claim to knowledge that can be validated by procedures devised by the appropriate scholarly community.[38]

Foucault's approach undermines not only any conception of objective science, but also what many consider the foundation of Christianity—God as Trinity, standing objectively over humanity, revealing truth both through general and specific revelation. This rejection of objectivity and

---

"Precisely that which is Christian in the ecclesiastical sense is anti-Christian, in essence: things and people instead of symbols; history instead of external facts; forms, rites, dogmas instead of a way of life. Utter indifference to dogmas, cults, priests, church, theology is Christian." Nietzsche, *The Will to Power*, 98. For a more complete understanding of the thought of Nietzsche, see his *Antichrist*. See also Williams, *The Shadow of the Antichrist*; Deleuze, *Nietzsche and Philosophy*; Danto, *Nietzsche as Philosopher*; and Allison, *New Nietzsche*, 1985.

36. Said, "Michel Foucault, 1926–1984," 1.

37. See Miller, *The Passion of Michel Foucault*.

38. Grenz, *A Primer on Postmodernism*, 131.

absolute truth, characterized by Foucault, betrays one of the more serious challenges presented by Postmodern thought to Christianity.

Jacques Derrida

Another significant philosopher in the Postmodern world is Jacques Derrida (1930–2004).[39] Educated in France, he had begun, by the early 1970s, to divide his teaching time between lecturing in Paris and in various American universities, including Johns Hopkins and Yale. He is most widely known for championing the movement of Deconstruction. His writings are extremely complex to decipher, as he forges new approaches and concepts in language, outside its traditional use. Deconstruction is exceedingly difficult to describe or characterize. Grenz explains that an explanation of it "involves the use of certain philosophical or philological assumptions to launch an assault on logocentrism, understood as the assumption that something lies beyond our system of linguistic signs to which a written work can refer to substantiate its claim to be an authentic statement."[40] At their core, Derrida's writings endeavor to dissuade the Western world from its notion that one can assume there is a meaning inherent in a text, and that it may be discovered. Grenz notes:

> In the wake of Derrida's work, avant-garde postmoderns conclude that we can no longer assume an ontological ground for certain knowledge. Derrida's attack on the "center," they declare, has forever shattered traditional appeals to the author's intention. In fact, it has undermined appeals to anything located beyond the text.
>
> What should we do in this situation? Derrida's followers counsel us simply to learn to live with the anxiety that results from his deconstruction of logocentrism and the demise of the metaphysics of presence. We must abandon the old understanding of reading as an attempt to gain entrance into the text in order to understand its meaning and embrace instead the idea that reading is a violent act of mastery over the text.[41]

39. See Derrida, *Of Grammatology*; *Margins of Philosophy*; *Of Spirit*; *A Derrida Reader*; *Acts of Religion*; and *The Gift of Death*. On Derrida and religion, see Caputo, *The Prayers and Tears of Jacques Derrida*.

40. Grenz, *A Primer on Postmodernism*, 148. See also Anderson, *Reality Isn't What It Used to Be*, 90.

41. Grenz, *A Primer on Postmodernism*, 150. See also Lentricchia, *After the New Criticism*, 179.

While Derrida never intended to create a specific theory to be applied in different situations, his strategy to dismantle logocentrism is profoundly troubling for Christian theology. Removing all possibility of unmediated truth in the written word, Derrida denies that language has a fixed meaning connected to a fixed reality, or that it unveils definitive truth. Those who choose to believe in the Christian Scriptures as God's Word, in any possible sense, also believe there is an ontological ground for certain knowledge. For the Christian, the words of Scripture do in fact point to a reality beyond the text—God himself.

Richard Rorty

Another scholar who provides philosophical underpinnings for Postmodernism is the American philosopher, Richard Rorty (1931–2007),[42] who aligned himself with many of the pragmatic ideas of John Dewey (1859–1952). In Rorty's pragmatist tradition, the specific nature of truth varies from that held in philosophy since the Enlightenment. Rather than embracing the correspondence theory of truth—statements are valuable and are either true or false, the veracity of which can be checked against the reality they describe—Rorty opts for a type of coherence theory. He declares that statements are "true" insofar as they cohere with the entire system of beliefs we hold. Essentially, pragmatists understand truth as that which works pragmatically, rather than that which is correct in theory only.[43]

Following the Postmodern assault on the Modern concept of the self, Rorty encourages us to view our lives as episodes within community narratives. "Everything one can say about truth or rationality is embedded in the understanding and concepts unique to the society in which one lives."[44] He argues that it is impossible to find a starting point for our discourse that is outside our own temporal context; impossible for us to rise above human communities. Therefore, we ought not to claim that any interpretation has universal, transcendent authority. He sees this as positive, however, for although we lose our perceived vantage point outside of ourselves, we gain a new appreciation for our community.

---

42. See Rorty, *Philosophy and the Mirror of Nature*; *Objectivity, Relativism, and Truth*; *The Consequences of Pragmatism*; and *Essays on Heidegger and Others*.

43. See Grenz, *A Primer on Postmodernism*, 154.

44. Ibid., 156. See also Rorty, "Science as Solidarity," 11.

If we give up this hope [to become a properly programmed machine], we shall lose what Nietzsche called "metaphysical comfort," but we may gain a renewed sense of community. Our identification with our community—our society, our political tradition, our intellectual heritage—is heightened when we see this community as *ours* rather than *nature's*, *shaped* rather than *found*, one among many which men have made. In the end, the pragmatists tell us, what matters is our loyalty to other human beings clinging together against the dark, not our hope of getting things right.[45]

For scholars exploring points of congruency between Postmodern thought and the Christian faith, Rorty's ideas are a double-edged sword. To be sure, Christian theologians must reject his insistence that an objective authority transcendent above humanity cannot be found. Christianity is predicated upon belief in a transcendent God and the metanarrative of God's dealings with humanity. In Rorty's proclamation of the importance of community, however, Christians may find common ground. The impact of individualism, which has arisen from the tenets of Modernity, has been especially negative within Western Christianity. Rorty's call to recognize that humanity exists primarily in community is closely aligned with scriptural teaching on believers as the Body of Christ.[46] Rorty's work serves as a strong correction to the unscriptural individualistic tendencies that run unfettered through the contemporary Western Church.

Summary

Through the writings of these various representatives of the philosophical underpinnings of Postmodernity, we can see the beginnings of the Postmodern movement. Lyotard brings clarity to the definition of Postmodernity, and suggests that Postmoderns would never accept metanarratives justified by way of Modernistic rationalistic principles. Foucault challenges the notion of the disinterested knower, and brings the subjectivism associated with existentialism to a new level. Derrida takes aim at the long-held assumptions of logocentrism, and leaves many wondering about the point of reading at all, if authorial intent is discarded entirely as a signpost for truth. Rorty assaults the recent Western focus on the individual with his emphasis on the place of the person within the community, and the importance of the individual story. Each of these

45. Rorty, "Pragmatism," 166. Emphasis in original.
46. See, for example, 1 Cor 12:12–31.

writers has contributed to the current trends of thought common within Postmodernism.

VARIETIES OF POSTMODERNISM

Some scholars have surveyed the vast array of ideas and concepts associated with Postmodernity and isolated the differing approaches based on the degree of change from Modernity. David Ray Griffin et al. have proposed four varieties of Postmodernism.[47]

Deconstructive Postmodernism, also referred to as *Ultramodernism*, holds that an objective approach to the facts of experience is impossible. All experience is, by nature, subjective. It therefore denies the objectivity of foundationalism, and refuses to acknowledge the presence of certain basic or foundational truths upon which humanity can objectively base reasoning. Language is not based upon, nor does it refer to, objective facts; it can refer only to other writings. Essentially, Deconstructive Postmodernism "overcomes the modern worldview through an anti-worldview: it deconstructs or eliminates the ingredients necessary for a worldview, such as God, self, purpose, meaning, a real world, and truth as correspondence."[48]

Liberationist Postmodernism focuses more upon the social and political form of Modernism rather than the philosophical foundation. In terms of social structures formed under Modernist thought, it is reactionary and seeks transformation. The liberation motif is found through a variety of modern struggles, and may be described as gay, black, feminist, or third world. Although not as insistent in its rejection of the search for absolute truth as the supporters of Deconstruction, it does not value consistency or normative truth, as did Modernism. According to David Ray Griffin, supporters of liberationist Postmodernism such as Harvey Cox may not debate "whether an objective analysis of the facts of experience undermines the modern worldview. But he does argue that theologians should not be constrained by the cultural mind-set that has been shaped by this worldview."[49]

---

47. Griffin, "Introduction: Varieties of Postmodern Theology," 1–7. See also Oden, *After Modernity . . . What?*; and Dockery, "The Challenge of Postmodernism."

48. Griffin, "Introduction to SUNY Series," xii.

49. Griffin, "Introduction: Varieties of Postmodern Theology," 4.

Constructive Postmodernism seeks to reconstruct the Modern world-view, largely via Process thought, attempting to integrate and reconcile the diverse facets of human experience (i.e., ethical, religious, aesthetic, and scientific intuitions) into one coherent explanatory scheme.[50] It calls for comprehensive thinking in the face of Modernity's inability to bring intelligible understanding of the world. Though rejecting metaphysics as a valid building block, constructive Postmodernists still strive for the construction of a new worldview. John B. Cobb states, "We disagree that the breakdown of the Enlightenment conceptuality displays the limits of conceptual thought in general. Before abandoning the wider quest for intelligibility and understanding, we propose that we should test the usefulness of other conceptualities."[51]

Conservative or Restorationist Postmodernism holds that there is much in the Pre-modern and Modern worldviews worth preserving. Perhaps more pragmatic than the other streams of Postmodernity, conservatives recognize that Modernity has changed aspects of our worldview that are difficult to ignore or move beyond. It often seeks to reconstruct theology by blending what is viewed as best in Modernity with the promise of Postmodern thought. While recognizing the importance of the individual and place of reason within society as trumpeted by Modernism, Conservative Postmodernism seeks to move beyond the abstract individual to the real human being, vested not only with reason, but also with the full sensory experience of life itself.[52]

POSTMODERNITY: THE KEY TENETS

As is apparent, the Christian approach to Postmodernity depends somewhat on the variety of the worldview under discussion. Despite the varying reactions to Modernity discernable within Postmodernity, however, there are several key themes present within almost all Postmodern conversation. I will now examine five such tenets before moving towards a more detailed appraisal of Postmodernity from a Christian perspective.[53]

50. Center for Process Studies, "What is Process Thought?"

51. Cobb, "Constructive Postmodernism."

52. Lawler, "Conservative Postmodernism, Postmodern Conservatism."

53. I am indebted in part for the breakdown of categories to Jaichandran and Madhav, "Pentecostal Spirituality in a Postmodern World," 45–49.

Anti-foundationalism[54]

In the Postmodern mind, knowledge is uncertain. It therefore abandons foundationalism—the idea that knowledge can be built upon the basis of irrefutable first principles and basic truths, which lead ultimately to God himself, and upon which rational thought and progress can be based.[55] The Moderns assume that values are not merely a product of the human intellect, but rather are embedded in a reality that transcends us. This transcendent reality guarantees that truth exists; humanity does not create truth, but discovers it through reason. Postmoderns discard the Enlightenment assumption that truth is certain and therefore entirely rational.[56] Grenz observes, "The postmodern mind refuses to limit truth to its rational dimension and thus dethrones the human intellect as the arbiter of truth. There are other valid paths to knowledge besides reason, say the postmoderns, including the emotions, experience, and the intuition."[57]

Deconstruction of Language

For the Postmodern, metanarratives are inherently suspect. As Jaichandran and Madhav note, "This is the essence of deconstructionism—the knocking down of would-be big stories (worldviews with universalistic pretensions), often through listening to the local understandings of truth of minority communities."[58] Overarching universal narratives, which connect with all of humankind (such as the biblical story of creation), are discarded out of hand. For the supporter of Deconstruction, all meaning is created by the individual; the reality of one is as real as that of another, for we create our own realities. Though rejecting metanarratives as the

54. Henry considers this "[t]he one epistemic premise shared by all postmodernists. . . ." "Postmodernism: The New Spectre?," 42.

55. See Erickson, *Truth or Consequences*, 252–72, for an excellent discussion of Foundationalism, Postmodernity, and Christianity. See also Depaul, *Resurrecting Old-Fashioned Foundationalism*.

56. Wallace asserts, "Concerning reason, postmodernists shun modernist views which inflate reason to the status of an entirely dependent, neutral, unbiased and objective instrument with which truth can and will be found." "The Real Issue."

57. Grenz, *A Primer on Postmodernism*, 7.

58. Jaichandran and Madhav, "Pentecostal Spirituality in a Postmodern World," 46. See also Grenz, who states: "[T]he community of participation is crucial to identity formation. A sense of personal identity develops through the telling of a personal narrative, which is always embedded in the story of the communities in which we participate." *A Primer on Postmodernism*, 168.

universal stories of humanity, many Postmoderns accentuate the place of oral traditions, narratives, and stories within the community as essential to ongoing human communication.[59]

In terms of communication, Deconstruction declares that contradictions are inherent in all discourse; the "true" meaning cannot be discovered. Readers must take an active role in determining subjective meaning. According to Veith, "Postmodernist theories begin with the assumption that language cannot render truths about the world in an objective way. Language, by its very nature, shapes what we think. Since language is a cultural creation, meaning is ultimately (again) a social construction."[60]

Inherent in the practice of Deconstruction is a hermeneutic of suspicion. Thomas C. Oden explains:

> By deconstruction, we mean the dogged application of a hermeneutic of suspicion to any given text, where one finds oneself always over against the text, always asking the sceptical question about the text, asking what self-deception or bad faith might be unconsciously motivating a particular conceptuality.[61]

The Denial of Absolute Truth: The Importance of Experience

In the Modern mind, absolute truth is simply "out there," available for discovery by the persistent truth-seeker. For the Postmodern, truth does not exist outside of subjective experience; therefore, no version of truth is greater than any other. Some forms of Postmodernism are inherently pluralistic—some Postmodernists believe absolute truth does not exist. The Postmodern mind rejects the Enlightenment notion that knowledge is objective. Grenz views Postmodern reality as "relative, indeterminate, and participatory."[62]

---

59. Erickson, *Truth or Consequences*, 202. Grigg suggests that "postmodernism [is] not a rejection of metanarrative itself, but [is] *a transitional phase rejecting the metanarratives of an integrated Western worldview for the emergence of new integrations in the global/local culture.*" "The Spirit of Christ and the Postmodern City," chapter 14, 7. Emphasis in original.

60. Veith, *Postmodern Times*, 51. See also Adams, "Toward a Theological Understanding of Postmodernism."

61. Oden, *Two Worlds*, 79.

62. Grenz, *A Primer on Postmodernism*, 7.

[handwritten marginalia: Reminiscent of Apophaticism]

Virtual Reality

Reflecting on the Postmodern view of human existence, Francis A. Schaeffer (1912–84) laments, "Since our existence has no meaning and we are not connected to history or its values by any binding truths, no one can be quite certain where reality and non-reality start and stop."[63] A key ingredient here is the blurring of fact with fiction, often through the participation by the individual in the virtual world via technology—all reality is virtual reality. Veith wryly observes:

> Thus the life of the mind has a new model—not Socrates searching for truth through dialogues in the marketplace, not Augustine contemplating his own life in light of Scripture, not Newton scrutinizing nature with mathematical rigor, not the scientist working in the lab or the historian sifting through archival evidence. The new model for intellectual achievement is a dazed couch potato watching TV.[64]

Decimation of Individuality/Promotion of Community

For Richard Rorty in particular, external forces create the self, to the extent that searching for one's inner self is pointless—it does not exist. Postmoderns have decreased the prominence of the individual in favor of the importance of community. Rorty's strong emphasis on community and society denies humanity its traditional place within Modernism as the center of the universe. Grenz notes:

> The postmodern worldview operates with a community-based understanding of truth. It affirms that whatever we accept as truth and even the way we envision truth are dependent on the community in which we participate. Further, and far more radically, the postmodern worldview affirms that this relativity extends beyond our *perceptions* of truth to its essence: there is no absolute truth; rather truth is relative to the community in which we participate.
>
> On the basis of this assumption, postmodern thinkers have given up the Enlightenment quest for any one universal, supracultural, timeless truth. They focus instead on what is held to be true within a specific community. They maintain that truth consists in

63. Jaichandran and Madhav, "Pentecostal Spirituality in a Postmodern World," 47. See also Veith, *Postmodern Times*, 61.

64. Veith, *Postmodern Times*, 61. See also Myers, *All God's Children and Blue Suede Shoes*, who demonstrates the impact of television culture on all aspects of society—even academia.

the ground rules that facilitate the well-being of the community in which one participates. In keeping with this emphasis, postmodern society tends to be a communal society.[65]

Veith concurs:

As the mass culture becomes more and more impersonal, individuals lose themselves in the mass mind or in highly segmented groups. The human is lost. . . . The anti-humanism of the postmodernists cannot sustain any of the so-called "human values." Freedom, individuality, self-worth, dignity—these are social constructions. Empathy, kindness, altruism, love—these are masks for oppression. The individual human being is swallowed up by culture; cultures are swallowed up by nature.[66]

With this philosophical presupposition, we may conclude that humanity becomes no more important than any other living thing—plant or animal. Naturally, the theological implications of human life without special significance are enormous.

POSTMODERNISM AND EVANGELICALISM: A CRITIQUE[67]

As one might expect, Evangelicalism (including Pentecostalism) has not responded enthusiastically to several of the basic tenets of Postmodernity.[68] At its core, Postmodern thought contradicts key Evangelical beliefs at crucial points. Some Postmodern individuals, for example, believe that all truth is relative and subjective; the foundation of the Evangelical Gospel is that absolute truth may be found in God himself, revealed through the life of Christ and the Scriptures. A key text here

65. Grenz, *A Primer on Postmodernism*, 8. Emphasis in original.

66. Veith, *Postmodern Times*, 72, 79.

67. Before delving into the more particular issues between Pentecostalism and Postmodernism, this section first explores the areas of compatibility and contrast between Postmodernism and conservative Christianity, of which Pentecostalism is a part. While I will not address concerns specific to Pentecostalism, much of this discussion will resonate with students of Pentecostalism.

68. On Postmodernism as a whole, some Evangelical scholars are more accepting. See, for example, Raschke, *The Next Reformation*, who argues: "[E]vangelical Christianity made its own unholy alliance with Cartesian rationalism and British evidentialism as far back as the seventeenth century, taking the wrong turn at a decisive juncture and thereby compromising the original spirit of the Reformation. . . . [T]he postmodern turn in Western thought widens the prospects for evangelical Christianity to flourish once again as a progressive rather than reactionary force in the present-day world." 9

So the issue for me is this: while knowledge is relative, Truth is not. Knowledge may be judged better or worse; informed or misinformed. The natural world is relevant in fact part of the scientific canons of validity obtain. But is this also so of values? The answer lies in our inner nature—which is in fact part of the natural order of validity obtain.

for many is John 14:6: "Jesus answered, 'I am the way and the truth and the life.'"

On other issues, such as the rejection of rationalism, Postmodern thought has something significant to contribute to segments of Evangelicalism largely overrun with rationalist tendencies. Given the prevalence of Postmodern thought within Western society and the tremendous impact of Christian values upon the same, it is inevitable that these two movements should intersect (and collide) at key junctures.

One may well ask, with Millard Erickson, whether Postmodern influence has pervaded Evangelical thought to the extent that an evaluation of the former by the latter is necessitated.[69] Quite apart from substantial anecdotal evidence, a variety of studies conducted by the Barna Research Group conclude that Postmodern thinking has made tremendous inroads into Evangelical thought. For example, a 1991 survey, in which the organization presented the statement, "There is no such thing as absolute truth; different people can define truth in conflicting ways and still be correct," found that a majority of those who identified themselves as Evangelical Christians either agreed or strongly agreed with the statement. As Erickson suggests, this reveals the striking impact of Postmodernity upon Evangelicalism.[70]

Areas of Beneficial Interaction[71]

To be sure, the impact of Postmodernity upon Evangelical Christianity is neither entirely positive nor negative. Despite calls in some Christian circles for a wholesale rejection of Postmodern thought, I believe we can learn much from the Postmodern critique of the Modernist thought so prevalent in much of Western Christianity. There is beneficial interaction between Evangelicalism and Postmodernism.

The Conditioned Nature of Knowledge. The supporters of deconstruction within Postmodernity have correctly observed that time, place, culture, and past experience influence our perception of truth and our interpretive conclusions. Many Christians, however, continue to pursue the Modern concept of truly objective knowledge. These individuals read

---

69. Erickson, *The Postmodern World*, 59.

70. Barna, *The Barna Report*, esp. 84–85. See Erickson, *The Postmodern World*, 62.

71. This section is loosely based on Erickson's observations. *Truth or Consequences*, chapter 10.

into the text what they are attempting to interpret objectively, as they are often unaware of their own presuppositions formed by culture and experience. The end result can be anything but truly objective.[72]

The Limitations of Foundationalism. Practically, Postmoderns are also correct in their rejection of Foundationalism as a common ground for communication about issues of faith and truth. Concepts that might be considered intuitive and self-evident by Evangelicals are in many cases no longer viewed as such by society as a whole. Christians must discover new means of finding common ground with others; natural theology based on a rational demonstration of God's existence will no longer suffice.

The Necessity of a Hermeneutic of Suspicion. Postmodernists often employ a hermeneutic of suspicion, asking whether persons have vested interest in the position they propose. Erickson suggests that in our interpretive methods we must apply a hermeneutic of suspicion to our own beliefs and doctrines, recognizing that we are far more likely to believe statements that concur with our belief systems than those that do not.[73] Postmodern thought, especially that of Jacques Derrida, is valuable, as it helps us recognize the inherent contradictions in many cherished arguments. While Modernity was often content to present summaries of debated issues as if there were no possible objections, an awareness of apparent contradictions within any argument or interpretation may be viewed as healthy, particularly in terms of academic integrity.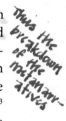

The Role of the Community. Postmodern thought has made a significant contribution to church life in particular through its emphasis on the importance of community. Reacting to the Modern exaltation of the individual, Postmodernists have once again placed the individual back in significant connection with others. A writer for the *Sydney Morning Herald* describes this trend among Australian youth:

> [Today's youth] are members of a generation who spend all day together at school, then get on the bus to go home and ring each other up on the mobile phone, or send a stream of text messages to each other. "Where are you now? Who are you with?" they inquire solicitously, while their parents pay the bill for this flow of continuous contact. Then, when they arrive home, they hop onto the

---

72. Erickson suggests that we should "be willing to allow ourselves to feel the full force of the postmodernists' contention. This includes the contention that there are alternative logics." *Truth or Consequences*, 189.

73. Ibid., 200.

internet to link up again in a chat room, or via email. . . . "They are the generation that beeps and hums," one of their fathers recently remarked, and so they are. They are the generation who, having grown up in an era of unprecedentedly rapid change, have intuitively understood that they are each other's most precious resource for coping with the inherent uncertainties of life. Their desire to connect, and to stay connected, will reshape this society. They are the harbingers of a new sense of community, a new tribalism, that will change everything from our old-fashioned respect for privacy to the way we conduct our relationships and build our houses. The era of individualism is not dead yet, but the intimations of its mortality are clear.[74]

Postmodernity strives to be aware of the impact of the community and our experiences with others on our own interpretation of issues and events. For the Christian, this concurs with the New Testament emphasis on the individual as part of the Body of Christ, and acknowledges the significant fact that most of Scripture was written not to individual believers, but to Christians who are part of a larger body of believers.[75]

The Importance of Narratives. For Pentecostals in particular, the Postmodern emphasis on the value of narratives rings true with what has historically been a Pentecostal focus. As Erickson notes, a majority of the world's cultures still prefer oral rather than written communication, and find it easier to remember key pieces of information in story form, rather than rational, well-argued discourse.[76] Having gleaned the "distinctive doctrines" of subsequence and initial evidence from the Acts narratives, Pentecostals as a whole will benefit from the Postmodern focus upon the importance of the story.

Areas of Incongruity[77]

As one might expect with an entity as challenging as Postmodernity, there are numerous points of contention with traditional Evangelical thought. Though the ideas presented below are seemingly contradictory to key

74. Mackay, "One for all and all for one."

75. See footnote 46 above.

76. Erickson, *Truth or Consequences*, 202.

77. See ibid., chapter 11. See also Davis, "Can There Be an 'Orthodox' Postmodern Theology?," 111–23; and McQuilkin and Mullen, "The Impact of Postmodern Thinking on Evangelical Hermeneutics, 69–82.

aspects of Evangelical dogma, each presents an opportunity for a fresh Evangelical look at the concept in question.

Deconstruction. Taken to their logical conclusion, many varieties of Deconstruction pose significant challenges for Christians. Based on the premise that there is contradiction inherent in each system of thought, this approach often presupposes that a logically consistent presentation of the system of truth embodied by the Christian faith is impossible. Through its efforts to make the reader aware of the inherent contradictions in final and absolute statements based on rationalism, all systems of thought are thus deconstructed, and collapse into the sum of their contradictions, rendering each meaningless. The challenge for the Postmodern thinker is to deconstruct the approach of deconstruction; this approach, like many others, must crumble beneath the weight of its apparent contradictions if it is believed to be credible.[78]

Linguistic Challenges and Relativism. According to Robert McQuilkin and Bradford Mullen, Postmodern thought, as it interacts with literary criticism, linguistics, and communications theory, has argued as follows:

> Language cannot accurately communicate thought to another person's mind, and with time and cultural distance the attempt becomes ever more futile. . . . The inadequacy of language is not necessarily bad because meaning is constituted of a combination of what is out there (objects and events, including the words of others) and what is in here (my own subjective sense.) Though the words of others play a formative role, the controlling element is what I bring to the text. And the outcome of that mix is all the reality there is. Thus meaning is relative, particularly relative to my present subjective perceptions.[79]

Evangelicals take exception to the Postmodern emphasis on the weakness of language to communicate, and the resultant rampant subjectivism. While the renewed recognition of the significant role our presuppositions play in our hermeneutics has been beneficial, many Christians

78. Erickson insists that the approach of deconstruction should itself be subject to deconstruction. He notes that Derrida disagrees, equating Deconstruction with justice, which can never be deconstructed. *Truth or Consequences*, 205. Derrida writes: "Justice in itself, if such a thing exists, outside or beyond law, is not deconstructable. No more than deconstruction itself, if such a thing exists. Deconstruction is justice." "Force of Law," 14–15.

79. McQuilkin and Mullen, "The Impact of Postmodern Thinking on Evangelical Hermeneutics," 71.

are uncomfortable with identifying our personal version of "meaning" with reality, which we believe exists independently of our perceptions.[80] Grenz notes:

> As Christians, we can go only so far with Derrida, for example, in his unrelenting attack on the "metaphysics of presence" and "logocentricism." In contrast to postmodern thought, we believe that there is a unifying center to reality. More specifically, we acknowledge that this center has appeared in Jesus of Nazareth, who is the eternal Word present among us.
>
> Therefore, we agree that in this world we will witness the struggle among conflicting narratives and interpretations of reality. But we add that although all interpretations are in some sense invalid, they cannot all be *equally* valid. We believe that conflicting interpretations can be evaluated according to a criterion that in some sense transcends them all.[81]

Rejection of Absolute Truth. With subjectivism raised to a new level, absolute truth is the logical casualty of the Postmodern system of thinking. A solid belief in absolute truth depends in part upon the presupposition that objectivity is possible in determining what is true. Contrary to the Modern perception of truth as static, objective, and waiting to be discovered, in the Postmodern mindset, truth is subjective. For the Evangelical, whose system of beliefs is based on the acceptance of God himself as Truth, as revealed both in Christ and through the Scriptures, the rejection of absolute truth by Postmoderns could not be more significant. Without joining themselves to the subjectivity of truth promoted by those of the Postmodern mindset, believers must nonetheless learn to present the absolute truth of the Gospel in a manner easily comprehended by those living with a more subjective frame of mind.

Rejection of the Metanarrative. The Bible presents the story of God and his interaction with creation and humanity. This universal story, or metanarrative, has been carefully recorded in Scripture, and is proclaimed to be relevant to all humanity, at all times, in all locations. Evangelicals believe this story to be the revelation of God himself, and he has thus inspired the writers of Scripture to record his thoughts. For Christians, there is an objective reality above all others—God himself. It is this reality, informed by the scriptural record of God's metanarrative, which in

---

80. Ibid.

81. Grenz, *A Primer on Postmodernism*, 164–5. Emphasis in original.

turn informs our ethics, morality, and understanding of truth. For some Postmodernists, however, no such metanarrative exists. Truth exists only as individuals within community find it subjectively. Again, the challenges of this Postmodern way of thinking are significant for Evangelicals who wish to promote the Gospel in a language relevant to Postmoderns, while not subscribing to all tenets of Postmodern thought. For scholars such as Millard Erickson, the Postmodern rejection of the Christian metanarrative is the most compelling reason to view the two as incompatible.

> I would contend that the universal element in the Christian message, the claim that there is one God, one creator, one ruler of the human race, is so deeply imbedded in the testimony of the biblical documents that it cannot be wrenched from Christianity without destroying the very organism. While postmodern evangelical Christians may think the marriage with postmodernism is possible, most non-Christian postmodernists do not share that sanguine understanding of the interrelationship.[82]

CONCLUSION

It has been shown that Postmodernity is the natural philosophical outcome of a generation of thinkers disillusioned by the empty promises of optimistic liberalism. By carefully tracing the development of Postmodern thought from Premodernity, through Modernity, and into Postmodernity, I have clearly shown the philosophical underpinnings of this movement.

The impact of several key philosophers on Postmodern thought has been explored. Jean-François Lyotard's rejection of metanarratives, based on the Modern principles of rationalism, has been influential, just as Michel Foucault's belief in the power of the subjective self and the impossibility of objectively discovering truth has been instrumental in shaping the Postmodern mindset. Jacques Derrida's objection to the use of language, as traditionally understood, led to his promotion of Deconstruction, with which all theologians must contend, specifically in the practice of hermeneutics. Richard Rorty's insistence that truth is simply based on what works, and not on any type of belief in absolutes, has

---

82. Erickson, *Postmodern World*, 78. I argue that Postmodern thought need not be accepted as a whole; indeed many of those who consider themselves Postmodern do not subscribe to the entire variety of Postmodern thought as outlined herein. One may well embrace the Postmodern tendency to value experience and community without surrendering the entire Christian metanarrative.

begun to permeate Western society. Christian theologians who hold to absolute truth as found in the revelation of Jesus Christ must be prepared to contend with this pragmatic theory of truth, or be deemed irrelevant to the thinking of this culture.

The key tenets of Postmodernity have been delineated. These include the rejection of Foundationalism, the concept that all knowledge and truth is founded upon key first principles ultimately leading to God himself. Metanarratives are inherently suspect, though smaller stories of life within community are applauded. The concept of absolute truth as attainable has been discarded; truth is purely subjective. The exalted place of the self so prevalent within Modernity has been replaced by the devaluing of the autonomous self in favor of both the human community and biological life as a whole.

Evangelical Christians have found much to celebrate within Postmodern thought, but also have observed areas that cause grave concern. The Postmodern tendency to highly view the role of existing presuppositions in our ultimate determination of meaning is instructive for believers, as is the inherent hermeneutic of suspicion. The insistence that language cannot be used to convey truth from one to another must be resisted, for the authority of Scripture as the guide for the life and faith of the believer thus hangs in the balance. Postmoderns speak the language of anti-foundationalism; Christians must learn new approaches to find common ground with others, while adhering to the foundation that has been laid in Jesus Christ.

The important place of community within Postmodernity is a valuable reminder to Evangelicals that the individualism so rampant in Western culture was never biblical; the value placed upon individual stories and narratives speaks to the essential oral traditions of Christianity itself. Evangelicals must persist in their belief in absolute truth, as found in God himself, and revealed in Christ and the Scriptures. Similarly, Christians cannot abandon their confidence in the story of God and humanity as presented in the Scriptures, despite the Postmodern rejection of metanarratives. Our understanding of both soteriology and eschatology rests upon the story of God and his plan for humanity.

Holding similar core doctrinal values as Evangelicals, Pentecostals would generally agree with the above assessment. For Pentecostals, however, Postmodern thought presents unique challenges and opportunities. In many ways, Pentecostalism may be observed holding to several key

Postmodern concepts—well before they were characterized and described by prominent Postmodern thinkers. While disregarding many of the more offensive Postmodern claims as they impact Christianity, Pentecostalism may still find within its roots key elements of Postmodern thought. Inasmuch as Pentecostalism arose as a reaction to Modernity, early Pentecostal hermeneutics typically eschewed Modern hermeneutics. Did early Pentecostal hermeneutics share approaches similar in focus to what is known today as Postmodern thought? Can Postmodern thought be found in early Pentecostalism? Chapter 3 addresses these and other issues.

In this ch. N— selects out important themes in the P/M mindset, then sets them against an Evangelical grid.

3

The Role of Experience, Rationalism, and Narratives in Early Pentecostal Hermeneutics

An ounce of testimony is often more helpful to hungry hearts than a pound of doctrinal teaching.[1]

A. S. COPLEY

God, the church, and the world are tired of listening to these modern preachers while they whittle intellectual shavings and theological chips. They want REALITY, a message from under the Throne, delivered by one who opens his mouth to be filled by God, with burning, clinching truth. This message is now going forth.[2]

CHARLES FOX PARHAM

The strength of Pentecostal traditioning lies in its powerful narratives. Through their "testimonies" of God's great work Pentecostals have quite successfully spread their experience to the masses. . . . Unfortunately, for much of their history Pentecostals have been better at telling their story than explaining it to their children.[3]

SIMON CHAN

THIS WORK HAS NOW explored several key attributes of Postmodernism, particularly as it relates to Christianity. In describing Postmodernity as a philosophical movement which has rejected rationalism and placed

1. Copley, in *Way of Faith*, 5.
2. Parham, *The Everlasting Gospel*, 76. Emphasis in original.
3. Chan, *Pentecostal Theology and the Christian Spiritual Tradition*, 20.

high value on the role of experience, as well as narratives as means of communicating that experience, I have necessarily begun the process of noting the convergent viewpoints between Postmodernity and Pentecostalism.

Undoubtedly all of human life is built upon experience, as we encounter our world, react to what we discover, and interact with those around us. Modernism has downplayed the importance of experience, particularly in terms of an epistemological approach to defining truth. Through Modernism, reason became king; truth could not be discovered, except through the brain's cerebral cortex. The reaction against Modern trends was in part the reason for the birth of Pentecostalism,[4] which therefore placed high value upon the role of experience in the Christian life and rejected the exaltation of reason as the arbiter of truth in the Christian context. Writing of the predecessors of Pentecostalism, Rick M. Nañez notes:

> [T]he giants of nineteenth-century evangelicalism preached to the masses, witnessing the rebirth of hundreds of thousands of souls. As the lost were wooed down sawdust trails, they deposited their sins—*and often their intellects*—at the foot of the altar, returning to their seats with the two commodities most prized among American believers—*Jesus* and their *feelings*.[5]

As will be further demonstrated, contra the Postmodernist, early Pentecostals employed the use of a metanarrative to bring coherence to their self-understanding, but, like Postmoderns, they also relied heavily upon community-based sharing of personal "stories" or "testimonies."

EARLY PENTECOSTAL EXPERIENCE AND REJECTION OF RATIONALISM

The late eighteenth century witnessed a dramatic increase of interest in the person and work of the Holy Spirit among Christians, who had previously expressed little interest in the third person of the Trinity. Indeed, as C. I. Scofield pointed out:

4. It is well documented that Pentecostalism arose from within a larger reaction by the Holiness movement to the excessive rationalism found in Protestant circles of the late 1800s. See, for example, Dayton, *The Theological Roots of Pentecostalism*; Nañez, *Full Gospel, Fractured Minds*, esp. 89–123; Noll, *The Scandal of the Evangelical Mind*; Hoftstader, *Anti-intellectualism in American Life*; and Marsden, *Fundamentalism and American Culture*.

5. Nañez, *Full Gospel, Fractured Minds*, 97. Emphasis in original.

> We are in the midst of a marked revival of interest in the Person and work of the Holy Spirit. More books, booklets and tracts upon that subject have issued from the press during the last eighty years than in all previous time since the invention of printing. Indeed, within the last twenty years more has been written and said upon the doctrine of the Holy Spirit than in the preceding eighteen hundred years.[6]

Early Pentecostals were not necessarily known as great theologians. In fact, many were anti-intellectual,[7] and were not shy about asserting the fact. However, some observers are surprised to note just how prolific these early Pentecostals were in terms of the various newspapers, magazines, and books, which they produced with the express purpose of explaining this new outpouring of the Holy Spirit.[8] In the years following the Azusa Street Revival, Pentecostals were concerned to make sense of their new experience, and were thoughtful in their responses to the question asked of them, as it was of Peter at Pentecost: "What does this mean?" (Acts 2:12). Significantly, there is therefore an abundance of primary literature available. For example, from 1906–8 William J. Seymour (1870–1922) edited a newsprint publication, *The Apostolic Faith*. This monthly offering included articles by several Pentecostal leaders, as well as testimonies of what God was doing at Azusa Street and throughout the world. In 1915 Seymour published *The Doctrines and Discipline of the Azusa Street Apostolic Mission of Los Angeles, Cal. with Scripture Readings*, a compendium of the theology and practices of the Mission to that point in history.[9]

Charles F. Parham (1873–1929) was equally prolific, publishing *Kol Kare Bomidbar: A Voice Crying in the Wilderness* (1902) and *The Everlasting Gospel* (c. 1919), to explain his views on Christian doctrine,

---

6. Scofield, *A Mighty Wind*, 9.

7. The Pentecostal, Rick M. Nañez, is the author of an excellent book on Pentecostalism and the life of the mind, *Full Gospel, Fractured Minds*. He convincingly argues that an anti-intellectual bias continues in contemporary Pentecostalism. While I argue that Pentecostals must abandon the wholesale acceptance of Evangelical hermeneutics as their own, this work does not contend that they must return to a pre-scholarly hermeneutic, nor does it support the latent anti-intellectualism still prevalent in the movement. Rather, I believe that one can reject the hegemony of reason as the determinant of truth and still develop with appreciation God's gift of the intellect.

8. See Wacker, *Heaven Below*, ix.

9. Seymour, *The Apostolic Faith* and *The Doctrines and Discipline*.

including the Pentecostal experience.[10] Others, such as George Floyd Taylor (1881–1934), David Wesley Myland (1858–1943), Ambrose Jessup Tomlinson (1865–1943), and Joseph Hillery King (1869–1946), each published works in the ten years following the initial Azusa outpouring, outlining his beliefs and practices associated with this new movement.[11]

Douglas Jacobsen, in *Thinking in the Spirit: Theologies of the Early Pentecostal Movement*, argues that early Pentecostals, while attempting to follow the predominant model of Protestant systematic theology in their explanations, recognized the need to bring experience and words together in a manner that was uniquely Pentecostal.

> Most leaders of the early Pentecostal movement were, of course, suspicious of theology done in the traditional way. Too often, they thought, theology had lost touch with the Spirit and had become dry and brittle, incapable of conveying the living truth of God's love to anyone. . . . At the same time, however, each [leader] was convinced that thought was a necessary part of Pentecostal faith— theology was necessary and unavoidable. . . .
>
> These authors never implied that they had to give up part of their pentecostal faith to write in a systematic and logical manner, and there is no evidence that their relatively systematic style of writing forced them to set aside certain pentecostal topics simply because they didn't logically fit with everything else. They were writing as pentecostals to pentecostals for pentecostal theological purposes while trying to be just as thorough and systematic as their non-pentecostal theological peers.[12]

From this early literature, we are able to determine the attitudes of early Pentecostal leadership towards the role of experience in the latest outpouring of the Holy Spirit, and the place of reason in determining truth from error, as differing doctrines and explanations swirled around the new movement. This chapter surveys the writings of some of the earliest Pentecostal leaders, presenting their views on the place of experience and reason within Pentecostalism.

10. Parham, *Kol Kare Bomidbar* and *The Everlasting Gospel*.

11. See Taylor, *The Spirit and the Bride*; Myland, *The Latter Rain Covenant*; Tomlinson, *The Last Great Conflict*; and King, *From Passover to Pentecost*.

12. Jacobsen, *Thinking in the Spirit*, 2, 7.

Charles Fox Parham

Charles Parham may rightly be called the founder of Pentecostal theology, for he first developed the distinctive Pentecostal doctrine of *glossolalia* as the initial evidence of Spirit Baptism.[13] For Parham, tongues speaking was the necessary evidence that one had been baptized in the Holy Spirit; without this evidence, one could not consider the experience valid.[14] He states: "[S]peaking in other tongues is an inseparable part of the Baptism of the Holy Spirit distinguishing it from all previous works; and . . . no one has received [the] Baptism of the Holy Spirit who has not a Bible evidence to show for it."[15]

Parham, who was born in Muscatine, Iowa, encountered numerous health problems early in life.[16] As an infant he contracted a virus, which permanently stunted his growth; at the age of nine, he was stricken with rheumatic fever, which weakened him for the rest of his life. Following several brief pastorates, he founded Bethel Bible School in Topeka, Kansas. He writes:

> Its unique features and teachings became subjects of the daily pa-
> pers throughout the land. Its only text-book was the Bible; its only
> object utter abandonment in obedience to the commandments of
> Jesus, however unconventional and impractical this might seem to
> the world today.[17]

Influenced by various Holiness teachers concerning the doctrine of Spirit Baptism, Parham directed his students to Acts 2, in search of a verifiable proof for the baptism in the Holy Spirit. "The main object of this study was to discover the real Bible evidence of this Baptism so that we might know and obtain it, instead of being confused by the chaotic claims

---

13. Ibid., 18. Letson disagrees, suggesting that it was William J. Seymour's "vision, leadership, teaching and drive," which "kept the whole thing on track." Letson concludes that while Seymour is the founder of modern Pentecostalism, Parham initiated a new paradigm shift within Christianity known as Pentecostalism. Letson, "Pentecostalism as a Paradigm Shift," 104–17.

14. Jacobsen, *Thinking in the Spirit*, 18–19.

15. Parham, *Kol Kare Bomidbar*, 35.

16. On Parham, see Goff, *Fields White Unto Harvest*.

17. Parham, *Kol Kare Bomidbar*, 32. The reader will note the sense of pride in referring to the Bible as the "only textbook," and the impracticality of this choice in the eyes of the world.

of modern Holy Ghost teachers."[18] On January 1, 1901, a female student at the school, Agnes N. Ozman (1870–1937), experienced *glossolalia* as the expected "Bible evidence" of the baptism in the Holy Spirit, recognized by many as the first person to speak with tongues in the modern Pentecostal movement.[19] Shortly after, Parham and thirty-four other students had a similar experience. By 1905 Parham had launched a second Bible school, this one in Houston, Texas, as an outlet for his Pentecostal preaching. Among his notable students was William J. Seymour, who was to become the leader of the Azusa Street Revival in Los Angeles one year later.[20]

Parham's thoughts on the place of experience within Pentecostalism and his rejection of rationalism are woven throughout his works. Having been raised with few books, he considered himself fortunate, for he grew up "with no preconceived ideas, with no knowledge of what creeds and doctrines meant, not having any traditional spectacles upon the eyes to see through."[21] Jacobsen notes that Parham

> . . . was convinced that he, unlike many of his peers, brought no interpretive scheme to the Bible at all. He simply believed what the scriptures actually said, and later in life he mused that his naive ability to read the Bible fairly and accurately without any warped preconceptions had helped him "weather the theological gales" that had driven so many others into error.[22]

One of Parham's contributions to Pentecostal theology, which speaks of his rejection of rationalism, is his strong belief in *xenolalia*. God would speak through believers, via tongues, in whatever human language was needed to complete the missionary thrust before Christ's soon return. All believers who were properly baptized in the Spirit received this ability in small measure, although only those who were called to foreign places of service would develop the full gift of a foreign language. Missionaries could cease wasting time with language courses, and minister directly to those in need. Parham explains:

---

18. Ibid., 33–34.

19. Ozman's testimony concerning these events is found in LaBerge, *What God Hath Wrought*, 28–39; and Goff, *The Topeka Outpouring of 1901*, 103–52.

20. See Goff, "Parham, Charles Fox," 955–57.

21. Parham, *Kol Kare Bomidbar*, 12.

22. Jacobsen, *Thinking in the Spirit*, 21.

> [H]ow much better it would be for our modern missionaries to obey
> the injunction of Jesus to tarry for the same power; instead of wast-
> ing thousands of dollars, and often their lives in the vain attempt to
> become conversant in almost impossible tongues which the Holy
> Ghost could so freely speak. Knowing all languages, He could as
> easily speak through us one language as another were our tongues
> and vocal chords fully surrendered to His domination. . . .[23]

Although subsequent Pentecostal missionary experience proved
Parham's theory of *xenolalia* to be misguided, his views show the extent to
which early Pentecostal leaders had shaken off the shackles of Modernity,
and embraced new forms of thought and doctrine entirely unsupported
by scientific evidence.

In the years following the Azusa Street Revival, Parham continued
his work as a tireless promoter of the baptism in the Holy Spirit with the
evidence of tongues. Those he described as well educated, belonging to
established and respected congregations, often challenged him. His description of such challenges is telling:

> A Baptist preacher said to a friend of mine: "Now, don't become
> crazy about this. I have been through college, and I know it is im-
> possible for anybody to speak in other or foreign languages, unless
> he has learned them." This preacher had a Ph.D., D.D., and L.L.D.,
> on the rear end of his name and a Rev. in front of it. My friend
> came to me in trouble and said: "What shall I do about this?"
>
> I challenged that preacher to come to my school for just one
> week. I promised him a post-graduate course that would enable
> him to put another degree on the end of his name. I would have
> gotten him so humble before God, and so willing to let God use
> him, that he would have come out of the post-graduate course
> with A.S.S. on the end of his name. Could I have gotten him to
> become as humble as was Balaam's mule, God would have talked
> through him in tongues.[24]

Parham felt little need to debate correct hermeneutical approaches
when discussing his "Bible evidence" for the baptism of the Holy Spirit.
Nor did he wring his hands because support for Spirit Baptism was found,
not in the didactic teaching of Paul, but in the narratives of Luke alone.
For this early Pentecostal leader, the proof of tongues as the sign of Spirit

23. Parham, *Kol Kare Bomidbar*, 28.
24. Parham, *The Everlasting Gospel*, 67.

Baptism could not have been more plainly defended than Scripture had already recorded. "Remember, that it is an incontrovertible fact in Scripture that the Holy Ghost of promise was, and is today, accompanied with speaking in other tongues."[25] While scholars today might smile at such a strong assertion with little or no theological support, this was typical of early Pentecostal leaders. After all, the Holy Spirit was given as a glorious tool of witness, not to provide scholars a new topic of debate:

> The present Pentecost is not only given as the sign of a believer, the sign to unbelievers, the power to witness (prophesy) only in your own language, but in other tongues as the Spirit giveth utterance; but in these last days the Holy Spirit is sealing in the forehead and bestowing the power so that we can sing, pray, and preach "in the Spirit" as a "gift of tongues," not a gift of brains.
>
> God, the church, and the world are tired of listening to these modern preachers while they whittle intellectual shavings and theological chips. They want REALITY, a message from under the Throne, delivered by one who opens his mouth to be filled by God, with burning, clinching truth. This message is now going forth.[26]

William J. Seymour

William Seymour was born in Centerville, Louisiana, the eldest son of Simon and Phillis Seymour. Raised in poverty, by the time of his father's death in 1891 he had left Louisiana for work up North, in cities such as Memphis and Indianapolis. Seymour worked at various jobs, including porter and bartender. During his stint as a waiter in Indianapolis, he was converted to Christ and joined the local Methodist-Episcopal church.[27] He appears to have spent a brief period in Chicago, where it is hard to imagine that he did not come into contact with the racially progressive teachings of the great faith healer, John Alexander Dowie (1847–1907).[28]

By 1905, after several years of evangelistic and other Christian ministry, Seymour connected with Charles Parham, who accepted him as a student in his Houston Bible school. Due to local segregation laws, Seymour was permitted to listen to the lectures only from the hallway

25. Ibid., 75.

26. Ibid., 75–76.

27. Martin, *The Life and Ministry of William J. Seymour*, 68–70. See also Borlase, *William Seymour: A Biography*; and Shumway, "A Critical Study of 'The Gift of Tongues.'"

28. Martin, *The Life and Ministry of William J. Seymour*, 74–5.

outside the classroom. In February 1906 he was invited to pastor a small Holiness mission in Los Angeles. Armed with Parham's Spirit Baptism theology, Seymour arrived in Los Angeles shortly after. Finding himself quickly locked out of the new church by its Holiness founder, who was unenthusiastic about Seymour's new teachings, Seymour began a series of Bible studies at the home of Richard and Ruth Asberry on Bonnie Bray Avenue. Within weeks, several of the participants, including Seymour, had experienced the baptism in the Holy Spirit with the "Bible evidence" of speaking in tongues.[29]

Soon Seymour was forced to seek more spacious accommodations, quickly settling upon the former sanctuary of an African Methodist Episcopal church at 312 Azusa Street. The revival at the small mission burned brightly until mid-1908, and arose again in 1911, thereafter ceasing forever. At its peak, the mission was packed to capacity by the faithful, those seeking their own Pentecostal baptism, and critics who had come to solidify their opposition to this noisy and undignified movement. From the mission, the Pentecostal message and experience spread rapidly throughout the earth.[30] As the pastor of the Mission, Seymour effectively oversaw the revival that spawned today's Pentecostal movement. As such, his thoughts on the role of experience and the place of reason within the Christian faith are extremely important.

In general, leaders of the Azusa Street Revival such as Seymour were not enamored with theology; indeed, the official Azusa Street Mission publication, *The Apostolic Faith*, explained that the new Pentecostal message had clearly not been given to the outstanding academics of the time, but was accessible to the most ordinary and uneducated seeker.

> There have been those who have sought for the baptism and could not get it, because they did not come humbly as a little babe. They did not give up their doctrines and opinions; they did not empty out so they could get the filling. This is not revealed to our great theologians.[31]

29. Robeck, Jr., "Seymour, William Joseph," 1053–57.

30. For more on the history and impact of the Azusa Street Revival and the subsequent Pentecostal movement, see Robeck, *The Azusa Street Mission and Revival*; Hunter and Robeck, *The Azusa Street Revival and Its Legacy*; Owens, *The Azusa Street Revival*; Anderson, *An Introduction to Pentecostalism*; Hyatt, *Fire on the Earth*; Dempster et al., *The Globalization of Pentecostalism*; Valdez, *Fire on Azusa Street*; and Dayton, *The Theological Roots of Pentecostalism*.

31. Untitled, *The Apostolic Faith* 1, no. 10: 3.

For his part, Seymour recognized that sound biblical doctrine was essential to the preservation of the Revival, but struggled with those who attempted to explain theologically something which, in his mind, was an experience given by God to the whosoever will. This barely-educated preacher was unwilling to join those who wished to abandon doctrinal purity, and simply experience unity through the workings of the Holy Spirit. "They say, 'Let us all come together; if we are not one in doctrine, we can be one in spirit.' But, dear ones, we cannot all be one, except through the word of God."[32] Again, "We are measuring everything by the Word, every experience must measure up with the Bible. Some say that is going too far, but if we have lived too close to the Word, we will settle that with the Lord when we meet Him in the air."[33]

While striving for doctrinal purity, Seymour nonetheless realized that the Pentecostal baptism was not a matter of knowledge or education, but ultimately of hunger and faith. Theology had its purpose, chiefly to ensure doctrinal purity. When it came to the baptism in the Holy Spirit, however, Seymour and the Azusa Street Mission leaders saw little need to analyze theologically what was taking place. Again, one can quickly see that discussions concerning the validity of supporting this new experience from the narratives of Acts were never entertained. In fact, many leaders were of the impression that too much analysis would actually hinder the Spirit from moving, as he desired.

> When we received the baptism of the Holy Ghost, the power came down in such a mighty way, and after a time people began to consider and got us to taking thought. But what are we that will put straps and bands on the Holy Ghost, when the Lord comes and finds and thrills us with the Holy Ghost? Just because it is not our power shall we quench it and hold it down? Let us be free in the Holy Ghost and let him have right of way.[34]

Seymour's personal preaching style betrayed a simple man with a hunger for God. An eyewitness described the preacher and his message: "He was meek and plain spoken and no orator. He spoke the common language of the uneducated class. . . . The only way to explain the results is this: that his teachings were so simple that people who were opposed

32. Seymour, "Christ's Messages to the Church," 3.
33. Untitled, *The Apostolic Faith* 1, no. 9: 1.
34. Ibid., 2.

to organized religion fell for it [*sic*]. It was the simplicity that attracted them."[35] Commenting in a sermon on those preachers who boasted of their credentials and new places of worship, Seymour declared:

> [T]he main credential is to be baptized with the Holy Ghost. Instead of new preachers from the theological schools and academies, the same old preachers, baptized with the Holy Ghost and fire, the same old deacons, the same old plain church buildings will do. When the Holy Ghost comes in He will cleanse out dead forms and ceremonies, and will give life and power to His ministers and preachers, in the same old church buildings. But without the Holy Ghost they are simply tombstones.[36]

George Floyd Taylor

George Floyd Taylor[37] was also a passionate spokesperson for the baptism in the Holy Spirit, with the special evidence of *glossolalia*. Originally a preacher in the Holiness movement, Taylor came into contact with G.B. Cashwell (1862–1916),[38] and accepted the testimony of his personal experience of Spirit Baptism at the Azusa Street Mission. Heavily involving himself in the Pentecostal Holiness Church, Taylor continued to preach and teach Pentecostal Spirit Baptism with a certainty, amid a clear lack of concrete proofs that would elicit shock from those of a rationalistic mindset. Again, in Taylor's writings, one does not read detailed exposition and exegesis from key passages of Acts to support the doctrine of *glossolalia* as initial evidence.

In a passage describing what Taylor believed were seven key operations of the Holy Spirit and the accompanying manifestations, he admits that errors might be found in his description of the first six manifestations; individual experiences may vary with his stated view. Readers should feel at "liberty to rearrange these manifestations if they choose." However, "When we come to the manifestation following the Baptism of the Spirit, we have a 'thus saith the Lord.' " In the view of this early Pentecostal leader, the Scriptures were clear, the testimony of the earliest believers was clear, and he had the correct interpretation: "We do not

---

35. In Martin, *The Life and Ministry of William J. Seymour*, 185.

36. Seymour, *Words that Changed the World*, 70.

37. See Synan, "Taylor, George Floyd," 1115–16.

38. See Synan, "Cashwell, Gaston Barnabas," 457–58.

teach that all will receive the gift of tongues, but we do teach that 'the manifestation of the Spirit is given to every man to profit withal,' and that, if the Scriptures are to be our guide, the manifestation following Pentecost always is the speaking with tongues."[39] In his discussion on Taylor, Jacobsen concludes:

> Taylor asserted, perhaps more unconditionally than any other pentecostal theologian, that everyone who received the baptism of the Holy Ghost would speak with other tongues as the Spirit gave them utterance. He allowed no room for dialogue on this matter, and he rejected the idea that any other corroborating criterion should be added to the mix.[40]

David Wesley Myland

David Wesley Myland[41] did not visit the Azusa Street Mission personally; his connection to Pentecostalism was independent of anyone there. However, his understanding and articulation of Pentecostal theology in the wake of the Azusa Revival is worth examining, for it bears the marks of the influence of experience and rejection of rationalism so prevalent among his Pentecostal peers.

Myland's *The Latter Rain Covenant with Pentecostal Power and Testimonies of Healings and Baptism* (1910)[42] provides an excellent introduction to this theology. "For Myland," Jacobsen observes, "theology was ultimately about life, not about logic. While he believed that Christian faith could be systematically analyzed to some degree, the more important goal was to experience God in one's life."[43] This was the core of Myland's teaching: God must be experienced in his fullness, and he was likely to be unpredictable in his approach. Myland typically disagreed with those who approached the experience of Spirit Baptism systematically. The real reason so few people truly understood the workings of Pentecost,

---

39. Taylor, *The Spirit and the Bride*, 54. This example is a clear testimony to the reliance upon experience and lack of rationalism present among early Pentecostals. Indeed, one is hard-pressed to find Taylor's "thus saith the Lord" regarding *glossolalia* as initial evidence. For the earliest Pentecostals, however, their experience with the Spirit amounted to clear proof of God's will for Spirit Baptism.

40. Jacobsen, *Thinking in the Spirit*, 96.

41. See Robinson, "Myland, David Wesley," 920–21.

42. Myland, *The Latter Rain Covenant*.

43. Jacobsen, *Thinking in the Spirit*, 112.

he wrote, was "because they [were] trying to work it out intellectually."[44] Those still caught in the debate over didactic versus narrative portions of Scripture would surely fall into this category.

Although Myland was perhaps more balanced in his approach to reason and emotionalism than many of his peers, his writing nonetheless shows the Pentecostal tendency to submit the mind to the experience of God. Myland clearly believed that the mind ought to be involved in Pentecostal faith and experience. To completely experience Pentecostal fullness, he suggested, you

> . . . have to have your imagination subdued, your reason adjusted, your perceptions clarified, and your judgment and will sanctified; otherwise you will be governed, not by knowledge, but by emotion and feeling. . . . No other ground is so dangerous. This is where warning is needed, because the enemy everlastingly seeks to play all kinds of tunes on our emotions and feelings and then laughs at us while we try to dance to his "piping," but cannot.[45]

Having warned his readers about the dangers of excessive emotionalism, Myland then turns his attention to intellectual issues. From his observations, those who had the most trouble acquiring the fullness of God did so because of the "intellectual nature." This so troubled him that he suggested "hard-headed fellows" may need to be "crucified at the place of a skull and then have [their] heads put to soak" under the influence of the Holy Spirit. He stated,

> Brains are good in their place, but they count for nothing unless the heart is set on fire with the sacrificing love of God. . . . If our service is only in the spiritual it leads to fanaticism; if it is in the physical only, the result is formalism. God save us from either of these awful extremes and enable us to worship Him with both the heart and mind.[46]

Another telling example of Myland's rejection of the characteristic tendencies of Modernity is found in his belief that Pentecostal missionaries should distinguish themselves on the mission field by their extraordinary faith. Unlike Parham and Taylor, however, this faith did not take the form of *xenolalia*, but a rejection of modern medical help. In fact,

44. Myland, *The Latter Rain Covenant*, 13–14, 64, 211.
45. Ibid., 14–16, 29–30.
46. Ibid., 13–16, 24. See also Jacobsen, *Thinking in the Spirit*, 122.

Myland often stated his reluctance to send into the mission field persons who requested medical supplies to accompany them. Trust in medicine and God were mutually incompatible for this early Pentecostal. When asked about those who might die on the mission field without appropriate medical assistance, Myland replied,

> Well, suppose they do die. I want to tell you this, that where one has died trusting God for healing, a half a dozen have died who were trusting in medicine. The missionaries who have trusted God the fullest come through the best. . . . If God has a purpose in a life over in Africa, He will keep that life until His work is done, if there is real trust. Let us pray for those who cannot fully trust.[47]

Donald Gee

Donald Gee (1891–1966), a British Pentecostal leader known as the "Apostle of Balance," was one of the more influential early Pentecostal writers.[48] His most lasting influence came from his early books, written during the 1930s, in which he strongly articulated and defended the largely misunderstood Pentecostal experience to both adherents and interested observers. Evidence of anti-rationalism is witnessed in the refusal to engage in clear hermeneutics; this doctrine should be evident to those with faith. Although Gee seemed to be aware of the importance of correct doctrine, and was therefore in favor of the study of theology itself, his solid preference was for experience over reason. Concerning the baptism in the Holy Spirit, he firmly states,

> To most of us, this has been a perfectly distinct experience from our conversion, and to this agrees the clear testimony of the Scriptures—Acts 8:16; 9:17; 19:2; etc. . . .
>
> When you are baptized in the Holy Ghost, you *know* it, and need no one to acquaint you with the fact. . . . In the final analysis, the Baptism in the Spirit is not a doctrine but an experience, and the test of whether I have received is not a cleverly woven doctrine that will include me within its borders, but whether I know the experience in burning *fact* in heart and life.[49]

47. Myland, *The Latter Rain Covenant*, 86–87.
48. Bundy, "Gee, Donald, " 662–63. See also Kay, "Donald Gee," 133–53.
49. Gee, *A New Discovery*, 20–21. See also Womack, *Pentecostal Experience*.

Gee's preference for experience over doctrine is further evidenced: "Doctrines about the Spirit are necessary and inevitable, but the all-important question is not what we mentally believe, but what we experientially enjoy."[50] Not one to mince words, he clearly stated:

> You may probably stumble at first over the teaching that the Scriptural evidence of the Baptism in the Holy Spirit is speaking with other tongues; and that it should always be expected in every case as an initial "sign". . . . Yet I firmly believe that if you ponder this with an open heart and mind before the Lord, you will come to see from the examples and significance of the recorded cases in the New Testament . . . that it is really so; and that . . . this strange sign unquestionably marks the divine choice for a simple, universal and supernatural evidence to seal the Baptism with the Spirit.[51]

Gee does not feel obligated to debate the passages Pentecostals use to support their theology. Rather, he confidently states that the Pentecostal position agrees with the "clear testimony of Scripture"—a telling insight into the mentality of this early Pentecostal teacher. The reader will not observe consternation on the part of Gee that his choice doctrine comes only from the narrative portions of Acts; indeed, it is his uncritical acceptance of the narratives of Acts 2, 8, 9, 10, and 19 that signifies his clean break with the Moderns, who would look for theology only in the didactic portions of Scripture.

Myer Pearlman

The American Myer Pearlman (1898–1943) was another influential figure in early Pentecostal theology.[52] As a convinced Pentecostal and educator, he undertook in 1937 to write a doctrinal summary, *Knowing the Doctrines of the Bible*.[53] This work provided his classes with a text that previously did not exist. No other Pentecostal work has matched its circulation or longevity. Since its appearance, this single volume of less than 300 pages has been continuously available. More than 125,000 copies have been sold in English alone. It served for many years as the standard Pentecostal Bible

---

50. Gee, *God's Grace and Power for Today*, 7.

51. Gee, *A New Discovery*, 16–17.

52. See Gohr, "Pearlman, Myer," 959.

53. Pearlman, *Knowing the Doctrines of the Bible*.

college theology text.[54] Considering his lack of training, Pearlman wrote a thorough summary of the work of the Holy Spirit. He notes the nature of the Spirit, the Spirit in the Old Testament, the Spirit in Christ, the Spirit in human experience, the gifts of the Spirit, and the Spirit in the Church.[55]

In his section on the Spirit in human experience, Pearlman discusses the Spirit's role in empowering believers for service. "[I]n addition and subsequent to conversion, a believer may experience an enduement of power whose initial oncoming is signalized by a miraculous utterance in a language never learned by the speaker."[56] Christians who know the Holy Spirit in regeneration and sanctification, yet fail to speak in tongues, have challenged the above conclusion, and Pearlman acknowledges as much. In his honest reply, we see Classical Pentecostalism at its best:

> It cannot be successfully denied that there is a real sense in which all truly regenerated persons have the Spirit. But the question naturally follows: What is there different and additional in the experience described as the Baptism with the Holy Spirit? We answer as follows:
>
> There is one Holy Spirit, but many operations of that Spirit, just as there is one electricity but many operations of that electricity. The same electricity propels streetcars, lights our houses, operates refrigerators, and performs many other tasks. In the same manner, the one Spirit regenerates, sanctifies, energizes, illumines, and imparts special gifts.
>
> The Spirit regenerates human nature in the crisis of conversion, and then, as the Spirit of holiness within, produces the "fruit of the Spirit," the distinctive feature of Christian character. . . .
>
> But in addition to these operations of the Holy Spirit, there is another, having for its special purpose the energizing of human nature for special service for God, and issuing in an outward expression of a supernatural character. . . . In the New Testament this experience is designated by such expressions as falling upon, coming upon, being poured out, being filled with, which expressions convey the thought of suddenness and supernaturalness. All these terms are connected with the experience known as the Baptism with the Holy Spirit.

54. Spittler, "Theological Style Among Pentecostals and Charismatics," 296–97.

55. Pearlman, *Knowing the Doctrines of the Bible*, 6.

56. Ibid., 310. For an insightful study of the initial evidence doctrine, see McGee, *Initial Evidence*; and Wiebe, "The Pentecostal Initial Evidence Doctrine," 465–72.

> Now while freely admitting that Christians have been born of
> the Spirit, and workers anointed with the Spirit, we maintain that
> not all Christians have experienced the charismatic operation of
> the Spirit. . . .[57]

Though not expounding in detail the Acts passages so cherished
by later Pentecostals, Pearlman seems content to refer the reader to Acts
2, 8, 10, and 19, where the truth of his teaching should be apparent.[58]
In this statement, Pearlman has expounded the traditional Pentecostal
theology on Spirit Baptism, corresponding closely to the second bless-
ing doctrine taught by both Dwight L. Moody (1837–99) and Reuben A.
Torrey (1856–1928). In Pearlman's view, Pentecostals do not dismiss the
role of the Spirit in conversion. They do, however, point to an additional
empowering for service available by the Spirit and witnessed by obvious
physical signs.

Carl Brumback

Carl Brumback (1917–87),[59] another early Pentecostal pastor and
speaker, expanded a series of radio sermons from 1942 to 1944 into his
significant defense of Pentecostalism, *What Meaneth This? A Pentecostal
Answer to a Pentecostal Question.*[60] A telling insight into the Pentecostal
mentality at this time is seen in Donald Dayton's suggestion that "Carl
Brumback's classic *apologia* for Pentecostalism . . . is basically a defense of
glossolalia."[61] The importance of this observation should not be missed.
At the time Brumback wrote, Pentecostals continued to forcefully defend
their understanding of tongues as evidence, while almost assuming the
validity of subsequence.

Brumback provides an excellent example of the continuity
Pentecostalism maintained in placing experience above rationalism
throughout the first five or six decades of the movement. He examines
five key passages from the book of Acts to support his position: Pentecost
(chapter 2); the Samaritans (8); the disciple at Damascus (9); Cornelius'
household (10); and the Ephesians (19). Brumback's "exegesis" of the pas-

---

57. Pearlman, *Knowing the Doctrines of the Bible*, 311–13.

58. Ibid.

59. See Wilson, "Brumback, Carl," 447.

60. Brumback, *What Meaneth This?*

61. Dayton, "The Limits of Evangelicalism," 37. Emphasis in original.

sages is, to the modern hermeneutical mind, rather incredible. Though space prevents an analysis of each passage, sufficient insight will be gained from an examination of Paul's conversion (Acts 9). Brumback refers neither to Greek nor to historical-critical questions. He notes simply that although Paul was sent to receive his sight and be filled with the Holy Spirit, no record was made of his reception of the Spirit, only of the return of his sight. His continued explanation is worth quoting verbatim:

> Of course, we all conclude that the will of the Lord was accomplished in this respect as well as in the restoration of [Paul's] sight. However, if our non-Pentecostal friends insist on emphasizing the absence in the record of Paul's speaking in tongues, we can say, just as logically, that he was not filled with the Holy Ghost at that hour. How could there possibly be any mention of tongues in the narrative, when there is a complete absence of mention of the experience of which the speaking with tongues is but a part?
>
> At the time that Paul was writing the First Epistle to the Corinthians it is certain that he possessed the gift of tongues (1 Corinthians 14:18). This being so, there must have been a first time when he was given this miracle of utterance. The logical place for this primary experience would have been, as in the case of all the other apostles, at the hour when he was filled with the Spirit.[62]

The manner in which Brumback explicates proof of initial evidence from this passage is a prime example of the pre-scholarly hermeneutic so often employed by Classical Pentecostals.

THE PENTECOSTAL STORY:
THE LATTER RAIN METANARRATIVE

As Eduard Schweizer has noted, Pentecostals were not the first to prioritize a passionate experience of the Holy Spirit: "Long before the Spirit was a theme of doctrine, He was a fact in the experience of the community."[63] Veli-Matti Kärkkäinen agrees: "It might well be the case that, in the first two centuries, charismatic, 'enthusiastic' spiritual life was a norm rather than a barely tolerated minority voice in the Church."[64] Pentecostals simply sought to "get back" to those early years of Christianity, complete

---

62. Brumback, *What Meaneth This?*, 216–17.

63. Schweizer, "pneuma," 396.

64. Kärkkäinen, *Pneumatology*, 39.

with the expectation of a powerful experience of the Holy Spirit in the everyday lives of believers.

Kenneth J. Archer argues that this restorationist desire within early Pentecostalism defined the Pentecostal "story." Further, the story Pentecostals so enjoyed telling was the benchmark of their hermeneutics:

> What distinguished the early Pentecostal exegetical method from the Holiness folk was not a different interpretive method, but a "distinct narrative" which held the similar methods together in a coherent and cohesive interpretive manner. . . . The Pentecostal hermeneutical strategy at the foundational interpretive level was a unique story.[65]

As Archer highlights, Alasdair MacIntyre has demonstrated that a community's narrative tradition will considerably impact its interpretive practices. "The narrative tradition provides the context in which moral reason, along with its interpretive practices can be understood."[66] For Pentecostals, this narrative tradition attempts to embody the larger Christian story of a created world without sin, the Fall, redemption through Christ, the subsequent Christian community, and the final restoration of believers at the end of time. Specifically, however, the story of Pentecostals is one of restoration, for they see themselves as an "authentic continuation of New Testament Christianity and . . . a faithful representation of New Testament Christianity in the present societies in which it exists."[67]

The importance of the story to Pentecostals can hardly be over-estimated, as Harvey Cox indicates in *Fire From Heaven: The Rise of Pentecostal Spirituality and the Reshaping of Religion in the Twenty-First Century*:

> As a theologian I had grown accustomed to studying religious movements by reading what their theologians wrote and trying to grasp their central ideas and most salient doctrines. But I soon found out that with pentecostalism this approach does not help much. As one Pentecostal scholar puts it, in his faith "the experience of God has absolute primacy over dogma and doctrine." Therefore the only theology that can give an account of this expe-

---

65. Archer, "Pentecostal Story," 1. Emphasis in original.

66. Ibid., 3. See MacIntyre, *After Virtue*, 193.

67. Archer, "Pentecostal Story," 5.

rience, he says, is "a narrative theology whose central expression is the testimony." I think that he is right. . . .[68]

Archer argues that "the Pentecostal community's identity is forged from its reading of the Biblical narratives of Acts and the Gospels. Pentecostals desire to live as the eschatological people of God."[69] As Pentecostals participate in the great story of God's redemption, they have seen themselves clearly as the restoration of the early Church in the twentieth century, awaiting final redemption. Among Christians, many Pentecostals believe only they truly recaptured the essence of life in the Spirit, as portrayed in the Acts narratives.

Notable Pentecostal scholars such as Edith L. Blumhofer, D. William Faupel, and Kenneth Archer, have observed that the key narrative for early Pentecostals was the "Latter Rain" motif, found in such scriptures as Deut 11:10–15; Job 29:29; Prov 16:15; Jer 3:3, 5:24; Hos 6:3; Joel 2:23; Zech 10:1; and Jas 5:7.[70] This is confirmed in the writings of early Pentecostals such as George Floyd Taylor, who dedicated an entire chapter of his work *The Spirit and the Bride* to explaining the early and latter rains.[71] A.B. Simpson (1844–1919) encouraged the readers of the *Christian and Missionary*

68. Cox, *Fire From Heaven*, 71.

69. Archer, "Pentecostal Story," 6.

70. Essentially, these verses speak of the weather cycle in Palestine, and God's promise to provide sufficient rain for a successful harvest, as Israel remained faithful to her covenant. Note the following: " 'And it shall be that if you earnestly obey My commandments which I command you today, to love the Lord your God and serve Him with all your heart and with all your soul, then I will give you the rain for your land in its season, *the early rain and the latter rain*, that you may gather in your grain, your new wine, and your oil. And I will send grass in your fields for your livestock, that you may eat and be filled.' Take heed to yourselves, lest your heart be deceived, and you turn aside and serve other gods and worship them, lest the Lord's anger be aroused against you, and He shut up the heavens so that there be no rain, and the land yield no produce, and you perish quickly from the good land which the Lord is giving you" (Deut 11:13–17, NKJV. Emphasis added.)

71. Taylor, *The Spirit and the Bride*, 90, writes: "God fashioned the land of Palestine to be the model land of all lands, to contain the produce of all zones and climes, to be a miniature world in itself, and so He arranged the coming and going of its rain clouds on a spiritual pattern, to beautifully adumbrate the movements of the Holy Spirit. So just what the rain is to the earth, the Holy Spirit is to the soul. God arranged the showers of rain in the land of Canaan, as a type of the operations of grace. Many scriptures allude to the early and Latter Rain, and these are used as types of the Holy Spirit."

Alliance magazine in 1907 to expect a "Latter Rain" outpouring.[72] Charles Parham also discussed this motif as early as 1911:

> A careful study of the subject in the Old Testament proves that the early rain fell upon newly sown seed, to sprout it and grow it; and that the latter rain fell on the fields at the time the grain was in the milk state to full it for the harvest.
>
> This is true of all Pentecostal work today. Christianity was in the milk state. . . .[A]t Topeka, God baptized his true ones with the real Pentecost. . . .
>
> [A]fterward the Holy Spirit fell in Pentecostal power. . . . [Captain Tuttle] saw above the building a great lake of fresh water. It overflowed until the whole earth was refreshed by its floods.
>
> This has been true of this Latter Rain. Wherever it has gone it has been like "rain upon new mown grass," filling the wheat for His "Glorious Harvest."
>
> The purpose of this Latter Rain is two-fold: The preaching of this "gospel of the kingdom" to all the world "as a witness," and the fulling of the grain for the harvest.[73]

Faupel argues that Pentecostals seized upon the motif of the latter rain, using it as a narrative to explain the importance of their movement in the Christian world. If Pentecost signified the early rain of the Holy Spirit upon the earth, how the world had longed for the latter rain during the drought caused by the "apostasy" of the Roman Catholic Church through the Dark and Middle Ages! The world had prayed for the Azusa Street Revival. According to Faupel, the Pentecostals became the people of the prophetically promised "Latter Rain," which meant that they had fully recovered not only the Apostolic faith, but also the Apostolic power, authority and practice.[74]

Early Pentecostals believed strongly that they were the restoration of the New Testament Church, the clearest expression of what God intended the Church to be since the days of the Apostles. As proof, Pentecostals often looked towards the occurrence of miracles within their ranks. In their

---

72. "We may . . . conclude that we are to expect a great outpouring of the Holy Spirit in connection with the second coming of Christ and one as much greater than the Pentecostal effusion of the Spirit as the rains of autumn were greater than the showers of spring. . . . We are in the time . . . when we may expect this latter rain." Simpson, "What is meant by the Latter Rain?," 38.

73. Parham, *The Everlasting Gospel*, 31.

74. See Faupel, *The Everlasting Gospel: The Significance of Eschatology*, 38–9.

view, signs and wonders had been a regular occurrence during the days of the Apostles, but as one would expect, had ceased during the apostate reign of the Roman Catholic Church. God had withdrawn the manifestation of miracles not permanently, as taught by Cessationists, but temporarily, to show his displeasure with the lack of faith and unbelief of the Church. Once the "true church" was again formed on the earth, miracles would naturally flow from the hand of God. Wesleyan Holiness leader John P. Brooks (1891) and early Pentecostal leader Bennett F. Lawrence (b. 1890) [1916] clearly outlined the rationale for this Pentecostal belief:

> The truth is that the marks of supernaturalism with which the Church was originally clothed were intended to abide with it, and to accredit its doctrine as Divine, just as Christ's own doctrine was accredited as Divine; because . . . the ministry of the church was to be a continuation of the ministry of Christ, and in his design, no doubt, was to be accompanied with the same phenomena of supernaturalism that verified his own ministry. . . . And as in the future that Church (the true Church) shall more and more emerge into notice from amidst the confusions and carnalities of sectarian Christendom, it cannot be doubted that there will be a reassertion of all the original gifts of which it was in the beginning made the possessor by its divine Lord, the gift of miracle included.[75]

> The honest-hearted thinking men and women of this great movement, have made it their endeavor to return to the faith and practice of our brethren who serve God prior to the apostasy. They have made the New Testament their rule of life. This effort, which is so general throughout the movement, has had a particular effect upon those who were exercised thereby. . . . The Pentecostal movement has no such history; it leaps the intervening years crying "*Back to Pentecost.*" In the minds of these honest-hearted, thinking men and women, this work of God is immediately connected with the work of God in the New Testament days. Built by the same hand, upon the same foundation of the apostles and prophets, after the same pattern, according to the same covenant, they too are a habitation of God through the Spirit. They do not recognize a doctrine or custom as authoritative unless it can be traced to that primal source of church instructions, the Lord and his apostles.[76]

75. Brooks, *The Divine Church*, 21.
76. Lawrence, *The Apostolic Faith Restored*, 11–12. Emphasis in original.

For these earliest Pentecostals, their manner and method of scriptural interpretation was not only correct, it was consistently witnessed by God himself as signs followed the correct preaching of his Word. One need not wonder whether Pentecostals had correctly interpreted their place in Christendom as recipients of the greater "Latter Rain" outpouring of the Holy Spirit; one need only witness the many miracles occurring within Pentecostalism to recognize the divine stamp of approval on this "full gospel" message. As one early Pentecostal noted, all miracles referred to in Mark 16:16–18 had occurred except the raising of the dead, and Pentecostals expected that to also happen shortly:

> The signs are following in Los Angeles. The eyes of the blind have been opened, the lame have been made to walk, and those who have accidentally drunk poison have been healed. One came suffering from poison and was healed instantly. Devils are cast out, and many speak in new tongues. All of the signs in Mark 16:16–18 have followed except raising the dead, and we believe God will have someone to receive that power. We want all the signs that it may prove God is true. It will result in the salvation of many souls.[77]

The importance of the Pentecostal story can hardly be overestimated. These earliest participants in this new movement saw themselves as the restoration of the presence of God as manifested through the Holy Spirit in New Testament days. The sign that their interpretation was correct came as God worked miracles among them, as testimony to the correct preaching of his Word.

> In sum, the "Latter Rain" motif provided the Pentecostals with a persuasive apologetic account for the existence of their community. The "Latter Rain" motif provided the basic structure for the Pentecostal story. The Pentecostal story brought together the Full Gospel message and extended the past biblical "Latter Rain" covenant of promise into the present Pentecostal movement. The Pentecostals, then, understood themselves as the prophetically promised eschatological movement, which would bring about the unity of Christianity and usher in the Second Coming of Christ.[78]

77. "Signs Follow," 4.

78. Archer, "Pentecostal Story," 10. On the importance of narratives to Pentecostals, see also idem, *A Pentecostal Hermeneutic*, esp. chapter 4, an update of his earlier article.

THE PENTECOSTAL STORY: THE IMPORTANCE
OF THE TESTIMONY

As noted in the introduction, while Pentecostals employ the decidedly non-Postmodern use of the metanarrative to inform their self-understanding and biblical interpretation, they have also relied heavily upon the personal stories of those within the congregation. Early Pentecostals were known for their "testimonies," declaring the work of God in their lives to whoever might attend a particular meeting.

Descriptions of the early Pentecostal movement almost always include the mention of testimonies within worship services. Noting that services at the Azusa Street Mission took place seven days a week between 1906 and 1909, Gastón Espinosa observes, "Despite the lack of an official liturgy, one could regularly expect to see enthusiastic prayer, song, testimony and preaching at almost every service."[79] Frank Bartleman, a participant in the Azusa Street Revival, noted:

> No subjects or sermons were announced ahead of time, and no special speakers for such an hour. No one knew what might be coming, what God would do. All was spontaneous, ordered by the Spirit. We wanted to hear from God, through whomever He might speak. . . . The meetings started themselves, spontaneously, in testimony, praise, and worship. The testimonies were never hurried by a call for "popcorn."[80]

Steven J. Land, author of *Pentecostal Spirituality: A Passion for the Kingdom*, observes:

> Like the New Testament days, communication and instruction were carried on through letters, tracts, testimonies and, most importantly, through an ethos growing out of and centered in revivalistic, participatory, populist-oriented worship. All those who had "gotten their Pentecost" were witnesses, tellers of good news. So there were no systematic treatises; that would be a kind of second-order activity removed from the atmosphere of prayer, praise and witness. Though most of the people were literate—some at Azusa even "highly educated"—they were overwhelmingly oral in their worship, witness, and work.[81]

79. Espinosa, "Ordinary Prophet," 39–40.
80. Bartleman, *Another Wave of Revival*, 58–59.
81. Land, *Pentecostal Spirituality*, 19.

Cecil M. Robeck, perhaps the leading Pentecostal historian of our time, supports the notion that Pentecostals placed tremendous importance on the role of individual testimonies in building the community of faith. Concerning the Azusa Street Mission meetings, Robeck notes that Seymour "created a climate in which anyone able to lead in a prayer, give a personal testimony, sing a song, manifest some charism, or exhort the saints was allowed to do so."[82] Further, testimonies were so valued that Clara E. Lum (d. 1946), William Seymour's secretary, spent considerable time recording oral testimonies for use in *The Apostolic Faith* newspaper. Lum was also responsible for selecting testimonies from among the thousands of letters arriving back at the Mission from those who had travelled abroad as missionaries, to be read aloud at the services.[83]

According to Robeck, the testimonies of the Mission became a "remarkable feature" of the worship during the revival.

> The testimonies of the faithful were not time-worn, tired retreads of something that had happened twenty or thirty years ago. They were new, vital vignettes—glimpses into the lives of people who came to the mission. Many visitors found themselves impressed enough with what they heard in these times of testimony that they called them the highlight of the meetings. People stood at the windows outside the mission just to hear the latest tale of God's working. People stood in line for an hour or more, eagerly waiting their turn. Many jumped to their feet, one right after the other, for the privilege of telling the crowd what God had just done in their lives. Their stories breathed excitement, and their voices rang with vitality. Sometimes testifiers could be heard for blocks in every direction.[84]

Walter J. Hollenweger (b. 1927), the "dean of Pentecostal studies," was one of the first to recognize that the oral nature of Pentecostalism contributed strongly to its worldwide growth. He believes its universal appeal can be largely explained by the contribution of black spirituality to Pentecostalism, including the following:

- narrative nature of theology and witness
- orality of liturgy

82. Robeck, *The Azusa Street Mission and Revival*, 115.
83. See ibid., 105.
84. Ibid., 154.

- maximum participation by the community in reflection, prayer, and decision-making, thereby creating a community that is reconciliatory

- inclusion of dreams and visions into personal and public forms of worship via the testimony.[85]

Reflecting on Pentecostalism's propensity towards oral communication, Hollenweger considers whether the movement might have something to contribute to the larger Christian Church in terms of theological method. Referring to the basis of Pentecostalism as the shared experience of the Holy Spirit, he notes:

> Taken seriously this offers a real possibility of discovering a methodology of theology in an *oral* culture where the medium of communication is—just as in biblical times—not the definition, but the description; not the statement, but the story; not the doctrine, but the testimony. . . . Whoever denies that one can do proper theology in these categories will have to prove that the Bible is not a theological book. Our way of doing theology is a culturally biased form (yet necessarily so, in our culture!). There are other equally relevant forms of doing theology. Pentecostalism offers raw materials and elements for such an alternative methodology.[86]

SUMMARY

From the early days of the Azusa Street Revival, Pentecostals were people of "the story," viewing themselves through the decidedly non-Postmodern vantage point of the Christian metanarrative. Their existence was explained through their understanding of God's Latter Rain outpouring, which would restore to the true Church the miracles and power of the Holy Spirit as first evidenced in the book of Acts. Pentecostals viewed themselves and their movement as God's last great outpouring of his Spirit upon the earth, and so interpreted their movement in general, and Scripture in particular, through the lens of this great narrative. In several other areas, however, the similarities between early Pentecostalism and current Postmodern thought are striking.

85. See Hollenweger, "The Black Roots of Pentecostalism," 36–40. See also idem, *The Pentecostals*; and *Pentecostalism*. Hollenweger considers the essence of Pentecostalism to be its black oral roots.

86. Hollenweger, "Charisma and *Oikumene*, 332–33. Emphasis in original.

From the earliest times, as evidenced by its initial leaders, Pentecostalism did not take the Modern approach to faith and Scripture. From William Seymour and Charles Parham, to George Taylor, Donald Gee, and Carl Brumback, these Pentecostal thinkers and writers each disavowed the reign of rationalism in favor of a faith lived as a partnership between the Word and one's experience. Like the Postmodernist reacting to the tenets of Modernism, Pentecostals could not apply a rationalistic outlook to their experience with the Holy Spirit. The early Pentecostals did not engage in debates over whether one portion of Scripture had more "instructional value" than others; the terms "narrative" and "didactic" were hardly in the vocabulary of most. As Frank D. Macchia observes, even today, "Pentecostals are . . . wary of critical approaches to the biblical text that alienate the readers from a life-transforming participation in the world of the scriptures. Hence, Pentecostal theology has tended to be oral, narrative, and devotional in nature rather than academic or philosophical. . . . The narrative world of the Bible in the context of the community of faith has formed the primary context for Pentecostal biblical interpretation."[87]

With the Bible in one hand and their "baptism in the Holy Spirit" in the other, the earliest Pentecostals set out to win others for Christ and teach them about the necessity of Spirit-baptism, but more importantly, assist in the reception of this exciting experience. Key to this process was the Pentecostal story on the individual level—the sharing of God's work in the lives of individual believers was an integral component of almost every early Pentecostal gathering. Pentecostals instinctively recognized the power of individual story as a means of connecting communities and communicating truth, much as contemporary Postmoderns value the same. For Pentecostals, however, the truth communicated was that of their place within the larger narrative of God's redemptive plan. Steven J. Land notes:

> Thus, the point of Pentecostal spirituality was not to have an experience or several experiences, though they spoke of discrete experiences. The point was to experience life as part of a biblical drama of participation in God's history. . . .
> Whether it was couched in terms of biblical dispensations, discrete personal experiences, or missionary travels, all of this language was meant to speak of the mighty acts of God's story of

87. Macchia, "The Spirit and the Text," 54.

redemption in Scripture, in their lives and in the world. . . . The narrative of salvation provided the structure for formation within the missionary movement.

The whole congregation was involved in the process of formation. The singing, preaching, witnessing, testifying, ordinances . . . altar calls, prayer meetings, gifts of the Spirit, all the elements of corporate worship prepared people for and called them to new birth, sanctification, Spirit baptism and a life of missionary witness.[88]

As the decades passed and Pentecostalism interacted on an increasing level with scholars of other backgrounds, a significant challenge arose. How were Pentecostals, with their pre-critical methods of biblical interpretation, to engage other theologians in scholarly debate, without appearing naïve and unlearned? How were Pentecostals to gain acceptance as equals into organizations such as the National Association of Evangelicals while still refusing to interpret Scripture according to generally accepted hermeneutical principles, such as the historical-critical method? How were Pentecostals to achieve academic respectability while still holding true to their cherished distinctive doctrines?

As Pentecostalism came of age, it became apparent that the approach of Pentecostal scholars would begin to mirror that of their Evangelical comrades as they began to employ the traditional Evangelical hermeneutics of Modernity to the core of Pentecostal theology.[89] While this "coming of age" was of academic significance and a positive step for Pentecostalism, the cost in terms of maintaining the essence of this revival movement must be counted. While those in the pew may not have significantly moved from their early Pentecostal roots, change of this sort in any movement begins with the scholars, who in turn educate the pastors. Have Pentecostal scholars begun to move away from some of the foundational precepts of the movement? In their drive for academic and denominational acceptability, have they surrendered hermeneutical presuppositions, which would today assist them greatly in speaking the lan-

---

88. Land, *Pentecostal Spirituality*, 74–5.

89. Ahn ("Various Debates in the Contemporary Pentecostal Hermeneutics," 21) notes, "Pentecostal theologians are no longer standing in the defensive position, rather they enthusiastically enter into meaningful dialogue with other traditions of Christianity, while they seek to re-evaluate their traditional hermeneutic. In fact, with a great appreciation for the early Pentecostal spirituality, contemporary Pentecostal scholars attempt to articulate Pentecostal experience and theology with various analytical methodologies in more sophisticated ways."

guage of Western youth? Have Pentecostals become wholly Evangelical in their approach to the Scriptures and, in doing so, hindered their abilities to present the one "supernatural" God to generations of youth desperately looking for such a Deity?

Chapter 4 examines these and other questions by focusing upon what is perhaps the premier debate within Pentecostalism concerning Pentecostal hermeneutics, that of Gordon D. Fee and his Pentecostal detractors.

4

Late Twentieth-Century Pentecostal Hermeneutics:
More Evangelical than Pentecostal?

The Test Case of Gordon D. Fee[1]

I do not throw out initial evidence, I throw out the language, because it is not biblical, and therefore irrelevant. From a reading of Luke and Paul I would expect people to speak in tongues when they are empowered by the Spirit. For most people this will be a subsequent experience, because they will have become Christians without realizing that this is for them.[2]

GORDON D. FEE

I would not want to say that Luke did not *intend us to understand the baptism of the Spirit to be distinct from and subsequent to conversion, intended for empowering, and always evidenced by speaking in tongues; I simply am less convinced than my Pentecostal forebears that Luke did so intend.*[3]

GORDON D. FEE

The obvious result of this reductionism is a willingness to permit repeatability of patterns, but not normativity. Hence, speaking in tongues associated with Spirit baptism may be normal, *and even desirable, possibly, but it cannot be proclaimed as a* normative model. . . . *This reductionist point of view . . . [is] somewhat short of a thorough-going Pentecostal theology, [and] is apparently a position held today by a number of evangelicals.*[4]

WILLIAM W. MENZIES

1. An earlier version of this chapter appeared as "Gordon Fee and the Challenge to Pentecostal Hermeneutics: Thirty Years Later."

2. Fee, interview with author, 5 December 1997.

3. Fee, *Gospel and Spirit*, 103–4. Emphasis in original.

4. Menzies, "The Methodology of Pentecostal Theology," 9. Emphasis in original.

WHEN ONE THINKS OF Gordon D. Fee, hermeneutics may come to mind as easily as New Testament studies *per se*, for throughout his career he has engaged the problems of interpretation and exegesis as readily as he has specific issues of biblical theology.[5] For Pentecostals, most significant have been his efforts to spark discussion on the hermeneutics behind two of Pentecostalism's most cherished doctrines, subsequence and initial evidence. This debate, essentially begun by Fee with a 1972[6] presentation on historical precedent, marks a clear turning point in Pentecostal hermeneutics, from the older Bible Reading Method to a more academically accepted approach. This chapter seeks to examine Fee's contribution to the discussion and survey the Pentecostal response.

Fee's challenge of traditional Pentecostal interpretations of Luke-Acts that have spawned the doctrines of subsequence and initial evidence, stems from his usage of some very Modern hermeneutical tools, the historical-critical method among them. Following the hermeneutics of E.D. Hirsch and others, Fee, as a Pentecostal, brings the standard hermeneutical methods of the Evangelical Protestant world of the time to bear upon the Pentecostal issues of the day. The reaction was one of fighting fire with fire, the Pentecostals responding with Modern Evangelical hermeneutics. This debate thus begins the shift in Pentecostal hermeneutics away from the Bible Reading Method to a more "accepted" Evangelical hermeneutic.

GENERAL HERMENEUTICAL PRINCIPLES OF GORDON FEE

When assessing Fee's understanding of a given subject, one must first delve into the hermeneutical guidelines he has set for himself. It is somewhat impossible to separate his theology from his hermeneutics, for in each instance his theological stance has come from following his own interpretive principles.

Fee has been influenced by many recent hermeneutical trends, from the work of Paul Ricoeur (1913–2005)[7] to Anthony C. Thiselton.[8] While

5. For the author's further thoughts on Fee, see Noel, "Gordon Fee's Contribution to Contemporary Pentecostalism's Theology of Baptism in the Holy Spirit" and "Gordon Fee and the Challenge to Pentecostal Hermeneutics."

6. Fee's "The Hermeneutics of Historical Precedent," originally written for the 1972 Annual meeting of the Society for Pentecostal Studies, was later published in Spittler, *Perspectives on the New Pentecostalism*.

7. See Ricoeur, *Interpretation Theory*.

8. See Thiselton, *New Horizons in Hermeneutics* and *The Two Horizons*.

preferring the approach of the older historical-critical method, and the focus on authorial intent by Hirsch,[9] Fee's work nonetheless shows an awareness of the variety of Modern approaches to hermeneutics, such as the emphasis on relevance in the New Hermeneutic. His willingness and ability to apply these hermeneutical approaches to Pentecostalism has been a hallmark of his work. He declares that "one does nothing more important in the formal training for Christian ministry than to wrestle with hermeneutics: the meaning and application of Scripture."[10]

The Inherent Ambiguity of Scripture:
A Hermeneutical Challenge

Fee maintains that the specific hermeneutical issues faced by Evangelicalism lie within its doctrine of inspiration. He notes that the Evangelical commitment to see Scripture as *both* divine and human creates its own set of tensions. The intersection of the divine with the human produces far more ambiguities than some feel comfortable with.

> But the buck stops there, at the text and its intent, as to what is infallible. God did not choose to give us a series of timeless, non-culture-bound theological propositions to be believed and imperatives to be obeyed. Rather he chose to speak his eternal word *this* way, in historically particular circumstances, and in every kind of literary genre. God himself, by the very way he gave us this word, locked in the ambiguity.[11]

In the debate between the natural unity and diversity of the text, Fee opts for what he terms the "radical middle." Our doctrine of inspiration suggests that Scripture inherently contains ambiguity, accommodation, and diversity, each to varying degrees. Since God chose to give us his Word in this manner, our task is to hold each end of the spectrum—historical particularity and eternality—with equal vigor. While we cannot generate the absolute certainty so sought by Fundamentalists, we can nonetheless move towards a higher level of commonality. The way towards this higher level is found at the crucial point of authorial intentionality—both human and divine. The task of the exegete and theologian is to discover and hear

---

9. See Hirsch, *Validity in Interpretation.*

10. Fee, *Gospel and Spirit,* 24.

11. Ibid., 33. Emphasis in original. See also Ladd, *The New Testament and Criticism,* 12.

the Word in terms of God's original intent. Only then may we begin to ascertain its meaning for our own historical setting.[12]

The Crucial Issue: Authorial Intentionality

Fee details why authorial intent is such a crucial issue, though it causes him great problems when dealing with Pentecostal distinctives, and generates the most tension among Evangelicals. Insisting on determining authorial intent provides several benefits. It serves as a corrective, limiting the possible meanings a text might be given,[13] and gives us a way forward to construct our theologies in a truly biblical fashion. It teaches us that apparent contradictions in the text need not always be resolved or harmonized, but may stand together in healthy tension. Unity is found in the diversity.[14]

Intentionality and Particularity/Eternality

Fee does not refrain from tackling perhaps the most difficult hermeneutical issue of all. The question is: Since God spoke his Word in historically particular circumstances, how much of the particularity itself is part of the eternal Word? If the texts call us to practice hospitality, do we agree that washing feet (the particular) is part of the eternal (showing hospitality)? It is obvious from the outset that this question is one of the most difficult for which to proscribe systematic solutions.

When faced with passages in Acts, where the eternality of the particulars is difficult to determine, Fee holds to what he believes is the purpose and overall point of the passage. Many hermeneutical difficulties lie in the manner with which one acknowledges—or fails to acknowledge—the immense role that tradition in terms of denominational heritage, and presuppositions, play in the interpretation of Scripture.[15] Fee believes the selectivity of hermeneutics is for the most part related to tradition, not

12. Fee, *Gospel and Spirit*, 35–36.

13. Ibid., 43. For example, Fee cites B. B. Warfield's (1851–1921) interpretation of "the perfect" in 1 Cor 13:10 as referring to the New Testament canon. Since neither Paul nor his audience could have possibly understood the text this way, it cannot be considered the "meaning."

14. Fee, *Gospel and Spirit*, 43.

15. One need only refer to Rudolf Bultmann's now famous essay on whether it is possible to do presuppositionless exegesis, and his resounding "No." See his "Is Exegesis Without Presuppositions Possible?," 289–96.

exegesis. Tradition may lead us to ask specific questions of the text, which are not otherwise legitimate. These questions then lead us towards the kind of hermeneutical posture to which we are predisposed. For example, to ask of the text of Acts "What is the evidence of Spirit Baptism?" may be asking a question the text was not written to answer. The answer found, of course, can scarcely be the proper one.[16]

Summary

Fee opts for the radical middle in the hermeneutical challenge associated with an inherent ambiguity of Scripture. This middle ground is the determination of authorial intent, both human and divine. With this is his insistence on a Spirit-centered approach to New Testament imperatives, and a constant awareness of the impact of tradition upon one's hermeneutics. These three principles are the foundation of Fee's reflection on Pentecostal hermeneutics and theology.

HERMENEUTICS AND PENTECOSTAL THEOLOGY

With Fee's hermeneutical principles in hand, I am now prepared to examine his theology on Spirit Baptism, particularly as it relates to his own denomination, the Assemblies of God (USA). Though Fee claims to be Pentecostal in every regard, he nonetheless takes considerable exception to the stated form of two key (some would argue distinctive) Pentecostal doctrines: the baptism in the Holy Spirit as an experience subsequent to conversion, and the declaration that the evidence of such baptism is speaking in tongues.[17]

---

16. Fee, *Gospel and Spirit*, 75.

17. "Statement of Fundamental Truths," Articles 7 and 8, 102. The official wording of the Assemblies of God position is as follows:

> 7. The Baptism of the Holy Ghost: All believers are entitled to and should ardently expect and earnestly seek the promise of the Father, the baptism of the Holy Ghost and Fire, according to the command of our Lord Jesus Christ. This was the normal experience of all in the early Christian church. . . . This experience is distinct from and subsequent to the experience of the new birth (Acts 8:12–17; 10:44–46; 11:14–16; 15:7–9). . . .

8. The Evidence of the Baptism in the Holy Ghost: The baptism of believers in the Holy Ghost is witnessed by the initial physical sign of speaking with other tongues as the Spirit of God gives them utterance (Acts 2:4). The speaking in tongues in this instance is the same in essence as the gift of tongues (1 Cor. 12:4–10, 28), but different in purpose and use.

Hermeneutics and Historical Precedent

Pentecostals admit to basing their theology of subsequence and initial evidence on historical precedent as found in Acts. With specific regard to Pentecostal theology, one must take the genre of the book seriously. Acts is historical narrative, and much of the scholarly debate with Pentecostalism first took place within this arena. Many have argued that one must distinguish between *didactic* and *historical* portions of Scripture, and that the didactic portions have primary importance for the formation of Christian doctrine.[18] It has been declared that what is clearly descriptive history in Acts must not be translated into normative experiences for the ongoing Church.[19] Fee does not deny that theology abounds in Luke's work. Rather, he simply pleads for one to remember that Luke cast his theology in historical narrative, and for anyone concerned with good hermeneutics, this must be taken seriously.[20] The key to determining what may be didactic within a framework of historical narrative is, for Fee, the role of authorial intent.

> Although Luke's "broader intent" may be a moot point for some, it is a defensible hypothesis that he was trying to show how the church emerged as a chiefly Gentile, worldwide phenomenon from its origins as a Jerusalem-based, Judaism-oriented sect of Jewish believers, and how the Holy Spirit was ultimately responsible for this phenomenon of universal salvation based on grace alone.[21]

18. For example, Guthrie (*New Testament Theology*, 548) declares, "We may observe at once that this evidence from the book of Acts does not provide us with any reflection on the theology of the Spirit. It is wholly concerned with his activity. . . . The theological exposition of the doctrine of the Spirit did not fit into Luke's purpose in Acts, but comes to fuller expression in the epistles."

19. See, for example, Pinnock and Osborne, "A Truce Proposal," 6–9; Stott, *The Baptism and Fullness of the Holy Spirit*, 8; and Hoekema, *Holy Spirit Baptism*, 23–24.

20. Fee, *Gospel and Spirit*, 90. Pentecostal scholars are quick to point out that there is renewed recognition of Luke as a theologian. Marshall's *Luke: Historian and Theologian* has been called "[a]n important shift in Evangelical thinking." See Menzies, "The Distinctive Character of Luke's Pneumatology," 20. Marshall writes, "Luke was entitled to his own views, and the fact that they differ in some respects from those of Paul should not be held against him at this point. On the contrary, he is a theologian in his own right, and must be treated as such." *Luke: Historian and Theologian*, 75. See also Marshall and Peterson, *Witness to the Gospel*. In addition, Gasque, *A History of the Interpretation of the Acts*, includes two chapters on Luke the Theologian, 136–63 and 251–305.

21. Fee, *Gospel and Spirit*, 91.

Three Key Principles

Fee outlines three specific principles regarding hermeneutics and historical narrative. First, authorial intent is the chief factor in determining normative values from narratives. Second, that which is incidental to the primary intent of a narrative cannot have the same didactic value as the intended teaching, though it may provide insight into the author's theology. Finally, for historical precedent to have normative value, it must be demonstrated that such was the specific intent of the author. If the author intended to establish precedent, then such should be regarded as normative.[22] As anyone familiar with Pentecostal hermeneutics and theology will quickly realize, the preceding "guidelines" commence the challenge of the Pentecostal position for subsequence and initial evidence, for both are based on the assumption that Luke intended to teach these doctrines from the related narratives in Acts. Further, Fee's guidelines are grounded in the standard starting point of Evangelical hermeneutics—the search for authorial intent.

Pentecostals have responded forcefully, yet creatively, to Fee's guidelines. Their response is detailed below.

Categories of Christian Theology

In general, Fee believes Christian theology may be divided into three (or four)[23] categories: Christian theology (what Christians believe), Christian ethics (how Christians ought to behave), and Christian experience (what Christians do in terms of religious practices). These must be further defined in terms of primary and secondary importance, depending on whether they are derived from imperatives, or incidentally by analogy or precedent.[24] Fee astutely notes that almost everything Christians derive

22. Ibid., 92.

23. This was one of the few changes from *Gospel and Spirit* to Fee and Stuart, *How to Read the Bible*, published several years later. The impetus came from a specific challenge by Roger Stronstad that the final category must be divided into two. See below.

24. Fee, *Gospel and Spirit*, 93. See also Fee and Stuart, *How to Read the Bible*, 106–8, for the same material rephrased for the layperson. By way of example, in the first category, we might consider the deity of Christ primary; how the two natures concur in unity is secondary. That Scripture is the inspired Word of God is primary; the precise nature of inspiration is secondary. With respect to Christian ethics, general maxims such as love for one's enemy and unlimited forgiveness are primary; concrete principles and application for specific situations are secondary.

from Scripture by way of precedent is in the third category, Christian experience or practice, and always at the secondary level. This is not to say that secondary statements are unimportant; we simply cannot treat them as identical to primary statements based upon clear imperatives.[25]

Fee wades further into the debate with his fellow Pentecostals:

> The doctrine of a baptism in the Holy Spirit as subsequent to conversion and accompanied by tongues seems to belong to the secondary level of doctrinal statements in my third category. That believers are to be (or keep) filled with the Spirit, that they are to walk and live in the Spirit is at the primary level and normative. When and how one enters the dimension of Christian experience, although not unimportant, is not of the same "normative" quality, because the "when and how" is based solely on precedent and/or analogy.[26]

Specific Principles Regarding Historical Precedent

With these general observations and principles in view, Fee offers the following specific principles for the use of historical precedent.[27]

First, the use of historical precedent as an analogy by which to establish a norm is never valid in itself. Such a process (drawing universal norms from particular events) produces a *non sequitur* and is therefore irrelevant.

Second, although it may not have been the author's primary purpose, historical narratives do have illustrative and, sometimes, "pattern" value. It should be noted, however, that especially in cases where the precedent justifies a present action, the precedent does not establish a norm for specific action. A caveat is in order here: for a biblical precedent to justify a present action, the principle of the action must be taught elsewhere, where it is the primary intent so to teach.

Third, in matters of Christian experience, and even more so of Christian practice, biblical precedents may be regarded as repeatable patterns—even if they are not to be regarded as normative.[28]

25. Fee, *Gospel and Spirit*, 93.

26. Ibid., 93–94.

27. It is important to list these principles just as Fee wrote them, for it is because of these that he has drawn much of the fire from his Pentecostal colleagues. Often the issue concerns the actual wording.

28. Fee, *Gospel and Spirit*, 93–4. The repeatable character of certain practices or pat-

Fee directly engages Pentecostal distinctives and historical precedent. He maintains that one is unable to prove authorial intent in the "patterns" of Pentecost, Samaria, Paul, and Ephesus. It is simply impossible to show that Luke *intended* to teach an experience of the Spirit as subsequent to conversion.[29] For Luke, the real evidence of Christian experience is the reception of the Spirit. What he is teaching in this narrative is the validation by the Jerusalem leaders of the spread of Christianity beyond Jerusalem.[30]

The Essence of Pentecostalism

Upon discovering that Fee does not subscribe to either subsequence or initial evidence as stated by his denomination,[31] the twin doctrines cherished by many Pentecostals as the true doctrinal essence of the movement, one may be drawn to inquire as to exactly *how* Fee still considers himself Pentecostal. The answer lies in his definition of the essence of Pentecostalism and the Pentecostal experience.[32] His attempt to articulate

terns should be guided by the following considerations: a) The strongest possible case can be made when only one pattern is found, and when the pattern is repeated within the New Testament itself. b) When there is an ambiguity of patterns, or when a pattern occurs but once, it is repeatable for later Christians only if it appears to have divine approbation or is in harmony with what is taught elsewhere in Scripture. c) What is culturally conditioned is either not repeatable at all, or must be translated into the new or differing culture.

29. On the other hand, one might respond with the equally correct assertion that it is also impossible to prove that Luke did *not* intend to teach subsequence from these patterns. The difficulty with demanding proof of authorial intent is that it attempts to place the burden of proof on one viewpoint and not the other.

30. This is widely agreed upon as Luke's intent for this narrative. With Fee, see Ladd, *A Theology of the New Testament*, 383–4; Johnson, *The Acts of the Apostles*, 150–3; Krodel, *Acts*; Bruce, *The Book of Acts*, 182–4; Stott, *The Spirit, the Church and the World*; and Marshall, *The Acts of the Apostles: An Introduction*, 157–8.

31. Fee dismisses (*Gospel and Spirit*, 98) the question of whether tongues is the initial evidence of Spirit-reception as a "moot point," and thus discusses it infrequently. Because tongues is seen as a repeated pattern in Acts, many Pentecostals have argued that it is *the* pattern. Fee disagrees by suggesting that to "insist that it is the only valid sign seems to place too much weight on the historical precedent of three (perhaps four) instances in Acts." He does not thereby downplay the role of tongues. He argues forcefully that Paul values tongues highly for personal edification ("Tongues—Least of the Gifts?," 3–14). His most recent comment on the issue (*God's Empowering Presence*, 890, 218–9), maintains this viewpoint, suggesting that personal edification is in no manner wrong, and is in fact viewed favorably by Paul, an avid tongues-speaker himself.

32. Some, such as Menzies ("The Methodology of Pentecostal Theology," 1–3), view

his understanding of what it means to be Pentecostal demonstrates his own strong commitment to Pentecostalism:

> In thus arguing, as a New Testament scholar, against some cherished Pentecostal interpretations, I have in no sense abandoned what is essential to Pentecostalism. I have only tried to point out some inherent flaws in some of our historic understanding of texts. The essential matter, after all, is neither subsequence, nor tongues, but the Spirit himself as a dynamic, empowering presence; and there seems to me to be little question that our way of initiation into that—through an experience of Spirit-baptism—has biblical validity. Whether all *must* go that route seems to me to be more moot; but in any case, the Pentecostal experience itself can be defended on exegetical grounds as a thoroughly biblical phenomenon.[33]

Summary

Based on Fee's principles, Pentecostals may say the following about their experience. In the New Testament, the presence of the Holy Spirit was the chief element in Christian conversion and the Christian life. In Acts, as well as in Paul's churches, the Spirit's presence involved a charismatic dimension normally associated with the reception of the Spirit. Although speaking in tongues may *not* have been normative, it *was* normally expected to accompany Spirit Baptism in the early Church. Modern believers, many of whom have not experienced a charismatic dimension to their conversion, may still, on the basis of the New Testament pattern, experience such a dimension of Christian life. This includes speaking in tongues, for it was the repeated expression of the dynamic dimension of

---

the essence of Pentecostalism to be the tying together of tongues as the initial evidence of Spirit Baptism as a subsequent event. The author asked Fee how he could still consider himself a Pentecostal and member of the Assemblies of God (USA), when he disagreed with statements 7 and 8 above of their fundamental truths. He told the Assemblies of God, "I cannot support the language used to articulate this, but I support what you *mean* by what you have written." At issue is the language used. Fee continued: "I do not throw out initial evidence, I throw out the language, because it is not biblical, and therefore irrelevant. From a reading of Luke and Paul I would expect people to speak in tongues when they are empowered by the Spirit. The reception of the Spirit is most commonly evidenced by speaking in tongues. It is very normal. I expect people to be empowered by the Spirit for witness. For most people this will be a subsequent experience, because they will have become Christians without realizing that this is for them." Fee, interview with author, 5 December 1997.

33. Fee, *Gospel and Spirit*, 110–11. Emphasis in original.

the coming of the Spirit. Fee notes, "If the Pentecostal may not say one *must* speak in tongues, the Pentecostal may surely say, why *not* speak in tongues? It does have repeated biblical precedent, it did have evidential value at Cornelius' household (Acts 10:45–46), and—in spite of much that has been written to the contrary—it does have value both for the edification of the believer (1 Cor 14:2–4) and, with interpretation, for the edification of the church (1 Cor 14:5, 26–28)."[34]

The unfortunate omission of this valid, biblical dimension of Christian life from the life of the Church is the backdrop against which we must understand the Pentecostal movement, deeply dissatisfied with life in Christ without life in the Spirit. Though their timing may have been off, what they sought to recapture for the Church was not.

> That this experience was for them usually a separate experience in the Holy Spirit and subsequent to their conversion is in itself probably irrelevant. Given their place in the history of the church, how else might it have happened? Thus the Pentecostal should probably not make a virtue out of necessity. At the same time, neither should others deny the validity of such experience on biblical grounds, unless, as some do, they wish to deny the reality of such an empowering dimension of life in the Spirit altogether. But such a denial, I would argue, is actually an exegeting *not* of the biblical texts but of one's own experience in this later point in church history and a making of that experience normative. I for one like the biblical norm better; at this point the Pentecostals have the New Testament clearly on their side.[35]

THE PENTECOSTAL RESPONSE

As might be expected, Pentecostal scholars have responded definitively to the hermeneutical and theological challenges put forward by Fee. While many Pentecostals have written on the topic, only three scholars have taken Fee's challenge seriously and provided appropriate responses: William W. Menzies, long-time Assemblies of God (USA) scholar and professor; Roger Stronstad, Academic Dean at Summit Pacific College, Abbotsford, BC; and Robert P. Menzies, Assemblies of God (USA) professor and missionary in Asia. In each section, Fee is given opportunity to respond to his

34. Ibid., 99. Emphasis in original. Also helpful are Fee's *The First Epistle to the Corinthians*, 569–713; and *God's Empowering Presence*, 863–8, 886–90.

35. Fee, *Gospel and Spirit*, 119. Emphasis in original.

critics.[36] Three issues in particular have been raised: authorial intent and the essence of Pentecostalism; Fee's categories of Christian theology; and historical precedent. The reader will quickly notice that these scholars do not debate the merits of presupposing authorial intent as the foundation of the argument, or appeal to experience as a qualified verifier of Pentecostal experience. Rather, those involved play by the rules of the Evangelical hermeneutics used by Fee, and set out to demonstrate Luke's charismatic intent.

Authorial Intent and the Essence of Pentecostalism

That Luke had specific theological intentions when writing his narratives is highly likely. Determining what his intent might have been remains one of the biggest issues separating Fee and other Pentecostal scholars. Fee's contention is that genre seriously affects biblical interpretation and, further, when narratives are used to derive theology, specific authorial intent must be shown. He does not, therefore, allow the critical passages of Acts to be used to establish normative patterns. Pentecostals recognize this, and get straight to the point. William Menzies declares:

> [I]f one can demonstrate that Luke did not intend to convey a theological message by his narratives, he has at that point effectively undercut the possibility of a clear Pentecostal theology. Pentecostal theology is dependent on a hermeneutical methodology that takes seriously the theological intention of Luke. Acts must be more than an interesting glimpse into the life of the early church. It must be more than mere historical resource. Since the only access we have to Spirit-baptism initiation experiences are mediated to us through the descriptive mode, and that limited to Acts, we are heavily indebted to Luke-as-theologian.[37]

Fee's hermeneutics raise several important questions. Who determines authorial intent, Pentecostals or non-Pentecostals? Who determines what is primary and what is secondary? Who is authorized to adjudicate between

36. The exception here will be Robert P. Menzies, to whom Fee has not responded. Asked about this, Fee replied that a response would have drawn him much further into the debate, for which he had neither the time nor passion. "By the time Bob published his thesis I had moved on to so many other projects that I simply abandoned the hermeneutical give and take. . . . I had read only enough of Menzies to know that . . . under the pressure of time [I wasn't] able to handle it adequately." Fee, email interview with author, 27 January 1998.

37. Menzies, "The Methodology of Pentecostal Theology," 7.

Pentecostals and their opponents as to whether or not Luke may teach twenty-first-century Christians about their experience of the Holy Spirit? Many Pentecostals believe that Fee's hermeneutics muzzle the important passages of Acts, leaving him in no position to answer the above questions. Though his work challenges the tendency to allegorize, moralize, and/or spiritualize historical narratives, as a whole it must be rejected.[38]

In focusing on Luke's theological intent, Fee consistently employs a basic presupposition: In the New Testament, the presence of the Spirit is the chief element in Christian conversion. Whereas others addressed Fee on his hermeneutical principles *per se*, Robert Menzies challenges the notion that Luke shares Paul's pneumatological emphasis in his writings on the Spirit's function. If Luke's basic intent in relating the activities of the Spirit is charismatic and not soteriological, the Pentecostal case concerning authorial intent in historical narratives is much stronger.

Fee's work has played an important role in the theological development of Pentecostalism since the 1970s. He clearly argues that Pentecostalism can no longer rely on nineteenth-century interpretive methods. But Robert Menzies maintains that this message is no longer relevant. Pentecostals have replaced their outdated hermeneutics with approaches that speak the Modern hermeneutical language. Fee's critique of Pentecostal hermeneutics, updated in 1991, now fails to address today's crucial question: "Does Luke, in a manner similar to Paul, present the Spirit as the source of new covenant existence?"[39] For Menzies, the answer is "No."

> I would suggest that the pneumatologies of Luke and Paul are different but compatible; and the difference should not be blurred, for both perspectives offer valuable insight into the dynamic work of the Holy Spirit. Clearly Paul has the more developed view, for he sees the full richness of the Spirit's work. . . . Paul attests to both the soteriological and the prophetic (as well as charismatic) dimensions of the Spirit's work. Luke's perspective is less developed and more limited. He bears witness solely to the prophetic dimension of the Spirit's work, and thus he gives us a glimpse of only a part of Paul's fuller view. Nevertheless, Luke, like Paul, has an important

38. See Stronstad, "The Biblical Precedent for Historical Precedent," 11.

39. Menzies, *Empowered for Witness*, 239. This question, which is the crux of Menzies' work, is answered in the negative through argument and exegesis. Although the specific proofs supporting the claim are outside the scope of this work, I will nonetheless explore the results and impact of his thesis. The interested reader may find a brief summary of his research in "The Distinctive Character of Luke's Pneumatology," 17–30.

contribution to make. He calls us to recognize that the church, by virtue of its reception of the Pentecostal gift, is a prophetic community empowered for a missionary task. In short, not only are the pneumatological perspectives of Paul and Luke compatible, they are complementary: both represent important contributions to a holistic and harmonious biblical theology of the Spirit.[40]

Further, Luke's intent is clearly subordinate to the above question. If Menzies' description of a "distinctive" pneumatology for Luke is correct, then Luke's intent to teach a Spirit Baptism as distinct from conversion is, he believes, easily demonstrated. "One need only establish that Luke's narrative was designed to encourage every Christian to receive the Pentecostal gift. And, since Luke highlights Pentecost as a fulfillment of Joel's prophecy concerning an outpouring of the Spirit upon 'all flesh' (Acts 2:17–21), this appears to be self-evident."[41]

Finally, Fee has been charged with "selling out" the essentials of Pentecostalism. After all, one who subscribes neither to the stated doctrines of subsequence nor initial evidence, and yet claims to be Pentecostal, will face some distrust. Some suggest Fee has simply reached for a hermeneutic acceptable to the Evangelical world. His reluctance to employ the concept of *normative*, when describing charismatic phenomena associated with Spirit Baptism, leaves one with an "impoverished" Pentecostal theology. "The use of *normal* in this connection is indeed compatible with the views of some contemporary evangelicals, but it is too weak to be made into a doctrine. Repeatability is hardly a preachable item."[42] William Menzies argues:

> The obvious result of this reductionism is a willingness to permit *repeatability* of patterns, but not *normativity*. Hence, speaking in tongues associated with Spirit baptism may be *normal*, and even desirable, possibly, but it cannot be proclaimed as a *normative* model. Hence, one is sorely pressed on exegetical grounds . . . if

40. Menzies, *Empowered for Witness*, 240–41.

41. Ibid., 239. Fee agrees that Luke's primary interest is in the Spirit and his missiological rule. It is less on initiating experiences than on the Spirit's role in the Church. The soteriological dimension is not his focus. Luke *assumes* the soteriological dimension. Fee does not believe that he reads Luke with Pauline lenses, anymore than in 1 Pet or John, where both assume that the reception of the Spirit is what makes one a Christian. It is a thoroughly New Testament viewpoint. "I do let Luke speak for himself. He just isn't saying what they are saying he says." Fee, interview with author, 5 December 1997.

42. Menzies, "The Methodology of Pentecostal Theology," 10. Emphasis in original.

this be true, to establish a clear doctrine either of subsequence or tongues as the accompanying Spirit baptism. This reduction-ist point of view . . . [is] somewhat short of a thorough-going Pentecostal theology, [and] is apparently a position held today by a number of evangelicals.[43]

Fee's belief that his proposals should not impact the essentials of Pentecostalism has also come under fire. To some, his message is theo-logically indistinguishable from that of James D.G. Dunn.[44] Fee's repu-diation of Pentecostal theology leaves him with nothing new to offer the theological world, and challenges the Pentecostal understanding of their Spirit Baptism experience at its deepest level. Fee agrees with most non-Pentecostals in affirming that Spirit Baptism is equated with conversion, although he does insist that the charismatic, empowering dimension is lacking and should be restored. For Robert Menzies, this still undercuts crucial aspects of Pentecostal theology:

> When the Pentecostal gift is confused with conversion, [the] mis-siological (and I would add, Lukan) focus is lost.

> The bottom line is this: If Fee is right, Pentecostals can no longer proclaim an enabling of the Spirit which is distinct from conver-sion and available to every believer, at least not with the same sense of expectation, nor can Pentecostals maintain that the prin-cipal purpose of this gift is to grant power for the task of mission. To sum up, the doctrine of subsequence articulates a conviction crucial for Pentecostal theology and practice: Spirit-baptism, in the Pentecostal sense, is distinct from . . . conversion. This convic-tion, I would add, is integral to Pentecostalism's continued sense of expectation and effectiveness in mission.[45]

---

43. Ibid., 9. Emphasis in original. Cargal ("Beyond the Fundamentalist–Modernist Controversy," 183) agrees: "In one of the first responses by Pentecostals to these chal-lenges, Fee essentially conceded the case by joining didactic value with authorial intent."

44. Dunn, *Baptism in the Holy Spirit*. In one of the first challenges to Pentecostal theology, Dunn forcefully challenged the Pentecostal position on subsequence by firmly equating the experience of Spirit Baptism with conversion.

45. Menzies, *Empowered for Witness*, 9.

Fee's Response[46]

Fee has responded with some clarification. He concurs on the charismatic nature of Luke's writings, and that his primary concern was charismatic and not soteriological. It is not "theology" in the larger sense that concerns him when discussing Acts, but the concept of "didactic" as it relates to the question of establishing Christian norms. He believes that part of the problem lies in his usage of "norms" and "normative." By "normal," Fee understands that this is the way it was in the early Church. The dynamic, empowering dimension of life in the Spirit was a normal, expected, recurring experience. Precisely because it was so "normal," it was presupposed; there was no compulsion to talk about it at every turn. By "normative," however, he means something that must be adhered to by all Christians at all times and in all places, if they are truly obedient to God's Word. It becomes a matter of obedience, no questions asked.[47]

Fee acknowledges the concern that this transition, from "normative" to "normal," waters down the Pentecostal position. He disagrees with William Menzies' assertion that "[r]epeatability is hardly a preachable item."[48] Fee points to the millions of believers worldwide that have and are experiencing the Pentecostal reality of dynamic life in the Spirit, many of whom have never heard of subsequence or initial evidence.[49] He concludes:

> Precisely because I understand this dimension of life in the Spirit to be the New Testament norm, I think it is repeatable, and should be so, as the norm of the later church. Where I would tend to disagree with my tradition in the articulation of this norm is when they use language that seems more obligatory to me than I find in the New Testament documents themselves.[50]

46. With the republication in 1991 of the two key articles from 1976 and 1985, Fee includes a brief postscript in *Gospel and Spirit*, 100–4, containing his response to William Menzies and Roger Stronstad.

47. Fee, *Gospel and Spirit*, 102.

48. Menzies, "The Methodology of Pentecostal Theology," 10.

49. Fee, interview with author, 5 December 1997.

50. Fee, *Gospel and Spirit*, 103.

Categories of Christian Theology

Roger Stronstad takes issue with Fee's threefold classification of doctrinal statements. He believes that Fee is guilty of "a confusion of categories" when he places the experience of Spirit Baptism, and the Pentecostal explanation of the same, into the third category. According to Stronstad, Spirit Baptism is not something Christians "do." Rather, it is an experience. The third category ought to be spiritual experience, with a fourth category needed for Christian practice. The essence of this argument is the hope that the hermeneutics appropriate for Christian practice somehow do not apply to Christian experience. By challenging the placement of Spirit Baptism into Fee's third category, Stronstad hopes to bypass his more difficult hermeneutical guidelines. Thus Fee's entire hermeneutical scheme, suggested for the category of Christian practice, may not apply to the Pentecostal doctrine of Spirit Baptism.

> As a spiritual experience it is akin to, say, the spiritual experience of being born again. Both the experiences of Spirit-baptism and of being born again are experiences in which God causes something to happen to the person. In neither case is it something that Christians do. . . . Consequently, the principles which apply to the fourth category, Christian practice, are irrelevant for this new third category, spiritual experience.[51]

Fee's Response

Fee's use of three and not four categories is "more descriptive than definite." While Stronstad correctly observes that there is a fundamental difference in spiritual experience and Christian practice, Fee acknowledges that he put them together because he perceived the hermeneutical issues to be similar for each category. Whether or not this is actually true remains open for further examination and dialogue. Fee admits that he might well be wrong in his assumption. His main concern is not to establish a hermeneutical axiom, but to make the hermeneutical observation that most differences among Christians occur in this third (and fourth) category.[52] Neither Fee nor Stronstad has actually examined what differences, if any, occur hermeneutically between the two categories.

---

51. Stronstad, "The Biblical Precedent for Historical Precedent," 5.
52. See Fee, "Response to Roger Stronstad's 'The Biblical Precedent,' " 12.

The Merits of Historical Precedent

Fee maintains that Pentecostals employ the key passages in Acts on the basis of historical precedent alone. For historical precedent to function with didactic merit, he argues that it must be taught elsewhere in Scripture. Herein lies the sore spot between most Pentecostal scholars and Fee. No other part of Scripture teaches subsequence or initial evidence. Thus, for Pentecostals, Fee has undercut their theology at the root. Roger Stronstad complains:

> Ultimately, this methodology means that Jesus, or Paul, or Peter, or John may instruct the contemporary Christian, but that Luke, because he chose to write historical narrative, neither intended to instruct the church nor will be allowed to instruct the contemporary church, whatever his intention might or might not have been.
>
> It is a monumental irony that Luke, the author of 25 percent of the New Testament, is allowed no independent status among the recognized teachers in the New Testament by Reformed hermeneutics and so-called scientific exegesis.[53]

Robert Menzies accurately captures the essence of Fee's dilemma concerning how the normative aspects of Luke's narrative may be clearly identified. "Unless we are prepared to choose church leaders by the casting of lots, or are willing to encourage church members to sell all of their possessions, we cannot simply assume that a particular historical narrative provides the basis for normative theology."[54] Fee's concern is therefore legitimate. His solution is to tie historical precedent to authorial intent. On the basis of this, he has rejected the formulation of Pentecostal theology, though he maintains the validity of their experience. Menzies agrees with Fee on this point, focusing instead on the charismatic theology of Luke, with the promotion of the charismatic thus intrinsically implied in any discussion of Lukan intent.

Others take a different approach, suggesting that the hermeneutical "rules" laid out by Fee border on the arbitrary, and that care must be exercised to avoid limiting the theological enterprise.[55] Stronstad argues that Fee's three principles for the use of historical precedent are "fundamentally flawed." In particular, he takes issue with the first principle—the

53. Stronstad, "The Hermeneutics of Lukan Historiography," 10–11.

54. Menzies, *Empowered for Witness*, 233.

55. See Menzies, "The Methodology of Pentecostal Theology," 10.

use of historical precedent as an analogy by which to establish a norm is never valid—and gives three examples from Acts to illustrate the use of historical precedent by the early Church for a variety of purposes, including the establishment of norms.

The first biblical example is at the beginning of Jesus' public ministry. He anticipates the scepticism of the people when he visits Nazareth, declaring that "no prophet is accepted in his hometown" (Luke 4:24). He then appeals to Elijah (Luke 4:25–26) and Elisha (Luke 4:27), both of whom turn away from their own community to minister to others. Thus, on the basis of the historical precedent of Elijah and Elisha, Jesus leaves Nazareth and goes down to Capernaum (Luke 4:30). Luke also reports Jesus' use of historical precedent when the disciples are charged with Sabbath violations, i.e., picking and eating wheat on the Sabbath (Luke 6:2). Jesus defends his disciples on the precedent set by David when he and his companions were hungry and ate the consecrated bread, lawful only for the priests (Luke 6:4). Historical precedent is used at the so-called Jerusalem Council of Acts 15, when the Apostles are deciding the fate of Gentile Christians. On the basis of Peter's vision concerning the Gentiles, the Apostles decide that God's purpose is met in making the Gentiles his people. Further, their decision to refrain from insisting upon Gentile circumcision establishes a normative doctrine in the Church.[56]

Despite his arguments against the validity of Fee's dictums, Stronstad recognizes his predicament:

> The impasse in this debate is that whereas it is possible to expose the flaws in Fee's hermeneutic of historical precedent it is impossible to prove that there is a biblical precedent for historical precedent. In other words, although it is possible to demonstrate that there are examples in the Book of Acts where the church used historical precedent to establish a norm, it is impossible to prove that Luke intended for his readers to interpret his narratives by the same principle. It is impossible to prove because Luke never tells his readers to do this.[57]

Stronstad concludes that the validity of the use of biblical precedent must either commend itself as self-evident, or it does not. A Pentecostal hermeneutic affirms that normative beliefs and practices may properly be derived from narratives on the basis of historical precedent. Though

56. Stronstad, "The Biblical Precedent for Historical Precedent," 6–7.
57. Ibid., 9.

often criticized for this approach, other New Testament scholars tacitly agree.[58] The real issue for Stronstad, then, is not whether Pentecostals are justified in using historical precedent hermeneutically, but whether they have done so correctly.

Fee's Response

Fee responds by confessing that in all the criticism directed towards his articulation, he has failed to find another hermeneutical approach "that took me by the hand and showed me how one goes about doing this—that is, establishing something normative on the basis of historical precedent alone."[59] Regarding the criticism of his first principle, he notes that the key word for him is "analogy." His point is that anything based on analogies is sure to fail hermeneutically when establishing norms, for they open up too many possibilities.[60] As for Stronstad's pointed questions concerning exactly who has the authority to decide authorial intent, Fee has two suggestions. First, scholars must work to discover whether Luke actually *had* a doctrinal/theological imperative in his narratives, with regard to repeating the specifics. Second, with the evident diversity of patterns within Acts itself, how does one determine which are normative? If Luke's concern and intent was to provide patterns for the establishment of normative doctrine, Fee wonders, how does one explain one's failure to narrate similar events in the same way? Luke's fondness for great variety, as he reports the experience of the early believers, leads Fee to conclude that the establishment of normative patterns is not his chief objective.

> I would not want to say that Luke did *not* intend us to understand the baptism of the Spirit to be distinct from and subsequent to conversion, intended for empowering, and always evidenced by speaking in tongues; I simply am less convinced than my Pentecostal forebears that Luke did so intend. And chiefly because, even though this pattern can be found in three (probably four, and perhaps five) instances, it is clearly not expressly narrated in this way in every instance. Although I am quite open on this question, I do not find . . . the kinds of criteria that help me to think otherwise on this matter.[61]

58. Stronstad (ibid.) quotes Michaels ("Evidences of the Spirit," 203), "There is nothing wrong in principle with deriving normative beliefs and practices from narratives."

59. Fee, "Response to Roger Stronstad's 'The Biblical Precedent,'" 11.

60. Ibid., 13.

61. Fee, *Gospel and Spirit*, 103–4. Emphasis in original.

Fee wholeheartedly agrees that Jesus justified and defended his and other's actions on the basis of historical precedent. He also supports Stronstad's use of his third illustration, the Gentile mission in Acts. For Fee, however, there is a difference between defending one's actions and establishing a norm. It is certain that Jesus defended the right of his disciples to pluck grain on the Sabbath from historical precedent. But did he thereby establish a norm for all generations following? Jesus moved from his hometown to another location on the basis of the historical actions of two Old Testament prophets. Did he thus establish a norm? Must we do the same? In both cases, the answer is undoubtedly negative.[62]

> All of this to say, then, that I am an advocate of the "biblical precedent for historical precedent"; I always have been, and undoubtedly always will be. My roots are deep within restorationism, after all. But on the issue of "biblical precedent as historical precedent for establishing what is normative"—as I understand that word—I need more dialogue with the larger Pentecostal community, not with the aim of scoring points in a debate, but with the aim of helping me to understand so that I would be able to articulate such a perspective with personal integrity within my own present historical context.[63]

CONCLUSION

Fee's contributions to hermeneutics, both for Pentecostalism and the Christian world in general, are significant. Rarely does one read material so concerned to integrate the practical with the theoretical, the "exegesis" with the "spirituality." For him, the inherent tension in Scripture can be alleviated only through the discovery of authorial intent. This focus, however, seri-

---

62. Fee, "Response to Roger Stronstad's 'The Biblical Precedent,' " 13–14. Holman agrees. Further, he notes that the third example used—the Gentile mission—is only valid because it meets certain finely stated criteria. He questions what criteria Stronstad would offer to distinguish between historical precedent that is intended to serve as a norm, and that which is not. "It does us no good to perceive Luke as a theologian and then be unable to arrive at criteria by which his historical narrative becomes authoritative for us in experience and practice." ("A Response to Roger Stronstad's 'The Biblical Precedent,' " 13). Holman suggests that consideration be given to the broad literary structure of a document, the consistent recurrence of themes, the place of emphasis such themes occupies in the document as a whole, and the distinction between sub themes and the more prominent themes and the relation of the two (14).

63. Fee, "Response to Roger Stronstad's 'The Biblical Precedent,' " 14.

ously challenges the traditional Pentecostal practice of relying on perceived patterns in Luke's narratives. In addition, his atypical views concerning the core of Pentecostalism have been highly objectionable to those holding to subsequence and initial evidence as the essence of the movement.

For Pentecostals, the opportunity to interact theologically with Fee's proposals over the past four decades has been a goldmine of self-discovery, provoking a new awareness of their own hermeneutical issues. Pentecostals have responded forcefully to Fee's challenge. They have taken considerable exception to his understanding of authorial intent and historical precedent. In each case, they have argued with some success for their own view of these issues, employing far more sophisticated and scholarly arguments than had been the case with their forefathers.

Though many of these issues will be resolved largely on the basis of theological presupposition, the fact that this debate has occurred is significant in demonstrating Pentecostalism's increased academic interests, and the coming of age of Pentecostal hermeneutics and theology. The Pentecostal scholars who responded to Fee did so by employing accepted Evangelical hermeneutical practices. None of the scholars in the debate proposed a distinctively Pentecostal approach to the hermeneutical issues, but rather played by the rules set down by Fee. For example, when discussing the importance of authorial intent and whether Luke thus intended to teach initial evidence, the response is to propose the "charismatic theology" of Luke, making the argument that all of Luke-Acts intends to teach charismatic theology. One notes that the debate does not include a discussion of whether authorial intent is the deciding factor in determining accurate Pentecostal theology—this Modernistic foundation of hermeneutics is assumed. The debate is thus doubly significant, both for the theological discussion itself, but perhaps more importantly, for the tremendous hermeneutical shift towards Evangelical hermeneutics demonstrated by both sides. As Robert Menzies has noted,

> Now, almost a century after its genesis, the Pentecostal movement finds itself in a new environment: American revivalism has given way to modern Evangelicalism. The major tenets of Pentecostal theology remain the same; but the way we as Pentecostals approach Scripture—the hermeneutic, which supports our theology—has been significantly altered. *The hermeneutic of Evangelicalism has become our hermeneutic.*[64]

64. Menzies, "Evidential Tongues," 111. Italics added.

The focus of this work now shifts from hermeneutical issues *per se* to the wider question of how the hermeneutical model chosen by Pentecostalism will impact the youngest generations of Pentecostals, who find themselves living and serving God with a mindset strongly influenced by Postmodern thought. The old adage intones that no denomination is able to sustain the passion and creativity of its founders beyond the third generation. As Pentecostalism witnesses the fourth and fifth generations of its offspring on the world stage, few topics ought to be of greater importance to the Pentecostal community than their ability to translate its essence into the minds and experience of children, youth, and young adults. As statistics prove, the old adage may well be as accurate for Pentecostalism as for any previous mainline denomination.

In chapter 5, I will survey the work of Rudolf Bultmann and his more recent followers as an example of the use of the more extreme Modern hermeneutical methods in an effort to speak to Modern culture. I will investigate Bultmann's proposals, along with the findings of *The Jesus Seminar*, inquiring into possible similarities between their approach and Evangelical trends in hermeneutics. Further, I will survey the current cultural landscape for the appropriate Pentecostal response to this ultra-Modern presentation of the Gospel. There is a demonstrable shift in secular society from the precepts of Modernity to Postmodernity, acutely felt in the younger generations who most readily accept change.

Should Pentecostalism desire to see the newest generations of believers embracing and living in the full experience of the Holy Spirit, as their forbearers intended, the movement must resist the trend in some circles to further align Pentecostal hermeneutics with those of modern Evangelicalism. Rather, it must push towards methods of interpreting Scripture that allow for the use of some Postmodern concepts—the role of community and personal experience—within the Pentecostal hermeneutical process.

5

Postmodernity, Pentecostalism, and Rudolf Bultmann

We cannot use electric lights and radios and, in the event of illness, avail ourselves of modern medical and clinical means and at the same time believe in the spirit and wonder world of the New Testament.[1]

RUDOLF BULTMANN

All I want is reality. Show me God. Tell me what he is really like. Help me to understand why life is the way it is, and how I can experience it more fully and with greater joy. I don't want the empty promises. I want the real thing. And I'll go wherever I find that truth system.[2]

ANONYMOUS TEENAGER

I personally believe that the age-old wisdom in the Bible can affirm my generation in all its complexity, while pointing us to a greater, eternal harmony. But will the church be able to communicate this to us?[3]

RUDOLPHO CARRASCO (GENX)

PENTECOSTALISM IS, AT ITS core, an evangelistic movement. The early Pentecostal passion surrounding the soon return of Christ led the new revival movement to present the Gospel earnestly to the world in the experiential and supernatural manner in which it had been received. To connect with their generation, early Pentecostals portrayed Scripture as a "living Word" which must be experienced by the hearer. Other groups

1. Bultmann, *New Testament and Mythology*, 4.
2. Quoted in Barna, *Baby Busters*, 144.
3. Quoted in Beaudoin, *Virtual Faith*, 93.

felt differently, suggesting that the Gospel, as the Bible presents it, is full of "myths" the Modern mind finds unbelievable. By way of remedy, we ought to demythologize the Gospel accounts, re-explaining those portions recording the "supernatural" or "mythical."

In the discussion concerning Scripture and the perceived need to demythologize, no name figures more prominently than that of Rudolf Bultmann. His desire to facilitate a better understanding of the Gospel by a rational and "enlightened" Modern humanity led him to advocate the above hermeneutic. While one, living in the time of Bultmann, was hardly described as having promoted a "Modern" or "Postmodern" hermeneutic, his approach to the interpretation of Scripture has much in common with typical Modern objectives. Further, it has spawned a new twentieth-century hermeneutic that is decidedly Modern in nature. In theological and evangelistic terms, Pentecostalism was birthed from a desire to pursue God through the Scriptures in a manner exactly opposite to that which Bultmann championed. It is therefore useful to examine his proposed hermeneutic, along with those that have arisen in its wake, for they stand in stark contrast to the methodological approach to scriptural interpretation that Pentecostals should seek to employ.

The precepts of Postmodernity are making their way into the academic institutions of our time. The newest generations on the grand stage of history are significantly more open to, and more consciously searching for, the supernatural than any generation in several centuries. As Pentecostals, we must not only refuse to "demyth" Scripture's supernatural accounts, we must emphasize and explain them to a generation seeking God in his realm—the supernatural.

While demythologization may have had some small merit in the world with which Bultmann dealt, the pursuit of such an agenda today is among the most destructive and detrimental that could be undertaken. Pentecostals must carefully evaluate the place of Evangelical hermeneutics in the Pentecostal understanding of Scripture, and continue to stand firmly against the more extreme expressions of a new generation of scholars wishing to demythologize the Scriptures, such as *The Jesus Seminar*. Understanding the approach of Bultmann and *The Jesus Seminar* as the hermeneutical extreme of Modernity, I will demonstrate the necessity of a Pentecostal hermeneutic, antithetical to the presuppositions of *The Jesus Seminar* and distinct from that of Evangelicalism, in both focus and priority, if not entirely in methodology. This demonstration will come, not from a theological or an epistemological argument, but from an examination of contemporary culture and attitudes among our youngest generations.

I will discuss and explain this thesis in several steps. A brief account of Bultmann's life and work will set the historical background. Some explanation of the concept of demythologization will be offered, as well as Bultmann's defence of the exigency for such an approach to Scripture, taken directly from an examination of his key work in this area. Some attention will be given to current hermeneutical approaches which follow in the spirit of Bultmann. Finally, a brief excursus into the Postmodern world of today's youth will bring the demythologization process into direct encounter with its greatest challenge as I inquire about the wisdom of such an approach today.

One would not suggest that the hermeneutics of Modernity employed by Evangelicalism would of necessity or design lead to the type of emasculation of supernaturalism proposed by Bultmann or his recent followers. The blind following of Evangelical hermeneutics by Pentecostals may in the end, however, lead away from the type of presentation of the Gospel that Pentecostals would wish to proclaim to this generation—a proclamation not just of words, but also with a demonstration of the Holy Spirit's power.[4]

THE LIFE AND TIMES OF BULTMANN

Rudolf Karl Bultmann was the son and grandson of Evangelical-Lutheran pastors. In 1903, at 19 years of age, Bultmann began theological studies at Tübingen University, completing three semesters before his final four semesters, split evenly between Berlin and Marburg. Several professors, including Martin Heidegger (1889–1976), Wilhelm Herrmann (1846–1922), and Johannes Weiss (1863–1914), made substantial contributions to Bultmann's academic development.[5]

---

4. See 1 Corinthians 2:4–5.

5. Kegley, *The Theology of Rudolf Bultmann*, xix–xx. Weiss, a member of the "history of religions school," was concerned to understand exactly what Jesus and his followers meant by the "Kingdom of God." Weiss taught that the reference was to God erupting into history, in a "divine storm," to bring to violent end world history and powers. This influence can be seen clearly in Bultmann, as he always speaks of the "Reign of God" instead of the "Kingdom of God." This way, the stress is laid upon God and his action, rather than the actions of humanity. Herrmann was important for contemporary theology, for he influenced both Karl Barth (1886–1968) and Bultmann. Herrmann believed that revelation, while found generally in nature, is foremost in the "inner life" of the his-

Bultmann completed his doctoral studies in 1910 and post-doctoral research in 1912, qualifying him to teach New Testament studies. Interestingly, his student years, 1903–12, were permeated by the optimistic liberalism which dominated European culture and theology in the period leading up to World War I. Many theologians were immensely optimistic about mankind and the inevitability of spiritual and moral progress on the earth, leading ultimately to the establishment of the Kingdom of God. The onset of war in 1914 and the resultant horrors against humanity by humanity greatly decreased the number of voices in the choirs of liberal optimism.[6]

In 1912 Bultmann was appointed lecturer in New Testament at the University of Marburg, where he remained for four years, leaving to assume an Assistant Professorship at Breslau. In 1920 he taught at Giessen before assuming his prominent role as Professor of New Testament at Marburg, where he taught until his retirement in 1951.[7] During this time, the writings that established him as a major New Testament scholar first appeared. *The History of the Synoptic Tradition* and *Jesus and the Word* challenged the quest for the historical Jesus. These books radically altered New Testament studies by suggesting that the Synoptic Gospels were not concerned to give the kind of historical information that many scholars had to that point been seeking and, to Bultmann's consternation, finding.[8] "New Testament and Mythology" (1941), *Theology of the New Testament* (1948 and 1953), and *Jesus Christ and Mythology* (1958) served to solidify the Bultmannian case for demythologization.[9]

---

torical Jesus, and not in his biographical details such as the virgin birth, resurrection, and miracles. These are of secondary importance. It is the inner life of Jesus, as attested to in the Gospels, that puts its hold on us, even as it did on Jesus' disciples. While we cannot speak directly of God, we know him and may speak of him existentially in terms of the impact of Jesus' inner life on our life. The impact of the existentialist views of Heidegger, professor of philosophy at Marburg with Bultmann (1923–28), began to appear in Bultmann's work as early as 1925. Two years later, Heidegger published *Being and Time*, generally regarded as one of the most influential sources of existentialist philosophy of the twentieth century. Heidegger's views were appropriated by Bultmann because they fit his understanding of New Testament teaching on existence. God is "Wholly Other," apart from mankind and the universe, yet by him alone humanity exists. God must be known existentially; that is, we cannot speak of God objectively. What can be known and spoken of concerning God is found in human existence, for we cannot know him other than through our own experience of him, as the "inner life" of the Christ of Faith touches us individually. See also Johnson, *Rudolf Bultmann*; and Macquarrie, *Twentieth-century Religious Thought*.

6. Perrin, *The Promise of Bultmann*, 12.

7. Ibid.

8. Johnson, *Rudolf Bultmann*, 91.

9. For English translations of Bultmann's work, see his *The History of the Synoptic*

DEMYTHOLOGIZATION

Bultmann's most influential contribution to theology came as a result of his desire to communicate the Gospel more effectively to Modern minds and hearts. This is a vital point, which many of his more devastating critics have overlooked. On 4 June 1941, Bultmann addressed the Society of Evangelical Theology at Alpirsbach, Germany, on the topic, "New Testament and Mythology: The Problem of Demythologizing the New Testament Proclamation." Thus appeared what Schubert M. Ogden calls "perhaps the single most discussed and controversial theological writing of the century. . . ."[10] I will examine this key work as a succinct and direct overview of Bultmann's position.

Myth in Scripture

Bultmann begins by stating what he deems to be the problem: myth reigns supreme in Scripture. A proper definition of "myth," as he understands the term, is essential for a correct understanding of his views, for the term carries negative connotations of something that is simply false or a legend with no basis in reality. For Bultmann, according to James F. Kay, "myth embraces those reality claims that do not square with scientific understanding."[11] Marcus Barth (1915–94) observes that "myth is present wherever the unworldly is spoken of in a worldly way, where one speaks of the gods in a human way, where the transcendental is objectified."[12] The purpose of myth is not to make the gods human, but to show the dependence of humanity upon the gods. Again, according to Barth, myth is anthropocentric: "To explain and understand a myth means therefore, to translate or transpose its language and its contents into such words as are suitable to express man's plight, man's decisions, man's expectations."[13] Though we may wonder whether some New Testament myths intend simply to tell us about God and not about ourselves, this is nonetheless Bultmann's beginning position. Demythologization is the only way to do justice to the innermost meaning and intent of the myths of Scripture.

Tradition; *Jesus and the Word*; *New Testament and Mythology*; *Theology of the New Testament*; and *Jesus Christ and Mythology*.

10. In Bultmann, *New Testament and Mythology*, vii.

11. Kay, "Theological Table-Talk," 327.

12. Barth, "Introduction to Demythologizing," 148.

13. Ibid.

The worldview of the New Testament is mythical, located in a three-storied universe, with the earth in the middle of heaven and hell. On the earth, the forces that rule above and below actively battle for control of and influence on mankind. Supernaturalism is everywhere and very much a part of life, a blend of Jewish apocalypticism and the Gnostic myth of redemption. The question Bultmann poses is whether Christian proclamation, "when it demands faith from men and women . . . expects them to acknowledge this mythical world picture of the past."[14] Is this even realistic to expect? Bultmann asks whether mythical world truths have been lost during the Enlightenment, and if these ought to be recovered and rediscovered by Modern thinkers. Unfortunately, however, he dismissed this in a sentence, asserting that because all of our thinking is shaped by science, humanity can only now think in mythical terms through "sheer resolve," a process that would "reduce faith to a work" and "would be simply arbitrariness."[15] The veracity of this statement flies in the face of the millions of believers worldwide who, according even to the type of existential experience of which Bultmann would have approved, have found it possible to cast off the aspects of scientific thinking which are unhelpful, and have embraced the New Testament worldview without much apparent distress.

Unbelievable Biblical Myths

Bultmann proceeds to detail the various aspects of the New Testament myth that Modern mankind will no longer believe. The idea that heaven is above and hell below is challenged, and perhaps rightly so, for it is not as much the location of these places that matters to believers but their existence, about which Bultmann makes no comment. He states, "Also finished by knowledge of the forces and laws of nature is faith in spirits and demons"; "the wonders of the New Testament are also finished as wonders"; and "We cannot use electric lights and radios and, in the event of illness, avail ourselves of modern medical and clinical means and at the same time believe in the spirit and wonder world of the New Testament."[16] The question that arises by way of response, however, is: What greater difficulty lies in believing in angels, demons, and miracles, that does not

---

14. Bultmann, *New Testament and Mythology*, 3.

15. Ibid.

16. Ibid., 4.

lie in believing in God *a priori*, which Bultmann assumes is possible? If one can believe in God, it would seem that belief in various spirits and acts of God would follow easily, for one has already had to adjust one's epistemology past the limits of the scientifically verifiable in order to admit belief in God.

Mythical eschatology is finished by the obvious fact that Christ's Parousia did not occur as quickly as New Testament writers had hoped. Mankind cannot understand how a supernatural "something or other," such as the Holy Spirit, could intervene in our closed universe and influence us. The idea of grace made available to believers through water baptism or the Lord's Supper meets a similar fate in the Modern mind of which Bultmann speaks. Death as a punishment for sin is obsolete, for all know medically that individuals die at a certain point, regardless of the piety of a life or great talent displayed in sinning. Original sin and substitutionary atonement are dismissed on grounds too numerous to mention. That the resurrection of Christ somehow empowers people twenty centuries later to live better lives is beyond Modern thinking.[17]

Finally, Bultmann suggests that "the idea of a preexistent heavenly Christ and the correlative idea of our own translation into a heavenly world of light, in which the self is supposed to receive heavenly garments and a pneumatic body, are not only rationally incredible but also say nothing to us."[18] When one is limited to Bultmann's approach to Scripture, it is little wonder that something such as the pre-existent Christ is meaningless. At this point he might have contemplated more fully whether something of importance in humanity's worldview has been lost through the Enlightenment.

All or Nothing?

Bultmann rejects the idea that one may demythologize certain but not all portions of the New Testament. Some may wish to deem obsolete the spatial references to heaven and hell, for example, but still insist on their reality. Bultmann tolerates none of this. "We can only completely accept the mythical world picture or completely reject it."[19] However, he seems

---

17. "Beyond" may perhaps be the best choice here, though I am quite sure it is unintentional in this manner.

18. Bultmann, *New Testament and Mythology*, 8.

19. Ibid., 9.

not to follow his own proscription. Later in the essay he asserts that there is nothing "mysterious" or "supernatural" about Christianity, and that it is an original possibility of mankind.[20] He also maintains, on the other hand, that only as a consequence of the saving work of God in Christ is this possibility capable of being realized. Bultmann states, "The question naturally arises as to whether this appeal to a unique salvation occurrence does not constitute an important qualification of his original demand for a radical demythologization of the New Testament. Can one really make such an appeal without setting a limit to demythologization?"[21] We would answer that this is an example of the line of contradiction that runs throughout Bultmann's reasoning.

Bultmann teaches that in order for the New Testament to retain its validity it must be demythologized, for that is the very nature of myth. It wishes to teach something about humanity, which it cannot do if we fail to understand it. Earlier attempts by liberal theology attacked this problem by simply dismissing all myths. Unfortunately, the truths of these passages were dismissed with the mythological language itself. As Marcus Barth notes, "Elimination was the old way of demythologization."[22] The truths hidden in the wrappings of mythological language were not to be discarded, but made known. Bultmann wishes instead to *interpret* mythology for Modern minds, to interpret the mythology of the New Testament dualism in existentialist terms—by removing the supernatural elements.[23]

BULTMANN'S LEGACY: *THE JESUS SEMINAR*

Of the many theological endeavors that have followed in Bultmann's footsteps, none are more celebrated (and lamented) than *The Jesus Seminar*. Slightly more than twenty years old, this latest formal inquiry into the historical Jesus follows some two hundred years of similar exploration. Seeking to determine which of the Gospel records of Jesus' life and teaching are authentic in light of the many Modern forms of biblical criticism, *The Jesus Seminar* has made a great many friends—and perhaps even more enemies.

20. Ibid., 24.
21. Cited in Ogden, "Bultmann's Project of Demythologization," 164.
22. Barth, "Introduction to Demythologizing," 152.
23. See Bultmann, *New Testament and Mythology*, 15.

In his history of *The Jesus Seminar*, Perry V. Kea notes that the origins of the search for the historical Jesus can be traced back to the Enlightenment and the application of the scientific method to biblical history. "When scholars informed by the Enlightenment considered the figure of Jesus in the Gospels, they began to ask if the claims made for Jesus could be supported by rational evidence or arguments. So began the quest for the historical Jesus."[24] The nineteenth century produced many "lives" of Jesus, perhaps none better than Albert Schweitzer's (1875–1965) *The Quest of the Historical Jesus*, which applies literary criticism to the Gospel accounts of Jesus' life and determines him to be an apocalyptic prophet.[25] Birger A. Pearson notes:

> The story of the "Quest of the Historical Jesus," as told by Schweitzer, includes not only rationalist attempts at discrediting traditional Christian teaching, but also attempts by Christian theologians to fend off such critiques by creating an edifice of critical theological scholarship by which a believable "real Jesus" might emerge to view. The result, often enough, was a "modern-ized" Jesus, one whose ethical genius and message of a "spiritual kingdom" brought him close to the liberal ideas of 19th-century German Protestantism.[26]

The years following the end of World War I saw a shift in focus from the biblical records of Jesus' life to the oral traditions behind the written records. Applying form criticism to the Gospels, scholars such as Bultmann believed they were gaining a glimpse into the traditions about Jesus before they were recorded in writing. Further recognizing that the order and sequence of events as recorded in the New Testament were thus artificial, Bultmann and others argued that the "Jesus of History" was not as important as the "Christ of Faith." In this period, known as the "No Quest," Bultmann developed his system of hermeneutics, arguing for the demythologization of New Testament records as they pertain to the life and work of Jesus of Nazareth, and focusing upon the theological activity of early Christianity. Though several of his students would again bring renewed focus to the search for the historical Jesus (known as the "New Quest"),[27] Bultmann's

---

24. Kea, "The Road to the Jesus Seminar." See also Woodmorappe, "The Jesus Seminar Reeks with Rationalism."

25. Schweitzer, *The Quest of the Historical Jesus*.

26. Pearson, "The Gospel According to the Jesus Seminar."

27. See, for example, Käsemann, "The Problem of the Historical Jesus."

questioning of the relevance and veracity of specific New Testament records regarding Jesus Christ remains influential to this day.[28]

Through the 1960s and 1970s, scholars began to focus upon literary criticism once again, concentrating upon Jesus' use of parables and allegories. According to Perry Kea, Dan Otto Via's *The Parables*,[29] Robert W. Funk's *Language, Hermeneutic, and Word of God*,[30] and Robert C. Tannehill's *The Sword of His Mouth*[31] each "demonstrated that the aesthetic dimension of Jesus' language was not merely decorative or ornamental, but essential to the communication of his message. While these works were concerned to examine Jesus' speech forms for their literary qualities, they also had the effect of demonstrating that the author of these parables and aphorisms (namely, Jesus) had a rather subversive or unconventional view of reality."[32]

In the 1980s, the focus on Jesus' language as key to the communication of his message led to the creation of *The Jesus Seminar* by Robert Funk. Comprised of nearly two hundred scholars, *The Jesus Seminar* met twice yearly, with the goal of determining what Jesus actually said and did. Its findings were published in three reports, *The Five Gospels*,[33] *The Acts of Jesus*,[34] and *The Gospel of Jesus*.[35] The basic critical approach is presented in a discussion of seven "pillars of scholarly wisdom" in the Introduction to *The Five Gospels*:

1. The distinction between the historical Jesus and the Christ of Christian faith.

2. Preference for the Synoptic Gospels (Matthew, Mark, and Luke) over John as sources for the historical Jesus.

3. The chronological priority of the Gospel of Mark.

---

28. See Kea, "The Road to the Jesus Seminar."

29. Via, *The Parables*.

30. Funk, *Language, Hermeneutic, and Word of God*.

31. Tannehill, *The Sword of His Mouth*.

32. Kea, "The Road to the Jesus Seminar." See also Crossan, *In Parables* and *In Fragments*; Dodd, *The Parables of the Kingdom*; Perrin, *The Kingdom of God* and *Rediscovering the Teaching of Jesus*; and Wilder, *The Language of the Gospel*.

33. Funk, *The Five Gospels*.

34. Idem, *The Acts of Jesus*.

35. Idem, *The Gospel of Jesus*.

4. The hypothetical source "Q" used independently by Matthew and Luke.

5. "The liberation of the non-eschatological Jesus . . . from Schweitzer's eschatological Jesus."

6. The fundamental contrast between an oral culture, such as that of Jesus, and a print culture.

7. The "burden of proof" on those who argue for authenticity, rather than those who argue for inauthenticity. [36]

Basing its finding upon these key pillars, *The Jesus Seminar* examined each Gospel passage relative to Jesus' speech or deeds, and voted to determine authenticity by using colored marbles.

Much of the methodology of *The Jesus Seminar* is based on the results of two centuries of critical scholarship. The evidence of the Modern tendencies in *The Jesus Seminar* is quickly observed early in *The Five Gospels*:

> The contemporary religious controversy, epitomized in the Scopes trial and the continuing clamor for creationism as a viable alternative to the theory of evolution, turns on whether the worldview reflected in the Bible can be carried forward into this scientific age and retained as an article of faith. Jesus figures prominently in this debate. The Christ of creed and dogma, who had been firmly in place in the Middle Ages, can no longer command the assent of those who have seen the heavens through Galileo's telescope. The old deities and demons were swept from the skies by that remarkable glass.[37]

John Woodmorappe writes, "Note the equation of anti-supernaturalist preconceptions with a 'scientific' (actually rationalistic) worldview. Clearly, these modernist scholars do not distinguish reason from rationalism. . . . To them, a questioning of anti-supernaturalism—or a belief in the reality of divine action—is in itself an attack on reason, scholarship and science."[38]

Given the excessively Modern nature of the seven pillars, it is not surprising that only eighteen percent of the sayings and deeds of Jesus,

---

36. See *idem, The Five Gospels,* Introduction. See also Pearson, "The Gospel According to the Jesus Seminar."

37. Funk, *The Five Gospels,* 2.

38. Woodmorappe, "The Jesus Seminar Reeks with Rationalism."

as reported by the Synoptics, were found to be authentic; John fares even worse, as nearly the entire book was found to lack veracity.[39] Further, as one might expect, none of the records of Jesus' life, which portray him as divine or participating in the expression of the supernatural acts of God, have been retained.[40]

THE BULTMANNIAN LEGACY AND POSTMODERNS

Bultmann's desire to remove myth from the New Testament accounts of Jesus, along with the desire of *The Jesus Seminar* to further emasculate the records of Jesus' life and ministry, could hardly be more inappropriate in today's culture. My critique of Bultmann's position on demythologizing and the conclusions of *The Jesus Seminar* does not come as much from scholarly sources that have criticized their work from the viewpoint of theological appropriateness, for many have pursued this. Rather, I examine the usefulness of demythologization in reaching the generations of North American youth known as *Generation X* and the *Millennials*, by asking whether the attempt of Bultmann and *The Jesus Seminar* to make the Gospel more "believable" to the Modern mind, borne out in demythologization, is effective in reaching them.

The Impact of Postmodernism

It is clear that Postmodernity has impacted today's youth. Although the significance or permanence of Postmodernity may well be debated, it seems clear that certain of its presuppositions are making inroads into the thinking of the post-boomer generations. In terms of the rejection of the rationalism often espoused by organized religion and the importance of experience in particular, today's students and young adults are approach-

39. See Funk, *The Five Gospels*. Naturally, many New Testament scholars have written against the findings of *The Jesus Seminar*. See, for example, Johnson, *The Real Jesus*; Witherington, *The Jesus Quest*; Eddy and Boyd, *The Jesus Legend*; Wright, *Jesus and the Victory of God*; Wilkins and Moreland, *Jesus Under Fire*; and Evans, *Fabricating Jesus*.

40. Pearson ("The Gospel According to the Jesus Seminar") notes: "A group of secularized theologians and secular academics went seeking a secular Jesus, and they found him! They think they found him, but, in fact, they created him. Jesus the 'party animal,' whose zany wit and caustic humor would enliven an otherwise dull cocktail party—this is the product of the Jesus Seminar's six years' research. In a sense the Jesus Seminar, with its ideology of secularization, represents a 'shadow image' of the 'New Quest,' with its neo-orthodox theology—and its ultimate bankruptcy."

ing the Christian faith, and our attempts to propagate the Gospel, in ways not seen since pre-Enlightenment times.

In his excellent work, *The Younger Evangelicals*, Robert E. Webber (1933–2007) draws several conclusions regarding the differences between the youngest Evangelicals in North America and the generations preceding them. Webber emphasizes that today's youth are fully aware they are maturing in a Postmodern world. As such, they have a much broader concept of what constitutes "reason," for they acknowledge that all rationality, scientific and otherwise, has some inherent measure of faith.[41]

Webber lists several other characteristics of younger Evangelicals, including their:

1. Recovery of the biblical understanding of human nature, particularly in the post-9/11 era

2. Awareness of a new context for ministry that differs from the pragmatist approach, and includes a new paradigm of thought

3. Stance for the absolutes of the Christian faith in a new way, recognizing that the road to the future runs through the past

4. Commitment to the plight of the poor

5. Willingness to live by the rules

6. Familiarity with technology, particularly that which is highly visual, and their ability to communicate through imaginative stories, appreciating the power of the symbol and of the arts

7. Longing for community and commitment to intergenerational and multicultural ministry

8. Attraction to absolutes that are not necessarily acquired by rationalism

9. Readiness to commit, search for shared wisdom, and recognize the unity between thought and action

10. Demand for authenticity in those with whom they interact.[42]

Walt Mueller notes with interest that J. I. Packer's classic work *Knowing God* has been replaced in many circles with Henry Blackaby's

---

41. See Webber, *The Younger Evangelicals*, 47–8.
42. Ibid., 47–54.

Experiencing God. The shift from knowing to experiencing clearly demonstrates the changing values of younger generations.[43]

Tony Jones succinctly states the impact of Postmodernity upon past, present, and future generations. In general, the Boomers studied under Modern professors, fully appreciative of the Enlightenment. Generation X studied during the transitional phase. "But the Millennials are getting full-blown, no-holds-barred Postmodern thought."[44] Little wonder then that the industries based directly on selling to youth, such as music, cinema, and advertising, are embracing the Postmodern ethos. Further, it is important to recognize that those working with today's youth were born into a culture of transition; those born today are entering a thoroughly Postmodern world. While not all will adopt Postmodern tenets as their own, Postmodernity will be the reigning culture in our institutions of higher learning.[45]

Other authors take this concept even further, acknowledging that what is learned from ministry to Generation X must soon be applied throughout culture. Brad Cecil challenges those who suggest that Postmodernity is simply another trend on the conference circuit, arguing instead that it is the most important cultural shift of the last 500 years. "It's not a generation issue exclusive to Gen-X or Millennials. In fact, it's fast becoming the adopted epistemology of all adults. Everyone in ministry—not just youth and young adult pastors—will have to wrestle with this phenomenon."[46]

Some observers note that the task of determining the spiritual values of Generation X has been considerably more difficult than for their parents, the Boomer generation. Concerning Generation X, Harvey Cox notes:

> [T]heir religious proclivities have remained a mystery almost as inscrutable as that of the Holy Trinity. Here is a generation that stays away from most churches in droves but loves songs about God and Jesus, a generation that would score very low on any standard piety scale but at times seems almost obsessed with saints, visions, and icons in all shapes and sizes. These are the young people who, Styrofoam cups of cappuccino in hand, crowd among the shelves

43. Mueller, *Engaging the Soul of Youth Culture*, 65. See Packer, *Knowing God*; and Blackaby, *Experiencing God*.

44. Jones, *Postmodern Youth Ministry*, 29. See also Twenge, *Generation Me*.

45. Jones, *Postmodern Youth Ministry*, 29.

46. Cecil, in ibid., preface.

of New Age spirituality titles in the local book market and post thousands of religious and quasi-religious notes on the bulletin boards in cyberspace.[47]

Anti-religious but Pro-spiritual

Tom Beaudoin suggests four themes implicit in GenX spirituality. First, this generation is inherently suspicious of Christianity as it has been presented by organized religious institutions. Second, GenXers wish to emphasize the sacred nature of their shared experiences, communal in nature, and lived daily in human existence. Third, today's youth identify with the scriptural theme of the suffering servant. Finally, GenX seeks unique ways of being religious and expressing faith. Students of Postmodernity will observe its impact on this generation throughout these themes.[48] Christians need not fear these, for in many ways they look back to Christian themes of the Pre-modern era. As Robert Webber asks, "Where do we go to find a Christianity that speaks meaningfully to a Postmodern world? . . . [O]ur challenge is not to reinvent Christianity, but to restore and then adapt classical Christianity to the Postmodern cultural situation."[49]

Paul Tyson observes very specific types of spirituality present in the youth he has studied:[50]

> At the conservative right end of the spectrum is the . . . **modern fundamentalist** spirituality. This spirituality seeks certainty, authoritative meaning and a clear moral framework. Next is . . . the blending of . . . fundamentalism with . . . **hypermodernism**. This blend is often seen where American fundamentalism combines with contemporary consumer culture. [Next] is **relationalism** which, to varying degrees, expresses discontent with the atomization, fragmentation and superficiality of consumer culture, and places high value on meaning derived from relationships. At the

47. Cox, in Beaudoin, *Virtual Faith*, ix.

48. Beaudoin, *Virtual Faith*, 26, 41–2.

49. Webber, *Ancient-Future Faith*, 24. See also Carroll, *The New Faithful*.

50. Although detailed study of these categories is outside the scope of this work, a basic understanding well serves the student of today's younger generations. As the reader will note, Tyson suggests that all youth are not fully affected by Postmodern thought, though this segment of youth is declining. While that might be true for Australia, I would suggest that few if any North American youth have failed to be impacted by Postmodern thought.

far end of the spirituality spectrum comes . . . **radical post-secularism**. These young people have no interest in modern certainty or postmodern irrealism, reject hypermodern consumerism and want more than relationally orientated metaphysical unbelief. These young people have a theological and religious thirst for spiritual water that reflects their sense of living in a very arid spiritual environment. They are typically highly critical of "church." Of these spirituality types, only modernist fundamentalism is "**secular**" in the sense that its belief world assumes "conservative" religious Biblical supernaturalism is in conflict with "progressive" atheistic scientific naturalism. All other spiritualities are in some manner **post-secular** and this has revolutionary implications.[51]

Organized religion and religious groups have fallen into some disfavor with those most impacted by Postmodernity, precisely for the reasons mentioned above.[52] Many churches have watched with alarm the great decline in attendance among all ages (and many appear not to have noticed), with teenagers and young adults leading the way.[53] Canadian sociologist Reginald W. Bibby, who has tracked the attitudes of Canadian teens towards religion for more than three decades,[54] has discovered that increasing numbers of teens would be classified in the relationalism or radical post-secularism categories outlined above. In *Canada's Teens*, Bibby reveals the results of two national surveys completed in 2000. The dichotomy between identity and practice is readily apparent: among Canadian teens, a full 76% identify with some religious group, while only 22% attend weekly services.[55]

51. Tyson, "Contemporary Australian Youth Spiritualities." Emphasis in original. Tyson continues by suggesting specific ways youth ministry must be tailored to each group in his spectrum.

52. See Bibby and Posterski, *Teen Trends*, 50–51.

53. Weekly church attendance in Canada by all ages declined from 61% in 1956 to 35% in 1985, according to Gallup Canada, one of the country's largest polling organizations. Cited in Bibby, *Restless Gods*, 12–3. The most recent surveys by Bibby, however, suggest that a recovery may be in the works: from a low of 21% of Canadians reporting weekly church attendance in 2000, numbers for 2003 seem to indicate a rebound to 1985 levels, at 27%. Bibby, *Restless Churches*, 12.

54. Bibby has tracked the social and religious trends among Canadian adults through a series of national surveys every five years since 1975, and has complemented these with *Project Teen Canada* national youth surveys in 1984, 1992, and 2000. Bibby, *Restless Churches*.

55. Bibby, *Canada's Teens*, 118. See also Bibby, *The Emerging Millennials*, released as this work was going to print.

Most interesting here is the admission of 43% who said they would be open to increased connection with organized religion, agreeing with this statement: "I would be open to more involvement with religious groups if I found it to be worthwhile."[56] For Generation X and the Millennials, the Church ought to be practical and useful in helping people deal with life and life's issues. It must be more focused on helping those in the community than on keeping those in the pews happy. Religion for religion's sake is out.[57]

Summing up his latest survey, Bibby notes, "Overall, these findings point to a paradox: many young people who are not involved in organized religion are nonetheless seemingly interested in many things that organized religion 'is about.' " He quotes religion writer Douglas Todd of the *Vancouver Sun*:

> Most young people probably would appreciate a safe, accepting—even fun—place where they can ask hard religious questions, and where "doubt" is not a dirty word. . . . Either the clergy's genuine welcome is not getting out to teenagers, mass culture is just too hostile to faith institutions, or the spiritual message isn't one that clicks with most young people. Or all of the above.[58]

As many youth and young adults continue to avoid traditional denominations in particular, and organized Christianity in general, observers often inquire as to where, if anywhere, they are headed. In an interview in *The Twentysomething American Dream*, a typical GenX attitude is observed: "What the hell's going to church for? These days you've got to take religion into your own hands."[59] Tom Beaudoin notes that this has occurred in two ways. First, GenXers have a widespread regard for paganism, however vaguely defined. Second, they have a growing enchantment with mysticism. "As practiced by Xers, mysticism is defined broadly as paganism and is often expressed as religious eclecticism. Xers take symbols, values, and rituals from various religious traditions and combine them into their personal 'spirituality.' They see this spirituality as being far removed from 'religion,' which they frequently equate with a religious institution."[60]

---

56. Ibid, 117–8.

57. Barna, *Baby Busters*, 142.

58. Todd, in Bibby, *Canada's Teens*, 127–8.

59. Cohen, *The Twentysomething American Dream*, 183.

60. Beaudoin, *Virtual Faith*, 25.

Reginald Bibby and Donald Posterski agree, noting that paradoxically, youth are having difficulty relating to organized religion precisely as they exhibit a strong interest in the things that religion has traditionally focused upon—the supernatural, spirituality, ethics, morality, and meaning. Forty-six percent rate *the quest for truth* as "very important," and twenty-four per cent rate *spirituality* the same. Only ten percent of teens, however, rate *religious involvement* as very important. "Time and again, young people express an openness to things spiritual, and disinterest in things organizational."[61]

New Age teachings and others, which emphasize the interaction between the immanent and the transcendent, are becoming increasingly popular.[62] Bibby's research reveals that a majority of Canadian teens believe in conventional Christian values:

- Life after death—78%

- Heaven—75%

- The existence of God—73%

- Jesus was the divine Son of God—65%

These same teens, however, also believe in a variety of less conventional values:

- Near-death experiences—76%

- Extra Sensory Perception—59%

- Astrology—57%

- Individuals can possess psychic powers—55%[63]

Observing an "irreverent religiousness" in this generation, Tom Beaudoin disagrees with those who view Xers as "simply irreligious or generally indifferent towards spirituality." Rather, they possess a "unique religiousness," observed largely in their interaction with contemporary

61. Bibby and Posterski, *Teen Trends*, 53.

62. Ibid., 53–5.

63. Bibby, *Canada's Teens*, 123. Bibby's latest survey also demonstrates that a higher percentage of today's teens obtain moral guidance from what they have experienced personally than do their parents and grandparents, who rely on external sources such as the Church. This also points to the impact of Postmodern thought upon today's youth, who often see morality in relativistic terms. See Bibby, *Restless Gods*, 217.

culture.[64] Religious symbolism, even if used in an irreverent and improper manner, abounds in GenX culture, and can be used to clearly observe a generational theology. According to Beaudoin,

> Religious institutions, our elders, or other sceptics should not fear irreverence and popular culture. Paradoxically, interpreting pop culture theologically—especially with an eye to its irreverence—highlights the depth of Generation X's religious practice. The more popular culture is explored, and the more irreverence is viewed as a legitimate mode of religiosity (in all its illegitimacy), the more Generation X will be shown as having a real religious contribution to make. GenX can make great strides not only towards fostering its own spirituality but also toward reinvigorating religious institutions and challenging the faith of older generations.[65]

Beaudoin seeks to challenge the common assumption that youth are uninterested in spiritual issues, and raises the ante by suggesting that organized religion may even learn from their younger Postmodern critics. "GenX's suspicion or outright derision of institutions, which includes . . . a reclamation of Jesus against institutions, is a bedrock component of Xer's irreverent spirituality. Xer religiosity squarely challenges institutions to come to terms with their relevance or irrelevance, to question whether they have become institutionalized."[66] Further, "In general, GenX culture challenges Churches to preach and practice from a position of humility and weakness in the world. By shunning the trappings of privileged social status . . . and seeking to serve, not to be served, Churches will respond faithfully not only to the prophetic charge brought by GenX but, more important, to the example of Jesus."[67]

Today's youth may also effectively challenge the Church to revive spiritual or mystical tradition, to refocus upon spiritual growth and religious journey where there has been a lack of focus. Their emphasis upon silence and meditation may prove to be a needed correction for the many churches caught in the endless rush and busyness of programs and committees.[68]

---

64. Beaudoin, *Virtual Faith*, 175–6.
65. Ibid., 180.
66. Ibid., 161.
67. Ibid., 162.
68. Ibid., 165.

Tony Jones agrees that Postmodernism may well be a positive force in the Church, challenging those who would suggest that Postmodern thought is in some way inherently evil. For him, many of the Postmodern critiques of Modernism should be welcomed by the Church. "No longer are we beholden to the scientific proof model of evangelism—everything does not need to be explained and rationalized. This should come as a relief to Christian youth workers who have been attempting to *explain* great mysteries like the incarnation, the resurrection, and the Lord's Supper."[69]

Pentecostalism and the Postmodern

Although it has been demonstrated that some Pentecostal scholars have increasingly accepted an Evangelical hermeneutic borne out of Modernity, there is evidence that this shift in the academy has not yet made a significant impact in the Pentecostal pew. Various observers have noted the inherent emotionalism in Pentecostalism, and the typical Pentecostal openness to experience and the supernatural.

An article in *The Economist* notes the experiential dimension of this movement, suggesting that the most remarkable religious success story of the past century has been "the least intellectual (and most emotive)" religious movement of all. Though founded by a "one-eyed black preacher," who was convinced that God would send revival if people prayed hard enough, there are now "at least 400 million revivalists around the world." According to the Pew Forum on Religion, many of these adherents have witnessed healings and/or exorcisms, and have "received direct revelation from God."[70]

As has been established, many youth today are bypassing the Christian Church, the appointed herald of the only supernatural God, for cheap and deadly imitations elsewhere. Pentecostalism must take up this challenge, for its own sons and daughters are among this generation of Postmodern youth. Simply caring for those already in the pews has never been a part of the Pentecostal mandate; this is a missions-oriented movement. Reginald Bibby notes that the lifeblood of religious groups is their youth. Social scientists, who have studied those joining such organizations, have concluded that religious groups grow primarily by recruiting

69. Jones, *Postmodern Youth Ministry*, 39. See also Shepherd, "Postmodern Responses to Being Church."

70. "O Come All Ye Faithful." See also "Pentecostals: Christianity Reborn."

and retaining their own children, and adding a few outsiders along the way, primarily through friendship and marriage.[71]

Bibby and Posterski maintain that any attempt to present the Gospel to the minds of Postmodern youth will have to:

> . . . carefully explore the realm of the supernatural. Young people do not have God grudges on their shoulders. They are not anti-religious. Rather, out of the legacy of their heritage and the input of their world, they are supernaturalists. . . . Young people are predisposed to the supernatural, and although they don't intend to turn to organized religion to actively pursue their interest, they are not negative about spiritual realities.[72]

I would suggest that those who have followed Rudolf Bultmann's demythologization of the Gospel are not only ineffective, but are damaging the cause of the Good News in this generation. With Pentecostals historically in the lead, the Church as a whole must return to teaching and preaching about a God of miracles, who can be experienced as he continues to act in very real ways in the lives and world of his children. This is the God for whom today's youth hunger. Tom Beaudoin agrees: "The turn to experience in GenX pop culture encompasses not only personal and communal religious experience but also an emerging sensual spirituality, an experience of living faith in the world, and a desire for an encounter of the human and divine."[73]

Pentecostalism generally continues to place great emphasis on experiencing the supernatural. In her description of the variety of Pentecostal churches worldwide, sociologist Margaret M. Poloma notes, "What these churches share is not single structure, uniform doctrine, or ecclesiastical leadership, but a particular Christian world-view that reverts to a non-European epistemology from the European one that has dominated Christianity for centuries."[74] Paul W. Lewis agrees: "[T]he nature of Pentecostal experience within Biblical hermeneutics [is] tied with certain elements which inform Pentecostal experience, and ultimately, these beliefs, experiences, and hermeneutics demonstrate a Pentecostal epistemology. This Pentecostal epistemology is a non-Enlightenment

71. Bibby, *Canada's Teens*, 115.
72. Bibby and Posterski, *Teen Trends*, 261.
73. Beaudoin, *Virtual Faith*, 165.
74. Poloma, "The Spirit Bade Me Go," 5.

enterprise, and places Pentecostal thought in a very different framework from conservative Evangelicalism. . . ."[75]

Poloma quotes Pentecostal pastor and theologian Jackie David Johns to further illustrate this point: "At the heart of the Pentecostal world-view is a transforming experience with God. God is known through relational encounter which finds its penultimate expression in the experience of being filled with the Holy Spirit. This experience becomes the normative epistemological framework and thus shifts the structures by which the individual interprets the world."[76]

Johns lists six special foci of the Pentecostal worldview, several of which will be observed to have particular relevance to a Postmodern world:

- The Pentecostal world-view is experientially God-centered. All things relate to God and God relates to all things.

- The Pentecostal world-view is holistic and systemic. For the Spirit-filled person God is not only present in all events, he holds all things together and causes all things to work together.

- The Pentecostal world-view is transrational. Knowledge is relational and is not limited to the realms of reason and sensory experience.

- In conjunction with their holiness heritage, Pentecostals are concerned with truth, but not just propositional truth. Pentecostals were historically anti-creedal.

- The Pentecostal epistemology of encounter with God is closely aligned with the biblical understanding of how one comes to know. . . . This understanding is rooted in Hebrew thought and may be contrasted with Greek approaches to knowledge. The Hebrew word for "to know" is *yada*. In general, *yada* is knowledge that comes by experience.

- The Scriptures hold a special place and function within the Pentecostal world-view. Pentecostals differ from Evangelicals and Fundamentalists in their approach to the Bible. For Pentecostals the Bible is a living book in which the Holy Spirit is always active.[77]

75. Lewis, "Towards a Pentecostal Epistemology," 95.

76. Johns, "Yielding to the Spirit," 74–9.

77. Ibid. This succinct summary is taken from Poloma, "The Spirit Bade Me Go," 5–6.

Viv Grigg also argues that Pentecostalism is stylistically well-suited to reach a Postmodern generation. First, charismatic and Pentecostal theology, as expressed in transformational conversations, fits well with the multiple stories of Postmodernism, just as Evangelical theology is often heavily entwined with Modernist rationalism. Second, the experiential nature of Pentecostalism connects well with those seeking a spiritual experience. Third, holism in Pentecostal circles is expressed by narratives rather than following logical progressions towards universal truth.[78]

Grigg goes even further, arguing that Pentecostals are essentially "postmodern phenomena," for they have moved from integrating the voices of Western power centers to "listening to the multiple voices of the peoples." He suggests, "Pentecostals have rejected the language, the theology, and the style of Christianity of the 'official', 'powerful', churches."[79] There can be no doubt as to the appeal of this type of Christian denomination for today's Postmodern youth.

Neil Hudson concurs, suggesting that the emphasis on experience at the heart of Pentecostalism may well strategically place the movement to reach the youngest generations. At the heart of Pentecostalism, according to Hudson, is an emphasis on a God who does indeed intervene and do surprising things among his people; a God who is to be encountered, and who performs miracles, both as a sign to his own people and a cause of wonder for non-believers. Worship for Pentecostals is, therefore, "where one *experiences* something" as opposed to where one is *taught* something.[80]

If the classical format of the Evangelical service brings to the fore the didactic elements, including the centrality of the Scriptures, for contemporary Pentecostalism the worship band and worship song display are more central.[81] While the Bible is undoubtedly honored in Pentecostal circles, the goal and desire of Pentecostal services is that the God of the Bible might be experienced, not just appreciated intellectually. While this experience can occur during sermons, it more likely and most often occurs during sung worship or in a ministry time following the sermon where individuals receive prayer. Hudson concludes: "For some, grappling

78. See Grigg, "The Spirit of Christ and the Postmodern City."

79. Ibid.

80. Hudson, "British Pentecostalism's Past Development." Emphasis added.

81. I remember a seminary professor telling us that throughout Church History the layout of a church at the front was symbolic of where the believers located God's presence. For Roman Catholics, the Eucharistic table is front and center; for Protestants, it is the pulpit; for Pentecostals, it is a drum kit!

with evangelizing amongst the sensory nature of a postmodern generation, this emphasis on experience resonates with the desires expressed in society. It is no surprise that there is a growing feeling that Pentecostalism might succeed in evangelizing a postmodern generation more effectively than they ever did in the rationalistic modernist era."[82]

The practice of some to rid the Scriptures essentially of all references to miracles and divine intervention, and the refusal in many circles to acknowledge that God works in the same ways today, is forcing many youth, who seek an encounter with the true God, to look elsewhere. As Rodney Stark and William S. Bainbridge note, "In an endless cycle, faith is revived and new faiths born to take the places of those withered denominations *that lost their sense of the supernatural.*"[83] In the words of one teenager,

> All I want is reality. Show me God. Tell me what he is really like. Help me to understand why life is the way it is, and how I can experience it more fully and with greater joy. I don't want the empty promises. I want the real thing. And I'll go wherever I find that truth system.[84]

Reginald Bibby agrees:

> This is a generation of young people whose current involvement in religion is appreciable. Further, their terms for greater involvement in groups are reasonable; if they can find their participation "worthwhile," they are open to it. In light of their widespread interest in meaning and mystery, the supernatural and the spiritual, religious groups who have something to bring need to bring it—and, to put it bluntly, stop complaining about the apathy of youth.[85]

A PENTECOSTAL CONCLUSION

Rudolf Bultmann clearly desired to make the Gospel more accessible to the men and women of his time. In his thinking, Modern minds could no longer access many of the truths so cloaked in the mythological language of the New Testament. The Modern mentality would no longer accept as valid the many miracles and supernatural occurrences in Scripture

---

82. Hudson, "British Pentecostalism's Past Development."

83. Stark and Bainbridge, *The Future of Religion*, 529–30. Emphasis in original.

84. Anonymous teenager, in Barna, *Baby Busters*, 144.

85. Bibby, *Canada's Teens*, 131–2.

which can never be scientifically validated. To bring the Gospel back to the people, Bultmann demythologized it, explaining in existential terms the meaning of each myth. With similar intentions, more recent followers of the Bultmannian ideal, such as *The Jesus Seminar*, seek to rid the New Testament accounts of Jesus' life and ministry of all but the most scientifically verifiable records.

With recent research into the "Postmodern mind," however, we are forced to acknowledge that Bultmann's concerns are invalid for the newest generations of Western youth. It appears, in fact, that a reversal is necessary. Instead of diminishing the transcendent and supernatural component of the Gospel, it must be emphasized, for this generation correctly believes it to exist and will seek it out in whatever form it is offered.

Pentecostals have a key role to play in this effort, for the entire movement arose essentially out of a perceived need to go beyond the rational, scientific approaches to the Gospel so prevalent at the turn of the last century. Paul Lewis notes, "Pentecostal thought actually has an implied historiography, which emphasizes the inseparability of history from God's work in the world. In other words, contrary to Rudolf Bultmann and his demythological enterprise, God works in and through history, and God's work in and through history is not limited to the pre-scientific age nor is it essentially different today."[86] Early Pentecostals were eager to experience in their daily lives the power and person of God, through the Holy Spirit. Though it has been demonstrated that some Pentecostal scholars have drifted towards Evangelical hermeneutics, it is also true that, for the most part, Pentecostals in the pew have not lost their focus upon the importance of experiencing God personally, and continue to interpret Scripture in a corresponding manner.

For Pentecostals, therefore, the opportunity has never been greater, as they are now faced with a generation seeking the same experiential approach to God that they have held so dearly for almost a century. Tony Jones notes, "One of the most noteworthy characteristics of the postmodern/post-Christian world is the dramatic rise of spirituality. Propositional truth is out and mysticism is in. People are not necessarily put off by a religion that does not 'make sense'—they are more concerned with whether a religion can bring them into contact with God."[87]

86. Lewis, "Towards a Pentecostal Epistemology," 105.
87. Jones, *Postmodern Youth Ministry*, 63.

Pentecostals must be leaders as the Christian Church, the true heralds of the one God, rises to this challenge and presents to our searching youth the God who can be experienced. For the sake of this Postmodern generation, may they not become a church which has "a form of godliness but [denies] its power" (2 Tim 3:5). They must embrace a hermeneutic that preserves the clear foci of early Pentecostalism. Only with a Pentecostal hermeneutic will the distinctive Pentecostal focus on experiencing God be solidly preserved.

The next chapter explores trends in Pentecostal hermeneutics since the conclusion of the debate between Gordon D. Fee and various Pentecostal scholars, via the work of Kenneth J. Archer. Since that debate, some Pentecostal scholars have begun to seriously consider the need for a distinctively Pentecostal hermeneutic, though few have offered a thoroughgoing model for discussion. Archer has proposed a distinctive Pentecostal hermeneutic. He contends that the wholesale importing of Evangelical hermeneutical methods into Pentecostalism will not serve the movement well into the present century. His belief, that the unique nature of the Pentecostal movement requires a distinctive Pentecostal hermeneutic, is of great value to this work for, as has been shown, today's youth are open to, and searching for, a God who reveals himself in the supernatural.

There is a demonstrable shift in secular society from the precepts of Modernity to Postmodernity, acutely felt in the younger generations who most readily accept change. Should Pentecostals recognize that a distinctively Pentecostal approach to Scripture is needed, Archer's proposals are an important step in ensuring that the Pentecostal interpretation of Scripture will remain both relevant and accurate in the coming years.

6

Pentecostal Hermeneutics for the Twenty-first Century: Kenneth J. Archer's Proposal

The current hermeneutical approach of most academic Pentecostals has been to embrace Modern assumptions and practices about hermeneutics from an Evangelical perspective. I believe that this practice will only continue to transform Pentecostals into mainstream neo-fundamentalists, undermining Pentecostal identity and practice.

Today, some Pentecostals attempt to express themselves with an Evangelical and modernistic hermeneutic (the Historical Critical methods). Yet if Pentecostalism desires to continue in its missionary objective while keeping in tune with its early ethos, it must move beyond Modernity.

In other words, a Pentecostal hermeneutical strategy is needed which rejects the quest for a past determinate meaning of the author and embraces the reality that interpretation involves both the discovery of meaning and the creation of meaning.

A Pentecostal hermeneutical strategy should attempt to continue to forge an alternative path that neither entirely accepts the pluralistic relativism of Postmodernism nor entirely affirms the objectivism of Modernism—a pathway that began to be forged in early Pentecostalism.[1]

KENNETH J. ARCHER

W HAT OF PENTECOSTAL HERMENEUTICS since the debate between Gordon D. Fee and other Pentecostal scholars? The issue has received limited attention since the conclusion of the debate in the early

1. Archer, *A Pentecostal Hermeneutic*, 3, 146, 147, 153.

1990s. An issue each of *Pneuma: The Journal of the Society for Pentecostal Studies* and *The Spirit & Church* was devoted entirely to the topic of Pentecostal hermeneutics.[2] During that time, various journals published articles dealing with Pentecostal hermeneutics,[3] but few outlined a way forward or proposed a new hermeneutical approach for Pentecostals.

The question then remains, "Do Pentecostals need a distinct hermeneutic to firmly establish their beliefs and practices in Scripture?"[4] Most of the dialogue among modern Pentecostal scholars concerns whether there actually exists, or should exist, a distinct Pentecostal hermeneutic. Some, such as Robert P. Menzies, suggest that Pentecostalism has little need of a unique hermeneutic; Pentecostal distinctive doctrines can be derived from Scripture, using commonly accepted Evangelical hermeneutical methodology. Others, such as Howard M. Ervin, contend that the Pentecostal emphasis upon the Holy Spirit produces a pneumatological hermeneutic, resulting in theological distinctives concerning the Spirit's role in the life of the Church and individual believers.

One who concurs with the latter is Kenneth J. Archer. Originally submitted as a Ph.D. dissertation to the University of St. Andrews, Scotland, Archer's book, *A Pentecostal Hermeneutic for the Twenty-First Century: Spirit, Scripture and Community*, was published in 2004 as Volume 28 in the *Journal of Pentecostal Theology Supplement Series*. The author presents both a history of Pentecostal hermeneutics, and proposes a new hermeneutical system for Pentecostals in the twenty-first century. Because of the applicable nature of Archer's book to the present work, and the scarcity of similar proposals, this chapter examines Archer's work, which sheds light on possible solutions for Pentecostal hermeneutics in the present century. I will present a detailed overview of his work, enabling the reader to accurately follow the in-depth analysis of his prescribed hermeneutic, concluding with thoughts on its contribution to Pentecostal hermeneutics of the future.

---

2. See *Pneuma* 15.2 (Fall 1993); and *The Spirit & Church* 2.1 (May 2000). *Pneuma* published seventeen articles on hermeneutics in its first sixteen volumes between 1979 and 1994.

3. See, for example, Kärkkäinen, "Pentecostal Hermeneutics in the Making"; Baker, "Pentecostal Bible Reading"; Archer, "Pentecostal Hermeneutics: Retrospect and Prospect"; Brubaker, "Postmodernism and Pentecostals"; and Thomas, "Women, Pentecostals, and the Bible."

4. Archer, "Pentecostal Hermeneutics: Retrospect and Prospect," 74.

Archer's monograph on Pentecostal hermeneutics is significant both for Pentecostals and the present work, as an effort is made to move beyond the acceptance of the historical-critical method. If his hermeneutical approach is a valid enterprise, then Pentecostals may look forward to engaging the Scriptures in a manner methodologically different from Evangelicals as a whole—yet more in line with their own traditions. Pentecostals may reclaim their hermeneutical roots and again interpret Scripture in a manner less directly impacted by Modernity.

INTRODUCTORY REMARKS FOR THE READERS

The introductory chapter of Archer's book details the typical remarks one would expect to find at the beginning of such a work, including focus and limitation of study, a review of flow of argument and, interestingly, a section entitled "My Personal Hermeneutical Journey: Traveling through the First Naïveté and into the Second Naïveté."[5] Archer details his personal "story," a theme that finds frequent use in his book. He notes that, following his conversion experience and throughout his academic career, "I eventually crossed the desert of sceptical (Modern and/or Postmodern) criticism. I had journeyed through the wilderness of the first naïveté (both precritical and then modernistic scientific Biblicism) and entered into the 'second naïveté.'"[6] This "crossing of the desert" sets the stage for the journey his book follows.

DEFINING PENTECOSTALISM: A DIVERSE AND PARADOXICAL ENDEAVOR

The goal of chapter 1 is to define Pentecostalism, noted in the title as "A Diverse and Paradoxical Endeavor." After surveying Pentecostalism's well-established roots in both Topeka, Kansas, and the Azusa Street Mission in Los Angeles, California, Archer moves into the social and theological influences upon the Pentecostal movement. Beginning with the emphasis on emotionalism found within Revivalism, he notes the tremendous importance this movement played in emphasizing the necessity of a personal, conscious conversion experience. In addition, early Pentecostals were profoundly impacted by the various Holiness movements, which

---

5. Archer, *A Pentecostal Hermeneutic*, 5–8.

6. Ibid., 7.

figured so prominently on the Western religious landscape of the late nineteenth century.[7] With their Holiness brethren, Pentecostals believed in a second crisis experience of faith following conversion, an experience of sanctification, in which the heart and life were cleansed and made holy by divine transformation. As children, not of Reformed thought but of Wesleyan thinking, Pentecostals joined with the Holiness "movement *protesting* the evils of modernity and the cold cerebral Christianity of the mainline Protestant traditions."[8]

The Impact of Modernity Upon Pentecostalism

Archer examines the impact of Modernity upon traditional Christianity, and Pentecostalism in particular, noting that evolutionary theory diminished both the supernatural and personal aspects of God; higher criticism undermined the authority of Scripture, and comparative religion studies relativized Christianity in comparison to other world religions.[9] As has been well established, Pentecostalism strongly protested the secularizing influence of Modernity upon Christianity, and the spiritually sterile conditions created by the wedding of the two. Mark A. Noll agrees: "[A]n ardent desire for the unmediated experience of the Holy Spirit was a . . . universal characteristic of those who became Pentecostals."[10] Melvin E. Dieter declares that Pentecostals sought a personal experience of the Spirit's "direct, divine, incontrovertible intervention which did not rely on the intellect or feeling but on a sign of the presence of the Holy Ghost which both the individual experiencing it and all who were looking on would know that 'the work had been done.' "[11] Archer states:

> In sum, "Pentecostalism" emerged as an identifiable Christian restorational revivalistic movement within the first decade of the twentieth century. The major theological themes of renewal

---

7. Archer notes that respected Pentecostal scholars like Donald Dayton, Vinson Synan, and Robert Anderson view Pentecostalism as rising out of the Wesleyan/Holiness movements of the late nineteenth century. See Dayton, "The Limits of Evangelicalism," 36–56; idem, *The Theological Roots of Pentecostalism*; Synan, *The Holiness-Pentecostal Movement*; and Anderson, *Vision of the Disinherited*.

8. Archer, *A Pentecostal Hermeneutic*, 16. Emphasis in original. See also Cox, *Fire From Heaven*, 75.

9. See Archer, *A Pentecostal Hermeneutic*, 17.

10. Noll, *A History of Christianity*, 387.

11. Dieter, "The Wesleyan/Holiness and Pentecostal Movements," 13.

held by Holiness movements (Wesleyan and Keswickian) were absorbed and synthesized into the "Full Gospel message," which by 1919 became entirely identified with the Pentecostals.

The Pentecostals' social location was predominantly from the lower social and economic strata of American society. Yet . . . the most universal characteristic of early Pentecostals was their passionate desire for an unmediated experience with the Holy Spirit. . . . [T]hey saw themselves as scripturally sound and at odds with both Liberal theology and Protestant orthodoxy. The Pentecostal movement was a protest both against Modernity and against mainline Christianity.[12]

The Early Pentecostal Worldview

Archer argues against the Social Deprivation theory put forward by Robert Anderson and others as a means of explaining the incredible growth and success of Pentecostalism.[13] Though early Pentecostals came predominantly from the lower social positions of society, Archer does not believe this theory adequately explains the tremendous growth of Pentecostalism, but rather "reduces the early Pentecostals' quest for a deeper spiritual walk with Jesus as a personal weakness rather than a serious faith claim."[14] He continues:

Pentecostals were and continue to be motivated by the "Full Gospel message," which is in direct opposition to Modernity's conception of reality (the established order of society). People (predominantly Holiness Christians) were attracted to Pentecostalism because of its seemingly scriptural message and supernatural signs. Pentecostalism was not just a reinterpretation of the "old time religion." Pentecostal celebrative worship services, with tongues, trances, exorcisms, dancing, and healings, were transforming activities of commitment to a new movement, rather than simply attempting to preserve old ways. The Full Gospel message was birthed as marginalized Christian peoples from the Anglo and African slave Holiness communities read Scripture with revivalistic restorative lenses. Thus, Pentecostalism originated due to the logical coherence of the Five/Four Fold Pentecostal message validated by the supernatural signs amongst the community and in di-

---

12. Archer, *A Pentecostal Hermeneutic*, 22.

13. See Anderson, *Vision of the Disinherited*.

14. Archer, *A Pentecostal Hermeneutic*, 24.

rect opposition to the predominate worldview of Modernity. It was the collision of Scripture, signs (Spirit), and societal worldviews that caused and continues to cause the spread of the movement motivated by the passionate desire for an unmediated experiential encounter with Jesus.[15]

Chapter 1 concludes with a discussion of the early Pentecostal worldview. As has been shown, early Pentecostal belief and attitude clashed strongly with the prevailing Modernistic outlook of the times, both in secular society and in cessationist Christianity. Archer argues, however, that Pentecostalism should not be characterized as "pre-Modern," for it was born in the Modern age, and though challenging many Modern assumptions, still used Modern language and belief when necessary. Pentecostals insisted, for example, on an audible, clear sign of the Spirit's presence.

> "Paramodern" would be a better way to classify early Pentecostalism. This concept captures the fact that Pentecostalism emerged within Modernity . . . , yet existed on the fringes of Modernity . . . , (by its emphasis on physical evidence for the Spirit's presence—a modernistic slant on scientific experimentation language). . . . The Pentecostal movement began as a Paramodern movement protesting Modernity and cessationist Christianity.[16]

SHIFTING PARADIGMS: THE HERMENEUTICAL CONTEXT OF THE EARLY PENTECOSTALS

Chapter 2 of Archer's work describes the hermeneutical context of early Pentecostals, by first examining the historical context from which rose the Fundamentalist/Modernist debate of Scriptural interpretation. In the first section, "Common Sense Realism: The Dominant Hermeneutical Context of the Early-Nineteenth Century," the author argues that the impact of German Higher Criticism and the "new science" was significant in terms of biblical interpretation throughout America in particular, quickly dividing Evangelical scholars from their more Liberal counterparts. Furthering the work of Mark Noll, Robert Funk, and others, Archer maintains that "[t]he new scientific model of scholarship encouraged the 'rapid professionalization' of biblical scholars that required them to be-

15. Ibid., 28.
16. Ibid., 33.

come 'specialized' and accountable to their 'academic peers' instead of the Christian communities to which they once belonged."[17] Evangelical membership in the faculties of America's universities fell sharply as the Modern university rose to prominence in the United States.

Prior to this paradigm shift, most (particularly Protestant) Americans adhered to the tenets of Common Sense Realism and believed that one could look upon the evidence clearly provided in Scripture and, from this, determine the "facts," which were then classified. Archer quotes A. T. Pierson (1837–1911), a premillennial dispensationalist and anti-modernist who, in 1895, demonstrated the importance of the Baconian empirical method:

> I like Biblical theology that does not start with superficial Aristotelian methods of reason, that does not begin with an hypothesis, and then wrap the facts and philosophy to fit the crook of our dogma, but a Baconian system, which first gathers the teachings of the word of God, and then seeks to deduce some general law upon which the facts can be arranged.[18]

For many years, the Common Sense Baconian system had preserved in American religious thought the concept that the common person, acknowledging the self-evident principles of the existence of God and the veracity of his Word, could discover the facts of Scripture, as one could discover the facts of science. Archer believes that with the passing of the old Common Sense consensus, Protestants moved in one of three directions. Modernists or Liberals argued that the Bible's authority did not rest upon historical or scientific claims; rather, authenticity was found in personal experience. In the opposite direction, the "academically informed Fundamentalist group" continued to reaffirm the veracity and authority of Scripture by appealing to the older scientific Baconian Common Sense model. For these Fundamentalists, inerrancy became the key, and much effort was put into establishing the historical veracity of the Scriptures.[19]

---

17. Ibid., 36. See Funk, "The Watershed of the American Biblical Tradition"; and Noll, *Between Faith and Criticism*.

18. Pierson, in Archer, *A Pentecostal Hermeneutic*, 38.

19. Archer, *A Pentecostal Hermeneutic*, 39–40.

The Third Route

In Archer's view, however, Pentecostals and Wesleyan Holiness believers forged a third route, affirming both the objective nature of Scripture and the importance of personal experience as a means of reaffirming the inspiration of Scripture. Scripture was inspired in the sense of the historical document and as a present experience of the Spirit through the Scriptures.[20] While both conservative groups looked with disdain upon the new science imposed upon their beloved Scriptures by the Modernist Liberals, a significant rift developed first between the Fundamentalists and Modernists, and only later between the Fundamentalists and Pentecostals.

While the Fundamentalists built their arguments on the foundation of Common Sense Realism, the Modernists sought Higher Criticism as their underlying base. "Both theological communities were 'modernistic,' yet they came to antithetical conclusions about the authority and inspiration of Scripture."[21] Like the conservative Fundamentalists, Pentecostals relied on Common Sense reasoning, arguing that Scripture was supernaturally inspired and preserved, and full of power to change individual's lives. Their concern, however, ran deeper than simply proving facts from the Bible treated as a scientific textbook; Pentecostals, like the Liberals, sought to authenticate their Christianity via religious experience.

> But unlike the Liberals, who talked about "religion of the heart" and experiencing God through the divine elements in the natural, Pentecostals would point to the supernatural signs of divine intervention taking place in their worship services (tongues and healing). Hence, early Pentecostals were generating religious experience, whereas the Liberals were simply talking about it.
>
> The Pentecostals said yes to both the authority of Scripture and the authority of experience. . . . Pentecostalism's lived experience was coloring their understanding of Scripture and Scripture was shaping their lived experience.
>
> Unfortunately, after the 1920s the Pentecostals would leave this more para-modern route and attempt to follow the modern path laid down by the Fundamentalists.[22]

20. Ibid., 40.
21. Ibid., 63.
22. Ibid., 63–4.

EARLY PENTECOSTAL BIBLICAL INTERPRETATION

Archer begins this chapter by examining the contemporary explanations of early Pentecostal hermeneutics as given by several prominent Pentecostal scholars. The first, Russell P. Spittler, suggests that while Pentecostals and Fundamentalists differ significantly in terms of speaking in tongues and miracles in today's world, they differ little in their pre-critical, excessively literal approach to biblical interpretation. Archer disagrees, if only in part, stating that Spittler's analysis produces "too simplistic of a descriptive statement concerning the interpretive method."[23]

For Grant Wacker, Pentecostal interpretive methods arose primarily as a logical extension of their "ahistorical outlook," a term Wacker uses to suggest Pentecostalism's belief that those writing Scripture were largely uninfluenced by their historical surroundings. One should not suppose that the years of history since the writing of the Scriptures has contributed to the better understanding of Holy Writ. "In the mind of the typical convert. . .Scripture 'dropped from heaven as a sacred meteor.'"[24] Interpretation was thus wooden at best, holding "the conviction that exegesis is best when it is as rigidly literal as credibility can stand."[25] Archer observes, "In other words, Pentecostals were not like classical Protestants or Fundamentalists when it came to interpreting the Bible. Classical Protestants and Fundamentalists read the Bible as a past inspired revelatory document, but the Pentecostals read the Bible as a presently inspired story."[26] On the whole, however, Archer disagrees with Wacker's characterization of the Pentecostal approach as ahistorical, noting that it "does not adequately express the Pentecostal interpretive stance."[27] Rather, he believes that Pentecostals interpreted Scripture in a transhistorical manner simply because they

> . . . believed Scripture inherently possessed the ability to speak meaningfully in different social settings than the one from which it originated.

---

23. Ibid., 66. See Spittler, "Are Pentecostals and Charismatics Fundamentalists?"

24. Wacker, "Functions of Faith," 66. See Spittler, "Scripture and the Theological Enterprise," 63.

25. Wacker, "Functions of Faith," 365.

26. Archer, A Pentecostal Hermeneutic, 69.

27. Ibid., 70.

The Pentecostal reading did confuse biblical narrative with modernistic historiography. . . . [T]hey were convinced that the biblical stories. . .happened just the way that they were told and could happen again.[28]

Archer concludes this section by noting the position of Donald Dayton and David A. Reed, who have described the Pentecostal tendency towards a "subjectivizing hermeneutic" or "pietistic hermeneutic," which combined religious experience with biblical interpretation.[29] Indeed, Archer agrees with the notion that there is a "pietistic, experiential, heartfelt approach to interpretation" among Pentecostals, but "strongly disagrees" that this constitutes a subjectivism that possibly contaminates objective truth.[30]

The Bible Reading Method

Archer concludes chapter 3 with a lengthy section, "The Bible Reading Method: An Alternative Explanation." He analyzes descriptively the interpretive method used by early Pentecostals. This is accomplished by examining a variety of early Pentecostal writings, teachings, and sermons, focusing upon Spirit-baptism with the evidence of *glossolalia*, and the Oneness issue.[31] He notes:

The Bible Reading Method was an inductive and deductive commonsensical method, which required all of the "biblical data" on a particular topic to be gathered and then harmonized. Once this was accomplished, it could be formatted into a cohesive synthesis from a restorative revivalistic perspective.[32]

In terms of Spirit-baptism, Archer draws first upon Frank J. Ewart's (1876–1947) historiography of Pentecostalism. Concerning the hermeneutical approach of early Pentecostal teachers, Ewart writes: "Their adopted method was to select a subject, find all the references on it, and

28. Ibid.

29. Ibid., 71. See Dayton, *The Theological Roots of Pentecostalism*, 23; and Reed, "Origins and Development," 117.

30. Archer, *A Pentecostal Hermeneutic*, 72.

31. I will summarize Archer's discussion of Spirit-baptism, as it provides proof of one of the Bible Reading Methods. His examination of Oneness Pentecostalism follows a similar approach and reaches the same conclusions.

32. Archer, *A Pentecostal Hermeneutic*, 91.

present to the class a scriptural summary of what the Bible had to say about the theme."[33] As Archer rightly observes, this is perhaps the closest extant summary of the early Pentecostal hermeneutical approach. The oft-quoted account of Charles F. Parham suggests the same:

> Having heard so many different religious bodies claim different proofs as the evidence of their having the Pentecostal baptism, I set the students at work studying out diligently what was the Bible evidence of the baptism of the Holy Ghost, that we might go before the world with something that was indisputable because it tallied absolutely with the Word.[34]

As Parham's wife later confirmed, his students had no text but the Bible, and no method but observing everything the Scriptures had to say on a particular subject and, from there, with the help of the Holy Spirit, determining Truth.[35] Archer also traces the interpretive path of William J. Seymour, pastor of the Azusa Street Mission. As with other early Pentecostals, Seymour did not summarize his interpretive method; it may be deduced, however, from his explanation of Spirit-baptism within the pages of *The Apostolic Faith*. He simply traces the theme of Spirit-baptism through the pages of Acts (chapters 2, 8, 10, and 19), then summarizes the findings into the doctrines of subsequence and initial evidence.[36] Again, this approach testifies to the widespread use of the Bible Reading Method among the earliest Pentecostals.

PENTECOSTAL STORY: THE HERMENEUTICAL FILTER

In this chapter, Archer examines the chief distinguishing feature of early Pentecostal hermeneutics from that of their Holiness cousins. "What distinguished the early Pentecostal Bible Reading Method from the Holiness folk was not a different interpretive method but a '*distinct narrative*'. . . . The Pentecostal hermeneutical strategy at the foundational interpretive level was a unique story."[37] Drawing on the work of George

---

33. Ibid., 75. See Ewart, *The Phenomenon of Pentecost*, 60.

34. Parham, *The Life of Charles F. Parham*, 52.

35. See Thistlethwaite, "The Wonderful History of the Latter Rain," 82.

36. Archer, *A Pentecostal Hermeneutic*, 77–8. Archer (80–2) concludes this section by demonstrating that R.A. Torrey held the same approach to Scripture, while arriving at a different conclusion regarding initial evidence.

37. Archer, *A Pentecostal Hermeneutic*, 94. Emphasis in original.

Aichele,[38] Harry S. Stout,[39] Anthony C. Thiselton,[40] and others, Archer recognizes the link between the social cultural location of individuals and their interpretive method. "Reading involves using both the information that is present on the written page, as well as the information we already have in our minds."[41] Following Alasdair MacIntyre, Archer asserts that "interpretive practices of a community are always dependent upon the community's narrative tradition."[42] For Archer,

> The Pentecostal community is a part of the larger Christian community, and yet exists as a distinct coherent narrative tradition within Christianity. The Pentecostal community or a collection of communities is bound together by their "shared charismatic experiences" and "shared story." The Pentecostal narrative tradition attempts to embody the Christian metanarrative. . . .[43]

> The Pentecostal story is synonymous with the Pentecostal narrative tradition. The Pentecostal story is the primary hermeneutical context for the reading of Scripture, hence providing the context for the production of meaning. The Pentecostal narrative tradition provides the Pentecostals with an experiential, conceptual hermeneutical narrative that enables them to interpret Scripture and their experience of reality.[44]

The Latter Rain

Determining the nature of the Pentecostal story is the task of Archer's chapter 4. The stated goal is to demonstrate the significant impact of the Latter Rain movement upon early Pentecostalism, and how this, in turn, tied into the Pentecostal identity as a restorationist movement. William D.

---

38. Aichele et al., *The Postmodern Bible*, 1–8.

39. Stout, "Theological Commitment," 44–59.

40. Thiselton, *New Horizons in Hermeneutics*, 9.

41. Archer, *A Pentecostal Hermeneutic*, 94. See McQuillian, *The Literary Crisis*, 16.

42. Archer, *A Pentecostal Hermeneutic*, 96. See MacIntyre, *After Virtue*.

43. By "metanarrative," Archer refers to a grand story, by which human societies and their individual members live and organize their lives in meaningful ways. The Christian metanarrative refers to the general Christian story about the meaning of the world, the God who created it, and humanity's place within it. Archer, *A Pentecostal Hermeneutic*, 97–8, fn. 24.

44. Ibid., 97–8.

Faupel's work on Pentecostalism[45] is an important step in determining the Pentecostal story; indeed, Archer believes that Faupel has demonstrated that the Latter Rain movement "provides the primary organizational structure for the Pentecostal narrative tradition."[46]

Some of the earliest Pentecostals, such as George Floyd Taylor,[47] relying on passages from the Old Testament which speak of both a former and a latter rain,[48] interpreted their present reception of the Spirit's outpouring in terms of the Latter Rain; the former rain occurred at Pentecost. This motif provided Pentecostals with a framework by which to interpret Scripture and determine their place within its narrative. Pentecostals saw themselves as the Latter Rain outpouring of God's Spirit, enabling them to conclude the final great harvest of souls before the return of Christ.

> The biblical "Latter Rain" motif became an important contribution to the Pentecostal story. The "Latter Rain" motif enabled the Pentecostals to hold together the "Full Gospel message" because it provided a coherent explanation for the restoration of the gifts, while also providing the primary organizational structure for their story. The Pentecostals became the people of the prophetically promised "Latter Rain" which meant that they had fully recovered not only the Apostolic faith, but also the Apostolic power, authority and practice.[49]

Archer argues that the work of Wesleyan Holiness leader John P. Brooks was clearly influential in early Pentecostalism. Brooks taught that the New Testament contained all the necessary instruction and information for Christian belief and polity. Denominational structures and creeds, along with the traditions of the Church, were not needed. "Brooks advocated that the real Christians must withdraw from all forms of organized Christianity and band together in local congregations in order to form the

45. Faupel, *The Everlasting Gospel: The Significance of Eschatology*, esp. 19–43.

46. Archer, *A Pentecostal Hermeneutic*, 100.

47. Taylor, *The Spirit and the Bride*, 90–9.

48. Deut 11:10–15; Job 29:29; Prov 16:15; Jer 3:3, 4:24; Hos 6:3; and Zech 10:1. Representative of these passages is Joel 2:23, "Be glad then, ye children of Zion, and rejoice in the Lord your God: for he hath given you the former rain moderately, and he will cause to come down for you the rain, the former rain, and the latter rain in the first month" (KJV).

49. Archer, *A Pentecostal Hermeneutic*, 102. See also 103–10, in which Archer describes the contribution of David Wesley Myland to this motif. See also Faupel, *The Everlasting Gospel: The Significance of Eschatology*, 39.

authentic church. The authentic church must be patterned after the true church as revealed in the New Testament."[50] For Brooks and other non-cessationist holiness teachers, the fact that signs and wonders had ceased in the institutional Church between the Apostolic and the current era was proof that divine approval had been withdrawn, if only temporarily. These signs and wonders would return when the true Church once again sought the empowerment of the Holy Spirit. This framework became the standard explanation of the role of miracles and the gifts of the Spirit within Pentecostalism.

CURRENT PENTECOSTAL HERMENEUTICAL CONCERNS

This chapter begins with a summary of the themes essential to many Pentecostals, including initial evidence, belief in themselves as people of the "Latter Rain," and an emphasis on supernatural manifestations and charismatic gifts within the worshipping community. Early Pentecostals were eschatological in their outlook, and opposed to the death grip of Modernity on the Church.

The Modernization of Early Pentecostal Hermeneutics

The next section explores "The Modernization of the Early Pentecostal Hermeneutics," and notes that as more Pentecostals became academically trained, increasing numbers

> . . . accepted the basic principles of Historical Criticism while rejecting the naturalistic worldview of Modernity. . . . [T]he historical-grammatical method became the primary method used by many Pentecostals. . . . The Pentecostals moved from the margins into mainstream, from the Paramodern into the Modern. They embraced the modernistic foundations poured by the Enlightenment.[51]

Archer cites the plea by Gordon L. Anderson and other Pentecostal scholars[52] for Pentecostals to continue to adopt the historical-critical method of hermeneutics, widely used by other conservative Evangelicals. Overall, in Archer's estimation, the view of Anderson and others has won

---

50. Archer, *A Pentecostal Hermeneutic*, 111. See Brooks, *The Divine Church*, 283.

51. Archer, *A Pentecostal Hermeneutic*, 131.

52. Anderson, "Pentecostal Hermeneutics: Part 2"; Fee, *New Testament Exegesis*. See also Noel, "Gordon Fee's Contribution."

the day: "As can be seen, Pentecostals have firmly embraced conservative yet modernistic concerns about texts."[53] I would argue that while that is indeed true for a number of Pentecostal scholars, it has not yet occurred fully in the Pentecostal pew. Thus, time is of the essence, for as go the scholars, so goes the movement.

A Distinctive Pentecostal Hermeneutic?

The bulk of chapter 5 concerns the current debate within Pentecostalism as to whether Pentecostal hermeneutics are simply a subgroup of Evangelical hermeneutics, or whether there ought to be a distinctly Pentecostal hermeneutic. Beginning with the debate as initiated outside the Pentecostal community, Archer reviews the critiques of Pentecostalism, begun by F. Dale Bruner and James D.G. Dunn, with books on the topic published in 1970.[54] Dunn, who has continued to dialogue with Pentecostals through the *Journal of Pentecostal Theology*, has been a tremendous conversation partner for Pentecostal theologians. Archer focuses upon the debate between Dunn and Robert P. Menzies.[55]

Of particular interest to this work is the fact that both Menzies and Dunn used the Historical-Critical method to argue whether or not Luke separates "the outpouring of the Spirit on individuals from 'conversion initiation' and see[s] it as an empowering gift rather than a soteriological gift."[56] As Archer correctly observes, Dunn answers "no," while Menzies argues "yes." As these authors debate whether or not a distinctive Lukan pneumatology even exists, it is apparent that the commonality between them is their belief that the "meaning" is placed within a text by its author. This is significant for Archer, for it shows both Pentecostal and non-Pentecostal scholars alike, debating the key passages of Acts, using exactly the same hermeneutical methods. We have observed the same oc-

53. Archer, *A Pentecostal Hermeneutic*, 132.

54. See Dunn, *Baptism in the Holy Spirit*; and Bruner, *A Theology of the Holy Spirit*. Neither Dunn nor Bruner supports the Pentecostal understanding of subsequence and initial evidence, though Dunn is more sympathetic.

55. Dunn, "Baptism in the Spirit: A Response." See also Menzies, "Luke and the Spirit." Other Pentecostal scholars have responded to Dunn's challenge, as well: Hunter, *Spirit-Baptism*; Ervin, *Conversion-Initiation*; Stronstad, *The Charismatic Theology of St. Luke*; Arrington, *The Acts of the Apostles*; Shelton, *Mighty in Word and Deed*; and Menzies, *The Development of Early Christian Pneumatology*.

56. Dunn, "Baptism in the Spirit: A Response," 6; and Menzies, "Luke and the Spirit," 117.

currence in our exploration of the debate between Gordon D. Fee and other Pentecostal scholars.[57]

A CONTEMPORARY PENTECOSTAL HERMENEUTICAL STRATEGY

Archer concludes his work by suggesting his own narrative hermeneutical strategy. It focuses upon the tridactic negotiation for meaning between the biblical text, the Holy Spirit, and the Pentecostal community, and is based loosely on the work of John Christopher Thomas.

The Contribution of the Biblical Text

Drawing on the work of Semiotic practitioner Umberto Eco, Archer demonstrates the important contributions of both the text and reader in the making of meaning. Eco argues that the avoidance of improper interpretation of a text may be located within sensitivity to the intention of the text itself, while in no way collapsing the intention of the text back into the intention of the author.[58] Eco believes the intention of the author is "very difficult to find out and frequently irrelevant for the interpretation of a text."[59] For Archer, this is an important stance, for "Pentecostals would not want simply to produce meaning in a manner that places the community over and against the text but instead allow the text to be a full fledged participant in the making of meaning."[60]

Critical readers must be sensitive to the lexical system of the language of the text, as well as the genre of the written text, which will aid the reader in proper interpretation.

> The early Pentecostals attempted to interpret "Scripture in light of Scripture," hence emphasizing the world of the text as the means to understanding Scripture. They appreciated the cultural context in which a text was generated, thus they would look to commentaries to inform their understanding, but this was not the Historical Critical method. Because of this, a text centered approach from a Semiotic perspective is not only congenial to early Pentecostals,

---

57. Further examination of this discussion will follow in chapter 7 below.

58. Eco et al., *Interpretation and Overinterpretation*, 25.

59. Archer, *A Pentecostal Hermeneutic*, 160. See Eco, *Interpretation and Overinterpretation*, 30.

60. Archer, *A Pentecostal Hermeneutic*, 160–1.

but it also reinforces the contemporary hermeneutical concern for a critical interpretive strategy that allows for the participation of the reader in the making of meaning. Therefore a Semiotic interpretive strategy will be the most conducive for Pentecostals because it allows for an open interdependent dialectic interaction between the text and the reading community in the making of meaning.[61]

The Contribution of the Pentecostal Community

Foremost in this section is the proposal that the Pentecostal interpreter must be "entrenched" within a Pentecostal community. One must embrace the Pentecostal story, and be connected to the Central Narrative Convictions of Pentecostalism. One will need to be recognized as a Pentecostal by those within the community, and acknowledge that one's identity has been shaped and formed by participation in this community. As the community is a key part of the interpretive process, the interpreter must be a willing participant in the Pentecostal story. "The community actively participates in the Pentecostal hermeneutical strategy not passively but actively through discussion, testimony, and charismatic gifts."[62]

Archer gives four reasons why he believes the literary method of choice for Pentecostals is a Narrative Critical approach. First, traditional Historical Critical methods have not paid sufficient attention to the primary literary genre of Scripture, which is narrative. Second, Narrative Criticism is a text-centered approach that attempts to understand the biblical text on its own terms; the emphasis does not fall upon the world behind the text, but on the story world of the text itself. Third, a Narrative Critical approach benefits the Christian communities' understanding and use of the Bible as Scripture, by using it as the foundational story for belief and practice. Finally, Narrative Criticism insists on the role of the reader in the creation of meaning.[63] Archer concludes:

> In short, this Pentecostal hermeneutical strategy will embrace a modified Narrative critical methodology while simultaneously affirming the Pentecostal community as the arena for the making of meaning. Interpretation is the result of a creative transaction

61. Ibid., 162–3.
62. Ibid., 165.
63. Ibid., 166–71.

of meaning, and this meaning is always done from the particular context of an actual reader in community. . . .

The contemporary Pentecostal community needs to recapture the promise of God and what it means to live on the margins in relationship to Jesus as expressed through the Full Gospel. This is a praxis-oriented approach that encourages a pragmatic constraint on the interpretation. If the interpretation does not encourage or motivate the listeners to experience transformation through participating in God's eschatological community then it should be rejected.[64]

The Contribution of the Holy Spirit

As taught by Christ, particularly in John 13–17, the role of the Holy Spirit is to teach the Christian community, guiding them in a clear understanding of Scripture's meaning for the present. The community must therefore commit themselves to discerning the Spirit's voice as he speaks, guides, and directs. "The Christian community provides the dynamic context in which the Spirit is actively invited to participate because without the Holy Spirit's participation there is no authentic Christian community."[65] Because Pentecostals recognize the Spirit's work upon all humanity, however, they will not limit his speaking to within the community only, but discern what he is saying to them from outside the community, both through other Christian groups and Pentecostals worldwide. In terms of interpretation, Pentecostals invite the Holy Spirit to be involved in the hermeneutical process, and then dedicate themselves to properly discerning his voice.

Aware that the high level of reader-response called for in this hermeneutical model would generate queries regarding proper validation of constructed meaning, Archer concludes his work by addressing the testing process for the validation of meaning. Following the lead of Willard Swartley,[66] Archer lists four factors to be addressed by the validation of meaning. First, the community must consider the wider church body and the history of doctrinal development as it assesses the validation of the meaning. Second, the meaning must be validated through the "praxis of

64. Ibid., 181–2.
65. Ibid., 183.
66. Swartley, *Slavery, Sabbath, War and Women.*

faith." The concern here is whether the meaning can be embraced and lived out within the community. Swartley notes that while being livable does not make meaning correct, nor is it likely correct if it is not livable either.[67] Third, the validity of interpretation should be subjected to cross-cultural validation. This becomes especially important as Pentecostals attempt to understand Scripture on political, social, and economic issues. Finally, the validation of meaning should be open to the scrutiny of academic communities, both Christian and non-Christian. As the Christian community understands the Bible to be historically revealed claims of absolute truth, it must be open to public scrutiny.[68]

> Pentecostals require a hermeneutical strategy that involves an interdependent tridactic dialogue between Scripture, the Spirit and community resulting in a creative negotiated meaning. . . . This author has outlined a critical contemporary Pentecostal hermeneutical strategy that takes place through the interdependent dialogical and dialectic process. The readers in community, the story world of the text, and the leading of the Holy Spirit are participants in the tridactic negotiation for meaning.[69]

Archer's Contribution to Current Pentecostal Hermeneutics

Archer lists five contributions of his study to the Pentecostal hermeneutical debates. First, it argues that Pentecostals were a Paramodern movement, existing neither as pre-Modern nor Modern. Second, his work readdresses the interpretive method of early Pentecostals as the Bible Reading Method, and not the more restrictive literalistic fundamentalist interpretive method often assumed of Pentecostal hermeneutics. Third, his book places substantial emphasis on the role of the community in the hermeneutical process, outlining the Central Narrative Convictions of Pentecostalism, and demonstrating how essential these are to the interpretive process of Pentecostals. Fourth, in uncovering the Central Narrative Convictions of early Pentecostalism, Archer deals significantly with early Pentecostal identity, as well. Finally, he has "presented a contemporary and post-critical hermeneutical strategy which attempts to

---

67. See ibid., 179.

68. See Archer, *A Pentecostal Hermeneutic*, 189–91.

69. Ibid., 191.

move the Pentecostal academic community beyond the present impasse created by Modernity."[70]

EVALUATION[71] AND CONCLUSION

In my opinion, Kenneth J. Archer has met his stated goals. "Paramodern" is a useful term for understanding the place of early Pentecostals relative to Modern trends and thinking. While intentionally reactive to the perceived approach of Modernity to faith and the Scriptures, Pentecostalism nonetheless arose from within the Modern world. One need only explore the Pentecostal insistence upon *glossolalia* as the Bible "proof" of Spirit-baptism to recognize from whence the earliest Pentecostals arose, for the concept of proof itself is more Modern than Postmodern. Many Postmoderns would be content with experience as an end in itself, without the need to explicate proof from the experience.

Archer has correctly traced the roots of Pentecostalism both to a work of the Holy Spirit and to a reaction against the excessively rationalistic Protestantism of the era, rejecting many of the secular definitions applied by various historians. Pentecostals celebrated the place of experience within faith, and offered those tired of Christian rationalism a welcome respite and a holistic approach to life and faith. Drawing from the personal testimonies of early Pentecostals, Archer has convincingly demonstrated the Pentecostal acceptance of the Latter Rain motif and the understanding of the supernatural occurrences in their midst as divine confirmation of their historic role in Christian history. Noteworthy for this work is Archer's success in exposing Pentecostalism's rejection of the overly rationalistic and cessationistic presuppositions traditionally applied to both narrative discourse and didactic portions of the New Testament.

I join with Archer in lamenting the modification by Pentecostals of their initial understanding of Scripture as both authoritative and trustworthy to include "inerrant" upon their joining the National Association of Evangelicals in the 1940s. Pentecostals did not require the language of inerrancy to determine the authority of Scripture. As Paul W. Lewis has

---

70. Ibid., 196.

71. The interested reader may consult reviews of Archer's book. See Elbert, review of *A Pentecostal Hermeneutic*, 320–28; and Vickers, review of *A Pentecostal Hermeneutic*, 384–86.

noted, Pentecostal belief in the authority of Scripture was not found in cognitive constructs alone, but was largely determined by the Pentecostals' immediate experience of God in and through the text. Lewis observes:

> . . . it is possible to note that for Pentecostals there is a concomi-tant relationship between Pentecostal experience and the Bible. Pentecostal experience informs one's understanding of the text; yet the text testifies of the same experience among the early church and the apostles. However, the authenticity of the Scriptures is *a posteriori* to Pentecostals. Evangelical renderings of the Bible are likewise *a posteriori*. The major distinction is that for Evangelicals the authority of the Scripture is cognitively derived and learned, whereas Pentecostals by nature assume the authority of Scripture. Therefore, in a sense, for Pentecostals the authority of the Scripture is self-evident (i.e., the text testifies to the experience which in turn verifies the veracity of the text), while for many Evangelicals the authority of the Bible is logically derived.[72]

Archer notes, "Inspiration had to be worded in the language of 'verbal inspiration' and embrace inerrancy. Hence the Pentecostals attempted to move away from the paramodern and embrace the Modern. Pentecostals accepted the foundations of Modernity and began immersing themselves in the language and concerns of modernistic thought. . . . The Pentecostals simply had to be educated into the modernistic thought and argument of the more 'intellectual' tradition."[73] In my view, the move towards accepting inerrancy was not in and of itself the genesis of the challenge that persists to this day, but rather the acceptance of the Modernistic hermeneutical baggage that accompanied it. Still, the reception of inerrancy as a descrip-tive for Scripture served to emaciate early Pentecostalism's understanding of Scripture as given by God for orthopraxy first, and orthodoxy, second. In support of this conclusion, Paul Elbert notes:

> In considering the New Testament writers themselves, one does not get the impression that they wrote first and foremost just to convey propositional truth, but to encourage faith-response. Pressing on from the concepts of truth and reliability of Scriptures to that of "inerrancy" seems to have just emphasized the correct-ness of Protestant doctrines, those articulated and unarticulated as well, rather than to enhance the thoughtful study of Scripture

72. Lewis, "Towards a Pentecostal Epistemology," 110–1. See also Ellington, "Pentecostalism and the Authority of Scripture," 16–38.

73. Archer, *A Pentecostal Hermeneutic*, 64.

on its own terms. In any case, as far as Pentecostals are concerned, perhaps results of this evangelistically suppressing and shame-enhancing union with "inerrancy" and its rationalistically geared overtones may be observable today in the marginalizing of testimony, tarrying, and in the propensity of some to be led more by their own acquisition of academic history than by dreams, visions, and the Holy Spirit.[74]

Archer's exploration of the Bible Reading Method is constructive, for it conclusively summarizes the early Pentecostal approach to interpreting Scripture. More substantive than simple "proof-texting," Pentecostals relied heavily upon the Holy Spirit for illumination, and the community for guidance, as they used deductive and inductive reasoning skills to bring scriptural teaching to reality in the lives of believers. While I am not arguing that Pentecostals today should entirely replicate the hermeneutical methods of their forbearers, I conclude that this approach allowed Pentecostals to unite the biblical past with the present, in a manner often contradictory to traditional Protestant creeds and dogma. Early Pentecostals viewed the supernatural occurrences found within Scripture as a pattern for that which ought to occur today; I would suggest that this view continues to be essential to the present survival and growth of the movement.

Further, the Pentecostal acceptance of narratives is perhaps more important today than in early Pentecostal history, for the movement is facing a generation that values the human story. Elbert notes, "Archer suggests that an intuitive grasp of narrative features is probably facilitated among people who have a reliance on oral communication and who listen to how stories are told, perhaps being similarly cultural to hearers in the first century to whom New Testament documents were read (and to such hearers in the majority of the world today)."[75] I concur. The use and acceptance of narratives by Pentecostals, and their reliance upon personal testimony, are key to effectively communicating the Pentecostal message to the youngest generations of Western youth.

Archer has also attempted a penetrating critique of the interpretive agenda of five hundred years of Protestant scholastic reflection, which he has termed the "Evangelical Historical Critical Method." The work of

---

74. Elbert, "Toward a Pentecostal Hermeneutic," 321–2.
75. Ibid., 324.

I. Howard Marshall[76] and others notwithstanding, Protestants have long viewed Luke through Pauline lenses. Archer successfully demonstrates the natural incompatibility of the wholesale acceptance of Evangelical hermeneutics by Pentecostalism with its core values. Archer's proposals allow Luke to speak for Luke, de-emphasizing the overwhelming attention paid to authorial intent by Evangelical hermeneutics, and promoting "the reality that interpretation involves both the discovery and creation of meaning for the present."[77] For the Postmodern thinker, Archer's proposal resonates deeply, for the text of Scripture must be understood academically and experienced in reality.

Finally, Archer's tridactic proposal for a new Pentecostal hermeneutic is well suited to meet the needs of younger generations. His emphasis on the role of the community and the work of the Holy Spirit confirms what young Postmodern thinkers already believe: Scriptural interpretation should occur more among the community than by individuals, and a supernatural God will surely be present as one attempts to understand his supernatural book. Archer's continuing focus upon the text demonstrates his determination to avoid the rampant subjectivism of an approach fully devoted to reader-response, and insistence that the integrity of the text and locus of meaning in the present interpreter must be held in creative tension.

Archer has presented a model for Pentecostal hermeneutics that upholds Pentecostal values and is congruent with the orthodox doctrine of inspiration, yet engages both scholastic concerns and the role of experience within the community in the interpretive process. It cannot be successfully argued that the wholesale embrace of the Historical Critical method of hermeneutics by Pentecostals has bode well either for our understanding or practice of Pentecostal doctrine. While Archer's hermeneutical approach will likely be revised as the conversation continues, he has pointed the way forward from a Pentecostal reliance on the hermeneutical methods of Modernity.

Whether Pentecostals ultimately embrace the specifics of Archer's proposal, or join them to other similar offerings, he has demonstrated that Pentecostals can and must move beyond simply embracing Evangelical

---

76. Marshall's *Luke: Historian and Theologian* (1970) was a watershed work for understanding Lukan theology by Protestant scholars.

77. Archer, *A Pentecostal Hermeneutic*, 194. See also Elbert, "Possible Literary Links."

hermeneutics towards a method of interpreting Scripture that is more properly suited to the Pentecostal message and the newest generations impacted by Postmodern thought. While Pentecostals may well have become more palatable to their Evangelical friends and academic colleagues, they may miss an enormous opportunity to present the Pentecostal understanding of Scripture to a world that is more open to the Pentecostal ethos of a supernatural God who acts supernaturally in our world than ever before.

Aware that the wholesale acceptance of Evangelical hermeneutics will not serve Pentecostalism well into the future, and having been presented with a viable Pentecostal hermeneutical strategy upon which to build, in chapter 7 I inquire as to whether Pentecostals may in fact have something of value to offer traditional Evangelical hermeneutics. I will now focus on the role of the Holy Spirit in hermeneutics, an area long overdue for theological attention. Beginning with a discussion on why the Spirit's involvement is crucial, this chapter then seeks to describe how exactly the Spirit assists the believer in Scriptural interpretation. I will conclude my discussion on the necessity of a hermeneutical system distinctive to Pentecostalism, and ask if embracing the beneficial connections with Postmodern thought may well prove advantageous for Pentecostals. Finally, I will examine whether, as some writers claim, experiential verification gives Pentecostals a hermeneutical advantage over those who have not experienced particular manifestations of the Holy Spirit. Pentecostalism's approach to experiential verification may well prove to be its most significant contribution to the larger world of Evangelical hermeneutics.

7

The Role of the Holy Spirit in Hermeneutics: The Pentecostal Edge?

Pentecostal approaches to biblical interpretation are playing an increasingly important role in the contemporary hermeneutical debate. . . . [W]e want to acknowledge that Pentecostal approaches to biblical hermeneutics are in a better position to accept the possibility of a subjective and more experiential dimension in hermeneutics.[1]

ROBERT J. MAY

In other words, [the Pentecostals'] charismatic experience is an experiential presupposition, which enables them to understand the charismatic life of the Apostolic Church, as Luke reports it, better than those contemporary Christians who lack this experience.[2]

ROGER STRONSTAD

[We] cannot consider Pentecostalism to be a kind of aberration born out of experiential excesses but a 20th century revival of New Testament theology and religion. It has not only restored joy and power to the church but a clearer reading to the Bible as well.[3]

CLARK H. PINNOCK

EVANGELICALS HOLD THE AUTHORITY of the Scriptures to be fundamental to the Christian faith. Before doing theology, one must recognize the unrivalled nature of Scripture, and acknowledge the role of God

1. May, "The Role of the Holy Spirit."
2. Stronstad, "Pentecostal Experience and Hermeneutics," 17.
3. Pinnock, foreword to Stronstad, *The Charismatic Theology of St. Luke*, viii.

the Holy Spirit in its formation. Often debated, however, is the method by which the theologian or layperson is to interpret the Word of God. What hermeneutic is to be used? As has been shown above, Conservatives (including Pentecostals) disagree considerably about this, and the discussion concerning proper interpretive methods continues.

Throughout this conversation, a vital element has largely been lacking. Though most begin their work on hermeneutics by affirming the role of the Spirit in the creation and transmission of Scripture, few scholars find it necessary to include a detailed description of the Spirit's role in illumination. This chapter explores the reasons for the deficiency of discussion concerning the function of the Holy Spirit in hermeneutics, and then discusses why the involvement of the Spirit is inherently necessary. I will make an attempt, through a survey of current literature on the subject, to understand how the Spirit aids us in interpreting the Scriptures. The possibility of a convergence of Pentecostal hermeneutics with Postmodern thought was raised earlier in this work, and I will now examine four options in this regard. Arising from this is the question of whether Pentecostals and Charismatics, through their experience with the Holy Spirit, have an interpretive advantage in hermeneutics. Many Pentecostal scholars will be shown to favor just such a concept. This survey is intended to show a distinctly Pentecostal contribution to hermeneutics, on which the foundation of a truly Pentecostal hermeneutic can continue to be built, and which will properly serve the current generation of truth seekers.

THE HOLY SPIRIT AND HERMENEUTICS: A DEAFENING SILENCE

Beginning research on the role of the Holy Spirit in hermeneutics, one soon discovers a frustrating paucity of material on the subject. A brief survey of current hermeneutical textbooks by Robert J. May[4] reveals an amazing lack of attention to the Spirit's role in the hermeneutical process. A recent article in the *Journal of Pentecostal Theology* postulates the correct method of hermeneutics from a Pentecostal perspective, but scarcely mentions the role of the Spirit.[5] Clark H. Pinnock notes that a scholar such as Gordon D. Fee can write a book entitled *Gospel and Spirit: Issues*

---

4. May, "The Role of the Holy Spirit."

5. Autry, "Dimensions of Hermeneutics in Pentecostal Focus," 29–50.

in New Testament Hermeneutics, and say nothing about the Spirit's role in interpretation.[6] Fred H. Klooster comments, "The illumination of the Holy Spirit is regularly mentioned in the theological literature; yet detailed discussion of this subject is rare."[7]

To what can this neglect be attributed? Various explanations have been put forward. Bruce K. Waltke suggests that the Enlightenment, "with its emphasis on unaided human reason and the scientific method, saw no need for supernatural enlightenment for the accurate interpretation of the Bible."[8] Pinnock submits two other explanations. First, Liberal scholars have long been interested in illumination and the "second horizon" of Anthony C. Thiselton.[9] They gravitate towards reader-focused interpretations, and are generally unconcerned with the dangers of subjectivism. In reaction to this, Evangelicals focused strongly on historical exegesis, almost to the total negation of the reader's interpretative role.[10] In addition, the rationalism so prevalent in society since the Enlightenment translates into a preference for static propositions. Pinnock states, "It leads us to treat the Bible as a code book rather than a more flexible case book. When the Bible is approached as a codebook, the Spirit cannot open it up. No room is left for that. Our cultural presuppositions tend to distort the true purpose of the Bible and the nature of its text."[11]

WHY MUST THE HOLY SPIRIT BE INVOLVED?

Regardless of the manner in which we envisage the Holy Spirit to have inspired Scripture, we must nonetheless agree that he *did*. The work of the Spirit did not end, however, when the last letter of the New Testament had been written. Surely he was at work throughout history, guiding those who "formed" the canon, and ensuring the proper transmission of the Bible from the original autographs to our present-day copies.[12] Paul W. Lewis comments on the Pentecostal view of the Spirit's role in Scripture:

6. Pinnock, "The Work of the Holy Spirit in Hermeneutics," 7. See Fee, *Gospel and Spirit*.

7. Klooster, "The Role of the Holy Spirit in the Hermeneutic Process," 451.

8. Waltke, "Exegesis and the Spiritual Life," 29.

9. Thiselton, *New Horizons in Hermeneutics*.

10. Pinnock, "The Work of the Holy Spirit in Hermeneutics," 8–9.

11. Ibid., 8.

12. For an excellent discussion of the canon, see Bruce, *The Canon of Scripture*; and McDonald, *The Biblical Canon*.

The Pentecostal notes the ongoing work of the Holy Spirit through the whole process to the present day. Historically, God revealed Himself to the people through both deeds and word. The Spirit safeguarded these traditions perpetuated about the words and deeds of God, first oral and then written, as the Spirit also inspired the authors and editors who constructed the Biblical texts which were accepted as authoritative by the church. The Spirit through the canonization process led the acceptance and recognition of the Biblical texts by the church. The canonized scripture, which is accepted by all branches of orthodoxy, we read today as the Christian Bible. Today, the Holy Spirit illumines the mind and heart of the reader to receive the meaning of the Biblical text. . . . Further, the Holy Spirit also enables us to apply those things taught to our daily life.[13]

As John Wesley (1703–91) wrote, "The Spirit of God not only once inspired those who wrote [the Bible], but continually inspires (supernaturally assists) those that read it with earnest prayer."[14] I deal with the "how" question below. Perhaps equally important is the inquiry of *why* we ought to consider the Spirit's role. Truly, the Spirit's help is imperative for a correct interpretation of Scripture. Without exhausting the subject, I will explore five reasons.

The Nature of the Bible

First, we must contemplate the nature of Scripture itself. The Bible is a spiritual book that was "God-breathed." We are unable to believe that it is such without the inner witness of the Holy Spirit to its authenticity.[15] John Calvin, reacting against the Roman teaching of ecclesiastical testimony, wrote:

> Let it therefore be held as fixed, that those who are inwardly taught by the Holy Spirit acquiesce implicitly in Scripture; that Scripture, carrying its own evidence along with it, deigns not to submit to proofs and arguments, but owes the full conviction with which we ought to receive it to the testimony of the Spirit. For though in its own majesty it has enough to command reverence, nevertheless, it then begins to truly touch us when the Holy Spirit seals it in our hearts.[16]

13. Lewis, "Towards a Pentecostal Epistemology," 111–2.
14. Wesley, quoted in Pinnock, "The Role of the Spirit in Interpretation," 493.
15. For further discussion, see Ramm, *The Witness of the Spirit.*
16. Calvin, *Institutes of the Christian Religion,* 1:72.

God's Self Revelation

Second, God has chosen to reveal himself within the pages of Scripture. Christians believe the Bible is, therefore, a sacred book, one that is not naturally understood by mankind. Bruce Waltke asserts, "*The nature of the Revealer* . . . demands that the exegete has proper spiritual qualifications. God has hidden himself in Scripture and must sovereignly show himself to us. We cannot make God talk through the scientific method."[17] French L. Arrington states, "Scripture given by the Holy Spirit must be mediated interpretively by the Holy Spirit."[18] James I. Packer notes that Evangelicals have often failed to realize the full significance of the Spirit's role in enabling a believer to understand the Scriptures.[19] If the intent of Scripture is the self-revelation of God, we cannot expect to gain a true understanding of Scripture without the Spirit, who "will guide you into all truth" (John 16:13). Martin Luther noted that "Scripture is the sort of book which calls not only for right reading and preaching but also for the right Interpreter: the revelation of the Holy Spirit."[20]

The Depravity of the Reader

Third, mankind is as inherently sinful as the Bible is intrinsically holy. The depraved nature of the human subject must be acknowledged. Paul's words to the Corinthians are instructive on this point: "The man without the Spirit does not accept the things that come from the Spirit of God, for they are foolishness to him, and he cannot understand them, because they are spiritually discerned" (1 Cor 2:14). Bruce Waltke comments:

> Because of our innate depravity our minds have been darkened (Rom. 1:18–22; Eph. 4:17–18; 1 John 2:1). We suppress the truth (Rom. 1:18), and we aim to justify our behavior, including our unbelief and unethical conduct (Prov. 14:12; 16:26). Satan continues to deceive us with half-truths, calling into question God's goodness and truthfulness (Gen. 3). Sin has destroyed our ability to do what is right (Rom. 7:13–25). We must come to the text with a pure conscience. Thus, apart from God's regeneration and the work of the Holy Spirit we cannot hear the text clearly.[21]

17. Waltke, "Exegesis and the Spiritual Life," 34. Emphasis in original.
18. Arrington, "The Use of the Bible by Pentecostals," 105.
19. See Packer, "Infallible Scripture and the Role of Hermeneutics," 348.
20. Luther, *What Luther Says*, 76.
21. Waltke, "Exegesis and the Spiritual Life," 33.

The Transformation of the Individual Believer

Fourth, the goal of the text is to transform the lives of the readers. Inspired Scripture without the Spirit will remain a dead letter, and is useless in accomplishing this goal.[22] Clark Pinnock notes, "The goal of the Spirit as he works within our lives shedding light on the Word is to deepen our friendship with God. . . . We do not read the text out of mere historical interest but for the purposes of transformation, in order that the Scriptures might become a revelatory text for us. The Spirit must be at work for this to happen."[23] The Spirit is the One in whom the text of Scripture comes alive for present-day believers. Without the Spirit's work, lives will remain unchanged, for the power of the Word cannot be separated from the constant work of the Spirit in the life of each individual. Scott A. Ellington suggests: "It is the transformative action of the Holy Spirit which persistently intrudes on Christian experience and prevents our interpretations from becoming simply a process of reading our own needs and wants into the text and hearing only that which we want to hear."[24]

The Transformation of the Church

Finally, the Scriptures were given for the uplifting and furtherance of the Kingdom of God. God did not leave the Church without help when Christ left the earth, but sent the Comforter to be with his people. Larry Hart writes, "Through pointing the church back to her very life-breath, through the promotion of spiritual renewal, through reminding the church of the 'God-breathed' nature of the Bible, and through working signs and wonders, proponents of Holy Spirit renewal may be aiding the church in her quest to understand and apply Biblical truth in a fundamental way."[25] Clark Pinnock rightly observes that Evangelicals must reappropriate two notions of Scripture that are often stressed in Orthodox and Roman Catholic circles: The Bible is the book for the people of God, and the Church is the normal *locale* of illumination—even for Protestants. "Scripture originally arose from the life of the community and was meant to be interpreted in the ongoing life of that community."[26]

22. See Pinnock, "The Work of the Holy Spirit in Hermeneutics," 5.

23. Pinnock, "The Role of the Spirit in Interpretation," 493.

24. Ellington, "Pentecostalism and the Authority of Scripture, 22.

25. Hart, "Hermeneutics, Theology, and the Holy Spirit," 63.

26. Pinnock, "The Role of the Spirit in Interpretation," 495.

HOW DOES THE HOLY SPIRIT AID IN ILLUMINATION?

Having noted the importance of the Holy Spirit's work in our hermeneutics, reflection on exactly how he is involved is in order. Though the writing on this has been limited, some scholars have dared to speculate, and we will survey their suggestions.

French L. Arrington

French Arrington presents four ways in which interpreters rely on the Holy Spirit:

> 1) Submission of the mind to God so that the critical and analytical abilities are exercised under the guidance of the Holy Spirit; 2) a genuine openness to the witness of the Spirit as the text is examined; 3) the personal experience of faith as a part of the entire interpretive process; and, 4) response to the transforming call of God's Word.[27]

Each of these is indirectly connected to one of the situations described above, detailing the necessity of the Spirit's involvement.

John Goldingay

John Goldingay is first concerned with the intellectual work of exegesis, interpreting the original languages of ancient texts. Exegeting a passage of Scripture, to ascertain its message to both the reader and the hearer, can often be mentally laborious work. We are renewed mentally and spiritually as the Holy Spirit works with us, giving us strength for our task.[28] Russell P. Spittler states, "Exegesis puts one into the vestibule of truth; the Holy Spirit opens the inner door."[29]

Second, as has been noted above, the minds of humanity have been darkened by the Fall and no longer possess the mental purity and holiness to clearly discern the Word of God. The spiritual Word is foreign to us; the Holy Spirit opens our minds to receive the things of God. According to Richard B. Hays, 2 Corinthians 3 suggests that "only readers made competent by the Spirit can throw back the veil and perceive the sense of Scripture; those who have not turned to the Lord who is Spirit are neces-

---

27. Arrington, "The Use of the Bible by Pentecostals," 105.
28. Goldingay, *Models of Interpretation of Scripture*, 188.
29. Spittler, "Scripture and the Theological Enterprise," 76.

sarily trapped in the script, with minds hardened and veiled."[30] The Spirit both renews minds to understand, and sparks insight that the essential significance of the text for today might be determined.[31]

The Spirit is vitally important in the exercise of the *charism* that expounds how the ancient Word is to be lived in the present. That Scripture intends to transform the community of God is without question. The Spirit enables both the one who preaches and those who listen to receive the Word of God, and identify what Scripture signifies for them. Preaching is essentially the task of interpreting a text correctly, determining the relevant message for the believer today, and delivering that to the people of God. Without the Spirit, the sermon will be "mere antiquarianism."[32]

Mark J. Cartledge

Mark Cartledge has attempted to derive some insight into the role of the Holy Spirit in hermeneutics from the five "Paraclete sayings" of John's Gospel. In John 14:16–17 Jesus makes the connection between love and obedience, noting that the Spirit is given to enable his followers to live obedient lives. No doubt the Spirit also empowers believers today to obey those things in Scripture that we might rather overlook! John 14:26 states that the Holy Spirit will teach and remind the disciples of everything that Jesus had taught them. Surely he does the same today, bringing Scripture to the remembrance of believers in the most urgent times and situations. The Spirit is given to testify to the disciples concerning Jesus (15:26–27). Who among us can say that we do not need fresh revelation respecting the work of Christ in our own lives, and further help in testifying of Christ to others? John 16:7–11 tells us that when Jesus comes, the Spirit—the Counsellor—will convict the world of sin. Through whom will he do this, if not through his disciples? True enough, the Spirit's conviction will be felt directly on the heart of every person. But as believers, our search for personal holiness will be reflected outward to those who are seeking, convincing and convicting them of their own sin. Finally, the words of John 16:12–15 promised to all disciples the presence of the Spirit, who would lead and guide them into all truth. What more could the interpreter ask for?[33]

30. Hays, *Echoes of Scripture in the Letters of Paul*, 148.
31. Goldingay, *Models of Interpretation of Scripture*, 188.
32. Ibid. Cf. Craddock, *Preaching*, 135–6.
33. For the full discussion of John's five Paraclete sayings, see Cartledge, "Empirical

Clark H. Pinnock

In 1993 Clark Pinnock offered an eightfold proposal on the subject.[34] First, and significant for this work, he suggests that we must see interpretation more in the sense of a corporate exercise and not the purview of the individual alone. Second, we must recognize the dynamic nature of our interpretive journey, as we maintain an eschatological focus. Third, though the intellect has garnered much of the focus of this discussion, we should realize that God's purpose in unfolding the truth of his Word goes beyond our intellect, to word and deed. Fourth, biblical interpretation must function in the same context as the Church, world mission. Fifth, the Spirit helps the Church to recognize the "signs of the times" and to reflect biblically and theologically on current trends and issues within the Church, and in society at large. There is little doubt that Postmodernism would fall within this category. Sixth, following the Spirit's leading does not suggest infallibility. Mistakes will be made and corrected through the community and the Word. Seventh, our commitment to unity must be stronger than our desire to preserve denominational walls and paradigms. Finally, and most interesting for this work, we must be open to God's leading of individuals as we develop friendship with God through the Scriptures.

Pinnock's last point is particularly poignant:

> . . . the Spirit does open up the Scriptures for us as individuals with a view to developing our friendship with God (Ps. 25.14; Jn. 15.14). We experience it in the sacrament evangelicals call the "quiet time," a time when we daily read the Bible prayerfully. In such moments, we often experience God speaking to us, when we allow the Bible to convict and convert, to build up and to tear down, to comfort and to challenge us. Usually we try to take the text in its intended sense and apply it. But sometimes we hear God saying something different, where a text will be given a meaning different from the one intended. At such times, a text written in one context functions as a word of God with a different force in a new one. It seems that a text may be the occasion of an insight without being the cause of it. The method is to allow a historical exegesis to interact with a prophetic openness to the Spirit.[35]

Theology," 121–5.

34. Pinnock, "The Work of the Holy Spirit in Hermeneutics," 16–23.

35. Ibid., 22. Pinnock refers here to Dunn, *The Living Word*, 130–6.

Robert J. May

Robert May has offered a framework that moves towards a holistic understanding of the Holy Spirit's role in hermeneutics. Our biblical hermeneutics should be *reasonable*, acknowledging, on one hand, the work of the academy and our own rational abilities, and, on the other hand, the dynamics of a people in a supernatural relationship with God. Our interpretive methods should *resonate* with both the past history of the Church and historical interpretation, as well as the present church community. The work of the Spirit, as a member of the Godhead, will always be seen as *relevant*, no matter in which context the present Church might find herself. Finally, and admittedly most difficult to clearly describe, our reading of the Scriptures should be *revelatory*, bringing people into encounter with the living God, through which God speaks to his people.

> So where our hermeneutics is reasonable to the Christian mind, where there is a sense of resonance with both past and present church communities, where our hermeneutics is relevant to the context of the one who reads and where God ultimately is revealed, we suggest that there is a greater likelihood that the Holy Spirit is at work in our hermeneutics.[36]

Roy B. Zuck

One of the most thorough non-Pentecostal discussions of this issue comes from Roy Zuck. He addresses the issue of whether the Holy Spirit's involvement in hermeneutics ultimately leads to a subjective interpretive process.[37] Asking questions such as "Is the Bible not clear in its meanings? Can only a select few have insight into the meaning of Scripture? Are the 'deep things of God' and his 'thoughts' (1 Cor. 2:10–11) understood by only some Christians?," Zuck suggests fourteen propositions; I offer the pertinent ones here.[38]

36. May, "The Role of the Holy Spirit."
37. Zuck, "The Role of the Spirit in Hermeneutics," 120–9.
38. Ibid. The other points are as follows: The role of the Holy Spirit in interpreting the Bible does not mean that one's interpretations are infallible; does not mean that only scholars can interpret Scripture; requires spiritual devotion on the part of the interpreter; means that a lack of spiritual preparedness hinders accurate interpretation; is no substitute for diligent study; is included in but not identical with illumination; does not mean that all parts of the Bible are equally clear; and does not result in believers having a comprehensive and completely accurate understanding of the entire Scriptures.

1. The Spirit's ministry in Bible interpretation does not mean he gives new revelation. The Spirit's work is always in association with the Word of God, not beyond it or in addition to it.

2. The work of the Spirit in interpretation does not mean that he gives some interpreters a mental acuity for seeing truths under the surface that are not evident to any other dedicated Bible students.

3. The Spirit's work in biblical interpretation does not rule out the use of study helps such as commentaries and Bible dictionaries.

4. The role of the Spirit in interpretation is no substitute for diligent study.

5. The ministry of the Holy Spirit in Bible interpretation does not mean interpreters can ignore common sense and logic. The Spirit assists the Spirit-filled learner to think clearly and accurately.

6. The place of the Holy Spirit in interpreting the Bible means that he does not normally give sudden intuitive flashes of insight into the meaning of Scripture.

The suggestions from the various authors above are nonetheless helpful for a more complete understanding of the Holy Spirit's role in our work. It is important for Pentecostals to have a substantial grasp of the Spirit's role in hermeneutics, for we have always expected the Holy Spirit to be involved in our interpretation of Scripture, helping to determine what was meant then and what is meant today.

Before delving further into the discussion concerning a Pentecostal advantage in hermeneutics by virtue of experiences of the Spirit common to Pentecostals, I must first conclude my discussion on the necessity of a distinctively Pentecostal hermeneutic.

A DISTINCTIVE PENTECOSTAL (AND POSTMODERN) HERMENEUTIC?

The debate presently occurring within the Pentecostal community concerns whether Pentecostals need a specific Pentecostal hermeneutic, or whether one borrowed from Evangelicalism, albeit with some modification, is sufficient. Viewing the position of Robert P. Menzies as that of the majority of Anglo-Pentecostals, Kenneth J. Archer laments:

> Pentecostals who use Redaction Criticism and the historical-grammatical method are primarily concerned with historical

analysis in order to discover the author's intended meaning. They seek to unlock the passage's meaning by elucidating what cultural influences and beliefs lie behind the text. The primary focus, then, is the world behind the text and not the text itself. The importance of the horizon of the present reader has been ignored and furthermore the world of the text becomes secondary to the historically reconstructed world behind the text. . . . Hence, the majority of academically trained Pentecostals who embrace Historical Criticism have moved away from the early Pentecostals' emphasis upon the text and readers. They have embraced Modernity's critical approaches that have always been primarily concerned with the world behind the text. Thus, they have moved away from the early pre-critical Paramodern approach of early Pentecostals to the acceptable critical Modern approaches, and in doing so aligned themselves with conservative North American Evangelicalism whose roots are Reformed and modernistic.[39]

A minority of Pentecostal scholars, according to Archer, views this new assimilation into Evangelicalism as negative and destructive to Pentecostal identity and doctrine. Mark D. McLean is representative:

> . . . a strict adherence to traditional evangelical/fundamentalist hermeneutic principles leads to a position which, in its most positive forms, suggests the distinctives of the twentieth century Pentecostal movement are perhaps nice, but not necessary; important but not vital to the life of the Church in the twentieth century. In its more negative forms, it leads to a total rejection of Pentecostal phenomena.[40]

Can the philosophies of Postmodernity be synchronized in any manner with Pentecostal hermeneutics? Does Pentecostalism need a distinctive hermeneutic, to ensure the continued relevance of our presentation of the Gospel to Generation X and the Millennials? As I noted in chapter 1 above, there appear to be four responses to this question.[41] The first response is in the affirmative: we ought to build a distinctive Pentecostal hermeneutic based on Postmodern viewpoints, free from rationalistic Evangelicalism. The second response is in the negative: we should reject Postmodern influence and build upon the foundation of

---

39. Archer, *A Pentecostal Hermeneutic*, 141.

40. McLean, "Toward a Pentecostal Hermeneutic," 37.

41. The following categories are from Brubaker, "Postmodernism and Pentecostals," 39–44.

an Evangelical hermeneutic. The third response suggests we should join Pentecostalism's concerns with traditional Evangelical hermeneutics. The final response posits that we should cautiously proceed to develop a Postmodern Pentecostal hermeneutic.

Affirmative: The Connection is Beneficial[42]

One of the major supporters of this view is Timothy B. Cargal.[43] He has argued that not only is there a natural link between Pentecostalism and faiths that place high value on the role of experience in worship and hermeneutics, but that the link also extends to the rejection of the grammatico-historical hermeneutic by both groups. Although some Pentecostals have in fact moved towards the grammatico-historical method, as was shown in chapter 4 above, Cargal notes that in general the pastor in the field still relies on traditional pre-critical[44] methods of interpretation. Thus, the Pentecostal scholar could guide the pastor in this line of interpretation, each striving to make the text as applicable as possible to her respective audience.

Cargal argues that with its experiential focus, Pentecostalism shares some common ground with Postmodern thought, and is therefore naturally placed to engage Postmodern culture on its own terms. He dismisses the Modern construction that only what is historically and objectively true is meaningful; therefore, he naturally takes issue with the foundational principles of the historical-critical method of hermeneutics. Arguing that Pentecostals have always believed that reason and rationalism are important, but that hermeneutical processes must involve more, he welcomes the Postmodern openness to truth outside of traditional modernist (and perhaps Evangelical) perspectives. Cargal declares:

42. Poirier and Lewis ("Pentecostal and Postmodernist Hermeneutics," 3) believe that the majority of Pentecostal scholars have reacted positively to Postmodern thought. "Ancient historians often tell of a city's inhabitants streaming out of the gates to greet a liberating conqueror or visiting dignitary. No image better fits the reception that Pentecostal scholars and theologians have given to Postmodernism."

43. Cargal, "Beyond the Fundamentalist-Modernist Controversy," 163–87. In agreement with Cargal is Sheppard, "Biblical Interpretation After Gadamer," 120–35.

44. A method of biblical interpretation that relies heavily upon a plain reading of Scripture, without examination of the history or semantic meaning of a particular text. A common saying among those employing a pre-critical hermeneutic is, "If the plain sense of Scripture makes common sense, seek no other sense, or you'll end up with nonsense." Source unknown.

As a postmodern paradigm increasingly illuminates the thinking of our culture in general, any hermeneutic which does not account for its loci of meanings within that postmodern paradigm will become nonsensical and irrelevant. If for no other reason than that, we must . . . explore the possibilities of a Pentecostal hermeneutic in a postmodern age.[45]

Negative: The Connection is Detrimental

Among those resisting the idea of Postmodern influence in Pentecostalism is Robert P. Menzies. Responding to Timothy Cargal, Menzies argues for the return to the similarities inherent between Pentecostal and Evangelical hermeneutics, and suggests that Pentecostals might even contribute to existing Evangelical hermeneutics, though not in the vein that I discuss in the following section. Menzies writes:

I see the assimilation of the modern Pentecostal movement into the broader Evangelical world as an exciting and positive event. Looking back over the last fifty years, Pentecostals can affirm the strength they have found in their Evangelical heritage. This legacy from Evangelicalism has been especially helpful with respect to biblical interpretation. . . . Looking forward I see the potential for additional theological contributions to the larger Evangelical world and Christian community. The Pentecostal understanding of Spirit-baptism is important in this regard. . . . The hermeneutical climate within Evangelicalism is more conducive now than ever before to Pentecostal theological contributions.[46]

Menzies asserts that Cargal underestimates the ability of scholars to bridge the gap between the ancient and modern situations of the text. While we cannot gain absolute certainty regarding historical matters, we can nonetheless gain knowledge. Menzies believes the tendency of many Postmodern writers to shift the locus of determinant for meaning away from the text to the reader may be nothing more than a reactionary move against years of sterile, dry, biblical criticism, resulting from the tenets of Modernism consistently applied to hermeneutics. Pentecostalism has seen the importance of the reader in the interpretative process for entirely different reasons, as was demonstrated in chapter 3 above. Menzies also suggests that the influence of Evangelical hermeneutics upon Pentecostalism

45. Cargal, "Beyond the Fundamentalist-Modernist Controversy," 187.
46. Menzies, "Jumping Off the Postmodern Bandwagon," 119.

has been beneficial. The charge that Evangelical hermeneutics have been overly rationalistic is, accordingly to Menzies, too broad, and without serious support.[47]

For Menzies, the move towards a more reader-centered approach to the text, common to the Postmodern line of thought, is a dangerous one:

> These approaches strike me as the logical successors of a sterile biblical criticism which has so emasculated the text that it had nothing of significance to communicate. At some point, the question had to be asked: why bother with all of this? The solution to this dilemma was obvious: if significance cannot be found in the meaning of the text, then it must be imported from outside the text.[48]

The issue here is substantial. Robert J. May notes: "Pentecostal presuppositions about a supernatural and transcendent reality are not only a point of contact with a Postmodern worldview, but equally challenge modernist assumptions that are so dominant within traditional Evangelical critical methods."[49] To be sure, Menzies serves the Pentecostal community well when he raises concerns over the location of the final determinant of meaning. Traditional Evangelical (and increasingly Pentecostal) hermeneutics have leaned heavily upon the historical-critical method, inherent with its safety in locating meaning objectively in the text. Given the wide variety of "objective" opinions as to the authorial intent of particular texts, however, I question the inherent objectivity of relying upon authorial intent as a bulwark against reader-centered subjectivity. As has been noted, the transition towards a reader-centered hermeneutic can be risky, as the meaning may now be found subjectively with the reader. In my opinion, Menzies has reacted too strongly by describing Cargal's proposals as "ultimately disturbing."[50] Current trends in Pentecostal hermeneutics suggest that increasing numbers of Pentecostal scholars are uncomfortable with the "either-or" approach demonstrated by Menzies and others.

---

47. Ibid., 117–9.
48. Ibid., 118.
49. May, "The Role of the Holy Spirit."
50. Menzies, "Jumping Off the Postmodern Bandwagon," 115.

Pentecostals Should Add to Evangelical Hermeneutics

This approach sees the value of the grammatico-historical method, but acknowledges Pentecostal concerns that the meaning derived is not stripped of its experiential dimension. The chief proponent here is Roger Stronstad. His work on the charismatic language of Luke-Acts utilizes a critical methodology, which he believes combines the best of Evangelical scholarship with experiential verification.[51] Some scholars believe that by the very act of experiencing for themselves that which Scripture describes, Pentecostals may interpret those descriptive passages with greater clarity than those without such an experience. While Stronstad acknowledges the value of traditional Evangelical hermeneutics, he recognizes the importance of experience in the interpretive process. Thus, a harmonizing of experiential verification with Evangelical hermeneutics is, in his opinion, the best way forward.[52]

Pentecostals Should Develop a Unique Hermeneutic

Among the supporters of this view is Kenneth Archer,[53] who feels that if Pentecostalism is to remain the relevant missionary force it has been, elements of Postmodernism are essential. He notes with approval the efforts of some scholars to bring their Pentecostal spirituality and pneumatology to bear in their hermeneutical work.[54] As was shown in chapter 6 above, Archer would blend together the Postmodern emphasis on the interpreter's context with classical Pentecostal spirituality.

> Today some Pentecostals attempt to express themselves with a purely modernistic hermeneutic (the historical-critical method), yet if Pentecostalism desires to continue in its missionary objective while keeping in tune with its classical ethos, then Pentecostalism must have a postmodern accent; an accent which is both a protest against modernity as well as a proclamation to move beyond modernity; or better, after the modern.[55]

51. Stronstad, *The Charismatic Theology of St. Luke.*

52. See Stronstad, "Pentecostal Experience and Hermeneutics," 14–30; and "Trends in Pentecostal Hermeneutics," 1–11.

53. See, for example, Archer, "Pentecostal Hermeneutics: Retrospect and Prospect." This line of thinking may be found throughout his work.

54. For example, Thomas, "Women, Pentecostals, and the Bible," 41–56.

55. Archer, "Pentecostal Hermeneutics: Retrospect and Prospect," 80.

Accordingly, some Pentecostal scholars such as Roger Stronstad have begun to propose hermeneutical guidelines more in keeping with the early traditions and experience of Pentecostalism. On the role of experience within hermeneutics, for example, Stronstad proposes that it must enter the process at the beginning, rather than the end, as suggested by other Pentecostals scholars.[56]

> Stronstad contends that a Pentecostal hermeneutic will have a variety of cognitive (Protestant grammatico-historico exegesis) and experiential elements (salvation and charismatic experience . . .). Stronstad recognizes that charismatic experience in itself will not enable one to become "an infallible interpreter" of Scripture; yet, charismatic experience provides an important pre-understanding to the Scripture.[57]

In this manner, Stronstad has challenged those who claim that Pentecostals often create theology from their shared experiences. By promoting the importance of experience at the beginning of the hermeneutical process, Stronstad has taken the first steps towards a truly Pentecostal hermeneutic.

Other Pentecostal theologians have suggested further steps towards a holistic Pentecostal hermeneutic. John Christopher Thomas, drawing from the methodology of the Jerusalem Council (Acts 15), proposes a hermeneutic containing three key components: the community, the activity of the Holy Spirit, and Scripture.[58] Archer notes, "Thomas has thus far presented a hermeneutical approach that attempts to be consistent with early Pentecostal ethos and resists the complete adoption of an Evangelical and modernistic Historical Critical method."[59] Further:

> Today, some Pentecostals attempt to express themselves with an Evangelical and modernistic hermeneutic (the Historical Critical methods). Yet if Pentecostalism desires to continue its missionary objective while keeping in tune with its early ethos, it must move beyond Modernity. . . .

56. See MacDonald, "A Classical Viewpoint," 58–75. See also Menzies, "The Methodology of Pentecostal Theology," 1–14.

57. Archer, A Pentecostal Hermeneutic, 143. See Stronstad, "Pentecostal Experience and Hermeneutics," 16–26.

58. See Thomas, "Women, Pentecostals, and the Bible," esp. 49–50.

59. Archer, A Pentecostal Hermeneutic, 146.

In other words, a Pentecostal hermeneutical strategy is needed which rejects the quest for a past determinate meaning of the author and embraces the reality that interpretation involves both the discovery of meaning and the creation of meaning. . . .

A Pentecostal hermeneutical strategy should attempt to continue to forge an alternative path that neither entirely accepts the pluralistic relativism of Postmodernism nor entirely affirms the objectivism of Modernism—a pathway that began to be forged in early Pentecostalism.[60]

Summary

Pentecostals must employ distinctive hermeneutical principles, primarily to maintain the Pentecostal focus upon the present-day experience of the Holy Spirit in life and ministry, and further, to share this same expectation of supernatural experience with those Postmoderns looking to experience God for themselves. Of the four options presented above, I believe that Pentecostals cannot simply embrace a connection with Postmodern thought, as Timothy Cargal would seem to suggest, for there is much in Postmodern thinking that has been shown to be antithetical to core doctrines of Christianity. Avoiding Postmodern influence altogether, however, as Robert Menzies has proposed, is likewise unadvisable for Pentecostals, for it may well prove to alienate our presentation of the Gospel from those who need to accept and embrace it. "Jumping Off the Postmodern Bandwagon" is not an option for Pentecostals.

Rather, Pentecostals must develop a distinctive approach to hermeneutics in the vein proposed by Roger Stronstad and Kenneth Archer above. In my opinion, the differences between the approaches advocated by each are few, as neither would pretend to develop a uniquely Pentecostal hermeneutic completely devoid of the beneficial advances in Evangelical hermeneutical scholarship. Archer's focus on the text in his proposed hermeneutic, while different than the traditional text-centered Evangelical approach, nonetheless pays homage to the caution Evangelicals have exercised to avoid the rampant subjectivity often associated with a full reader-response hermeneutic.

60. Ibid., 146, 147, 153.

EXPERIENTIAL VERIFICATION:
THE PENTECOSTAL EDGE?

To be sure, Pentecostalism has become more academic in its defense, and its scholars have tended to align themselves recently with Evangelicals in their move towards adopting conservative methods of historical criticism.[61] Yet, a difference in focus remains. For the Pentecostal, Scripture must primarily speak to the modern reader; simply focusing on what the text may have originally meant is not enough. The Pentecostal insists on closing the gap between the two horizons. Archer notes:

> A hermeneutic that focuses only upon what the original inspired author meant . . . will not completely satisfy the requirements of a Pentecostal hermeneutic. The essence of Pentecostalism asserts that "the spiritual and extraordinary supernatural experiences of the biblical characters are possible for contemporary believers."[62]

Some Pentecostal scholars continue the tendency towards a hermeneutical system that is heavily slanted towards rationalism, and downplay the role of the Holy Spirit and/or experience.[63] Yongnan Jeon Ahn argues:

> . . . within the modernistic epistemological presupposition scholars, who utilize historical critical methodology, tend to intrinsically restrict the experiential dimension of the interpreter in hermeneutical enterprise that has formed the bedrock of the Pentecostal hermeneutics. As emphasizing the role of experience in Pentecostal hermeneutics, Pentecostals need to recognize the necessary involvement of the interpreter in hermeneutical process in order to understand the meaning of a text.[64]

French Arrington agrees: "The real issue in Pentecostalism has become hermeneutics, that is, the distinctive nature and function of Scripture and the roles of the Holy Spirit, the Christian community, grammatical-historical research, and personal experience in the interpretive process."[65] The Holy Spirit enables the reader to bridge the gap between the ancient

---

61. Archer, "Pentecostal Hermeneutics: Retrospect and Prospect," 74.

62. Ibid., 75.

63. Thomas, "Women, Pentecostals, and the Bible," 41.

64. Ahn, "Various Debates in the Contemporary Pentecostal Hermeneutics," 30–1.

65. Arrington, "The Use of the Bible by Pentecostals," 101.

authors of Scripture and the present interpreter.[66] Pentecostals contribute most substantially to hermeneutics in the area of experience and verification. Whereas Classical Pentecostalism tended to distinguish poorly between the horizons of reader and author, contemporary scholars rely on their own experience to bridge that gap.

In the discussion concerning whether Pentecostals may have an advantage in the interpretation of texts which describe experiences commonly occurring within Pentecostalism, readers may be surprised to discover how many Pentecostal scholars have written in support of such a notion.[67] Before surveying those who have written in the affirmative, however, I will consider the objections of one leading Pentecostal scholar, Gordon Anderson.

Gordon Anderson

Gordon Anderson believes that this approach leads to an apparent elitism that cannot well serve either Pentecostalism or the wider Evangelical community. Arguing for the substantial similarity in the Pentecostal and Evangelical approach to interpretation, Anderson states, "A Pentecostal hermeneutic is not special insight unavailable to others."[68] He differentiates between two schools of thought concerning how the Holy Spirit aids interpretation of the Scriptures. Commenting on Anderson's position, Robert May notes: "Either the Holy Spirit enables the human mind to intellectually grasp *the revelation* of Scripture, or alternatively, the human mind is quite capable of understanding the meaning of the scriptures without the aid of the Holy Spirit, it is rather *the will* of the one reading that is the object of the Holy Spirit's action."[69] For Anderson, Pentecostals ought to align themselves with the second position; the Spirit does not act upon the mind but rather upon the will of the individual. The Spirit's role is not to shed light upon the meaning of the text itself, but to move the will of the individual to a place of receptivity to the meaning of the Scriptures.

---

66. Ibid., 105.

67. What follows is a brief look at several Pentecostal scholars who have expressed thoughts on this subject.

68. Anderson, "Pentecostal Hermeneutics," 8.

69. May, "The Role of the Holy Spirit." Emphasis in original. See Anderson, "Pentecostal Hermeneutics," 11.

Naturally, by taking this position, Anderson does not believe Pentecostals have a superior opportunity to understand the Scriptures through their charismatic experience, but are empowered through the Spirit, along with all other believers, to act accordingly. Other Pentecostal scholars disagree, suggesting that Pentecostals may be in an advantageous position through the Spirit's work on the believing mind, as well.

William W. Menzies

William Menzies proposes that the crux of the hermeneutical issue is actually methodology. He suggests three levels of a Pentecostal hermeneutic. The first is the *inductive* level, which is comprised of three varieties of inductive listening: declarative, implicational, and descriptive. The second is the *deductive* level. He points out that after one has availed of inductive hermeneutics, certain patterns or theological motifs, common either to the whole of Scripture or to a particular author, begin to emerge. While not stated specifically in Scripture, these patterns and motifs are often essential for understanding the particular nuances of the text. Finally, he describes the *verification* level. While others chide Pentecostals for their dangerous practice of "exegeting" out of experience, Menzies argues that it is dangerous to develop theology and hermeneutics from *non-experience*. If a biblical truth is to be promulgated, then it certainly ought to be verifiable and demonstrable in life. When Peter stood on the Day of Pentecost and proclaimed, "this is that" (Acts 2:16, KJV), testimony about the experience and exposition of Joel's prophecy flowed together.[70]

Howard M. Ervin

Howard Ervin (1915–2009), a Baptist turned Pentecostal, suggests a *pneumatic* hermeneutic, based on the need for an epistemology firmly rooted in biblical faith, "with a phenomenology that meets the criteria of empirically verifiable sensory experience (healing, miracles, etc.) and does not violate the coherence of rational categories."[71] A pneumatic epistemology also "provides a resolution of (a) the dichotomy between faith and reason that existentialism consciously seeks to bridge, though at the expense of the pneumatic; (b) the antidote to a destructive rationalism that often accompanies a critical-historical exegesis; and (c) a rational ac-

70. Menzies, "The Methodology of Pentecostal Theology," 1–14.
71. Ervin, "Hermeneutics: A Pentecostal Option," 23.

countability for the mysticism by a piety grounded in *sola fidei.*"[72] Because Pentecostals allow the experiential immediacy of the Holy Spirit to inform their epistemology, this contact with the *pneumatic* enlightens their hermeneutics in a way that may be considered beyond the traditional view of illumination. Ervin writes:

> Pentecostal experience with the Holy Spirit gives existential awareness of the miraculous in the biblical worldview. These events as recorded are no longer "mythological," but "objectively" real. Contemporary experience of divine healing, prophecy, miracles, tongues, and exorcism are empirical evidence of the impingement of a sphere of non-material reality upon our time-space existence with which one can and does have immediate contact. Awareness of, and interaction with the presence of this spiritual continuum is axiomatic in a Pentecostal epistemology that affects decisively its hermeneutic.[73]

Roger Stronstad

Roger Stronstad believes there are five components to a Pentecostal hermeneutic: charismatic experiential presuppositions, the pneumatic, genres, exegesis, and experiential verification.[74] This is a clear wedding together of Pentecostal concerns with traditional Evangelical hermeneutics. If the five components are examined clearly, only the first and fifth are observed to be at all distinctive.

Stronstad is convinced that Pentecostals have much to offer traditional hermeneutics in the areas of pre-understanding and experiential verification. Summarizing Pinnock, Stronstad notes that "the charismatic experience of the Pentecostal—ministering in the power of the Holy Spirit, speaking in other tongues as the Spirit gives utterance, being led by the Spirit—enables him to understand Luke's record of the activity of the Holy Spirit in Acts better than the non-Pentecostal."[75] Clark H. Pinnock writes, "[W]e cannot consider Pentecostalism to be a kind of aberration born of experiential excesses but a 20th century revival of New Testament theology and religion. It has not only restored joy and power to

72. Ibid., 23–4.
73. Ibid., 35.
74. See Stronstad, "Pentecostal Experience and Hermeneutics," 28–9.
75. Ibid., 15. Badcock (*Light of Truth and Fire of Love*, 139–44) agrees.

the church but a clearer reading to the Bible as well."[76] Stronstad interprets this further:

> [C]harismatic experience in particular and spiritual experience in general give the interpreter of relevant biblical texts an experiential presupposition which transcends the rational or cognitive presuppositions of scientific exegesis.
>
> In other words, [the Pentecostals'] charismatic experience is an experiential presupposition which enables them to understand the charismatic life of the Apostolic Church, as Luke reports it, better than those contemporary Christians who lack this experience.[77]

John Christopher Thomas

John Christopher Thomas seeks to develop a Pentecostal hermeneutic from the Acts 15 record of the Jerusalem Council. For him, this passage records an example of hermeneutics based on the collective experience of the community, the Scriptures, and the primary role of the Holy Spirit in mediating these Scriptures to the context of the believers.[78] Contrary to the current Evangelical use of the historical-critical method, which regards authorial intent as a deciding factor in determining scriptural truth, Thomas suggests that the tridactic method used in Acts 15 might better satisfy Pentecostals in their search for suitable hermeneutical principles:

> [T]his study suggests that there may indeed be a distinctive hermeneutical approach to Scripture, contained in the New Testament itself, that is more in keeping with the ethos and worldview of the Pentecostal community than are many of the interpretive approaches currently being employed by a number of Pentecostal interpreters.[79]

Regarding the role of context and community, Thomas notes that "the methodology revealed in Acts 15 is far removed from the historical-critical or historical-grammatical approach where one moves from text to

---

76. Pinnock, in Stronstad, *The Charismatic Theology of St. Luke*, viii.

77. Stronstad, "Pentecostal Experience and Hermeneutics," 17. This concept is not new. Indeed, some scholars believe that the reference to "private spirits" in the Westminster Confession of Faith refers to charismata in terms of interpretive help. See Curtis, "Charismata as Hermeneutical Help?," 1–20.

78. Thomas, "Women, Pentecostals, and the Bible," 50.

79. Ibid., 54–5.

context. On this occasion, the interpreters moved from their context to the biblical text."[80] Participants in the Jerusalem Conference first related their various experiences as God demonstrated his desired inclusion of the Gentiles in the plan of salvation. Only after these testimonies did the Apostles refer to Scripture; with the guidance of the Holy Spirit, passages were then chosen which supported the testimonies relating God's activity within the community. Indeed, the reference to the Holy Spirit in verse 28 indicates a stronger link to the Spirit's role in the interpretive process than many conservatives (or Pentecostals) are willing to acknowledge.

Thomas acknowledges that this reliance on the Holy Spirit in the interpretive process can lead to "rampant subjectivism," but he argues that this model provides protection against this, for it "clearly regards Scripture as authoritative, for ultimately the experience of the church must be measured against the biblical text...."[81]

Robert May notes:

> Thomas is clearly dissatisfied with much of the contemporary discussion regarding the role of the Spirit in interpretation. For Thomas, there is a clear role for the Spirit, which is tangible and necessary for the believing community to function effectively. Thomas is also aware of the subjective element that is obvious when such a path is chosen. He has placed controls in the paradigm that he is proposing that would help limit the range of interpretations, but he refuses to stifle the Spirit's role through mere "academic lip service." And this is refreshing and challenging, if a little dangerous.[82]

Paul W. Lewis

Paul Lewis notes that Pentecostal experience is both unique and important in several ways. First, long before the debates over inerrancy, Pentecostals assumed the authority of Scripture, for they experienced that which the Scriptures described. Second, in the debate between the text and the reader as the locus of authority, Pentecostals assume "that the author and the interpreter are both necessary as sender and receiver

80. Ibid., 50.
81. Ibid., 55.
82. May, "The Role of the Holy Spirit."

of Divine assistance as both are 'inspired' by the Holy Spirit."[83] Further, in terms of the pre-understanding of the interpreter, "Pentecostal experience authenticates and provides reassurance that the pneumatological experiences of the Bible are also meant for today."[84] Pentecostal experience also impacts the application of the text, and how these applications are accepted within the Pentecostal community. Finally, Pentecostal hermeneutics are informed by a "third horizon," which refers to the customs and worldview of the members of the recipient culture, if different from that of the interpreter's. This third horizon can assist in understanding one's own cultural bias. "Theological reflection invites an experience through a practice, which in turn leads into more theological reflection. . . . So, not only does Pentecostal experience influence the pre-understanding directly as a person interprets the Bible, it also informs the theological framework, which itself forms part of the pre-understanding."[85] Lewis concludes:

> Pentecostal experience is fundamental to the whole process. It necessitates the need to focus upon the original authors, and thereby, the text. . . . Further, Pentecostals presuppose the authority of the Scripture due their Pentecostal experiences. Thereby, Pentecostals are placed within an [sic] unique position as Biblical exegetes, for Pentecostalism promotes the prophetic gifts and finds no philosophical problem of the inspired authors foretelling events prior to their occurrences (e.g., Daniel, Isaiah). . . . Therefore, the Pentecostal can enter the discussion with a more balanced perspective on the origins, aspects, and features of Biblical texts.[86]

John McKay

John McKay takes this concept further than many other scholars in his wedding together of charismatic Christianity and current hermeneutics.[87] He is highly critical of the tendency towards critical/analytical methods of scriptural study often found within academia, which does little to impart the truth of God to the student of the Scriptures. Instead, McKay argues

---

83. Lewis, "Towards a Pentecostal Epistemology," 112.
84. Ibid., 114.
85. Ibid., 117.
86. Ibid.
87. McKay, "When the Veil is Taken Away."

that charismatic readers must not let their involvement with the academy negatively impact their own interpretation of Scripture. McKay's personal experience with the baptism in the Holy Spirit effectively changed his outlook on Scripture from a purely academic interest to a subjective and life-changing one. Spirit-baptism thus changed his view of Scripture significantly, to the point that instead of embracing both "rational" and "spiritual" insight into Scripture as beneficial and complementary, he chooses the more radical approach of suggesting the latter is superior to the former.

> It is not that charismatics cease to think theologically; quite the contrary. However, their theological perspective has changed, and changed so radically that they find their views no longer fit with those of the majority of today's biblical theologians, and furthermore that they fail to find much satisfaction from participating in their debates. It is my convinced opinion that a charismatic's view of the Bible must be different from everyone else's, be they fundamentalists, conservatives, liberals, radicals, or whatever.[88]

Kenneth J. Archer

Other scholars take a less extreme position than John McKay's, recognizing the importance of both reason and the Holy Spirit in hermeneutics. Kenneth Archer, building upon the work of John Christopher Thomas, suggests that while the traditional Evangelical emphasis on the historical-critical method is important, it alone is insufficient. Readers may gain access to the original historical/cultural meaning of the text, but help is not available in terms of meaning for the present. "The traditional Evangelical historical-critical methods would be utilized in the hermeneutic process but would not monopolize the process. Contemporary Christian experience must also be included in the hermeneutical process."[89]

Arden C. Autry

Arden Autry agrees with Kenneth Archer's line of thinking in his focus on the role of the Holy Spirit in bringing the individual into encounter with God. For Autry, correct reading of the Scriptures must involve more than an accurate rendering of the author's intention. Reading the biblical

---

88. Ibid., 38–9.

89. Archer, "Pentecostal Hermeneutics: Retrospect and Prospect," 79.

text must bring the reader into contact with the transcendent reality that is God. Like Archer, Autry sees both the historical-critical methods of biblical study and spiritual experience at play in hermeneutics. The critical methods will objectively control the reader's conclusions and lead to a *correct reading*, and *creative readings*, which are context specific and may surpass the original authorial intent, will also be derived through the help of the Holy Spirit. "[T]he language of the Bible does seem to have a dynamic quality not always exhausted by the author's original intention. . . . The 'correct' reading serves the 'creative'; and the 'creative' measures itself by the 'correct.' "[90]

Summary

While the excessive subjectivism often prevalent in the reader-response model of hermeneutics is not desirable within Pentecostalism, neither is the frequently detached and sometimes esoteric objectivity found within the historical-critical method. Pentecostal hermeneutics ought to move towards the center of this debate, acknowledging and relying upon the historical-critical method with its objectivity on one hand, while remaining open to the more subjective verification of Pentecostal experience on the other. Referring to the title of Robert Menzies' rebuttal to Timothy Cargal—"Jumping Off the Postmodern Bandwagon"—May concludes: "It is the post-modern bandwagon of rampant subjectivism that we should jump off and not the possibility of the Christian experience of the transcendent."[91] William MacDonald agrees: "Does this holy experience result in an experience-centered theology? Hardly. The better way to label it is this: Christ-centered, experience-certified theology."[92]

CONCLUSION

This chapter has shown the important connection between Scripture and the Spirit of God. Active both in its inception and transmission, the Spirit has ensured that God's Word, the testimony to the incarnate Christ, has been written down and preserved for all generations. As scholars and interpreters of Scripture in the twenty-first century, we must be ever cognizant of the integral role the Spirit has already had in the transmission of Scripture. Furthermore, we must acknowledge the cardinal link between

90. Autry, "Dimensions of Hermeneutics in Pentecostal Focus," 37, 49.
91. May, "The Role of the Holy Spirit."
92. MacDonald, "A Classical Viewpoint," 64.

the author of the Scriptures we study, and the illumination of their meaning, which can only come from him. Without the Spirit working in our lives and hermeneutics, we are blind and truly unable to ever grasp the truths contained therein.

There is little doubt that Pentecostalism has changed significantly in the time since closer ties with the larger Evangelical community began. Although we acknowledge the increased acceptability of Pentecostalism and the maturing of Pentecostalism academically, we must inquire as to the price paid. This work agrees with Paul Lewis' suggestion that the

> . . . stark contrast between the more cognitive, Enlightenment influenced Evangelicalism and orality-pneumatologically based Pentecostals has somewhat diminished since the 1950's due to the "Evangelicalization" of the Pentecostals. The real issue was that the Pentecostals capitulated in several areas in order to be accepted, among other factors, in the conservative Evangelical community of the National Association of Evangelicals.[93]

Pentecostalism now appears to be in full debate over the necessity of a distinctive Pentecostal hermeneutic and what that entails. Those who have embraced the traditional Evangelical hermeneutical approaches are apprehensive about the subjectivism some suggest is required within a Pentecostal hermeneutic. Conversely, those who embrace the possibilities of a truly Pentecostal hermeneutic caution against the toll the traditional Modern approaches will take on distinctive Pentecostal theology. Paul A. Pomerville laments

> . . . the excessive impact of the western world view and scholastic theology on evangelicalism. Some evangelicals may be content with the unhappy combination of a warm conversion experience and a cold intellectual doctrine and apologetic, but the Pentecostal cannot afford that tension. The very center of his distinctive is jeopardized—the dynamic, charismatic experience of the Spirit in the Christian life.[94]

93. Lewis, "Towards a Pentecostal Epistemology," 119. In terms of specific areas in which Lewis believes we have capitulated, he lists pacifism, decline of eschatological vision, rejection of ecumenical concerns, development of racism, the move from the Holiness background and implied ethics, revision of our doctrine of Scripture, reversal of the role of women in ministry, and the demise of the belief of the Spirit's presence and work in the present age. While we may wish to debate certain of these examples, there is a strong case for the impact of Evangelicalism upon Pentecostalism in many of the above areas. See Hocken, "A Charismatic View," 96–106; and Smith, "The Closing of the Book," 49–71.

94. Pomerville, *The Third Force in Missions,* 14. See also Tarr, "Transcendence,

For Pentecostals, the link between hermeneutics and experience is well established; their contribution to the larger Evangelical hermeneutical world is perhaps just beginning to take shape. At issue is whether Pentecostals ought to solidify their affiliation with traditional Evangelical methods that rely so heavily on Modernist presuppositions, or chart a new hermeneutical path that strikes a balance between text-centered and reader-centered approaches. For many Pentecostal scholars, a new approach, encompassing a novel view of the role of the Holy Spirit, is needed. Robert May declares:

> Few evangelicals would deny that part of the Spirit's role is to bring believers into a relationship with and knowledge of God. This function for most is seen to be predominantly through prayer and Bible study. Questions about whether this is the Spirit's primary role in hermeneutics—the knowledge of God—or whether the Spirit's role is in relation to the mind or the will or the reader's context need to be placed to one side for now. The clear challenge that is being brought by Cargal, Thomas, McKay, Autry and others is that this particular aspect of the Spirit cannot be, on the one hand, freely acknowledged, and yet, on the other hand, restricted to human rational and objective categories. . . .
>
> For many Pentecostals, the Holy Spirit is active in a supernatural dimension and is quite capable of acting in ways that break the rules of more rational approaches and still bring people into a deeper knowledge of God. Pentecostal approaches to hermeneutics are well-placed to accept this dimension. The extent to which others within Pentecostalism are willing to actively recognize this element is debatable.[95]

Pentecostalism must pursue a distinctly Pentecostal hermeneutic, along the pattern established by Kenneth Archer's proposal, though not necessarily embracing his proposed hermeneutic as a whole. Pentecostal interests are best served by an approach to the interpretation of Scripture that combines recent advances in hermeneutical scholarship with a Pentecostal sensitivity to the roles of narratives, community, and experience in our hermeneutical methodology.

Further, Pentecostal scholars must recognize the possibilities of a distinctly Pentecostal contribution to the greater world of Evangelical

---

Immanence, and the Emerging Pentecostal Academy," 195–222.

95. May, "The Role of the Holy Spirit."

and Protestant hermeneutics. As I have demonstrated in this chapter, significant numbers of Pentecostal scholars believe that Pentecostalism has something to offer Evangelical hermeneutical methods by way of experiential verification. I agree. Pentecostals must embrace a hermeneutical method which strikes a balance between the text-centered and reader-centered approaches currently in vogue. As Archer demonstrates, it is possible to adhere to a hermeneutical structure, which does not eliminate either of these important parameters. In so doing, Pentecostals will contribute significantly to the hermeneutical methodology of other Protestant groups who are also facing an increasingly Postmodern society which is less inclined to accept any presentation of the Gospel truncated by Modernity. As Pentecostalism of the past served the Christian Church by renewing her awareness of the Holy Spirit, both in theology and practice, Pentecostals today may contribute much to a methodology of hermeneutics that holds to the best of the historical-critical method, yet is open to the role of experience, narratives, and community in the interpretive process.

8

Conclusion and Contribution

Where do we go to find a Christianity that speaks meaningfully to a postmodern world?. . . . [O]ur challenge is not to reinvent Christianity, but to restore and then adapt classical Christianity to the postmodern cultural situation.[1]

ROBERT E. WEBBER

This is a generation of young people whose current involvement in religion is appreciable. Further, their terms for greater involvement in groups are reasonable; if they can find their participation "worthwhile," they are open to it. In light of their widespread interest in meaning and mystery, the supernatural and the spiritual, religious groups who have something to bring need to bring it—and, to put it bluntly, stop complaining about the apathy of youth.[2]

REGINALD W. BIBBY

THIS WORK DEMONSTRATES THAT Pentecostalism must refrain from embracing a fully Modern approach to hermeneutics, but instead interpret Scripture with an ear to Postmodern thought. This approach allows for a full recognition of the "supernatural"[3] inherent within the

1. Webber, *Ancient-Future Faith*, 24.

2. Bibby, *Canada's Teens*, 131–32.

3. As noted in chapter 1 above, various scholars have observed that the term "supernatural" has been imported into theology from philosophy, and did not gain widespread acceptance into the theological world until the sixteenth century.

Gospel message, and enhances the relevance of the Pentecostal (and Gospel) message to the newest generations of North American youth.

To accomplish this task, it was first necessary to define Postmodern thought, particularly as it relates to the anti-Modern tendencies in early Pentecostalism. The work of four key philosophers—Jean-François Lyotard, Richard Rorty, Jacques Derrida, and Michel Foucault—was examined, which provided the philosophical underpinning for the majority of Postmodern thought. The major varieties of Postmodernism were acknowledged, as well as five common Postmodern themes, including anti-foundationalism and deconstruction of language. Chapter 2 concluded with a critique of Postmodernism from an Evangelical/Pentecostal perspective.

Chapter 3 sought to demonstrate that early Pentecostal methods of interpreting the Scriptures contained many elements of Postmodern thought, some seventy-five years before these ideas became commonplace in academic circles. This was applicable particularly in terms of the importance of narratives, the role of experience in determining veracity, and the significance of community. While Pentecostals employ the decidedly non-Postmodern use of the metanarrative to inform their self-understanding and biblical interpretation, they have also relied heavily upon the personal stories of those within the congregation. Pentecostal reliance upon shared experience as a tool in the interpretation of Scripture is an oft-derided, but key component of, Pentecostal praxis.

Chapter 4 sought to show that since the Azusa Street Revival, Pentecostal scholars and, in turn, Pentecostalism, became increasingly Modern in their approach to hermeneutics. The debate between Gordon D. Fee, an Assemblies of God (USA) scholar, and other Pentecostal theologians, was highlighted as an example of the increasingly Modern tendencies of hermeneutics among Pentecostals. Fee's approach to interpretation, which includes strong focus upon authorial intent, necessarily led him to challenge traditional Pentecostal belief in subsequence and initial evidence. Interestingly, the Pentecostal scholars who engaged Fee also used similar Modern hermeneutical techniques.

Via our exploration of the demythologization urged by Rudolph Bultmann, chapter 5 explored current youth culture. Representing Modern hermeneutical principles taken to the extreme, Bultmann's work (and modern programs such as *The Jesus Seminar*), argues for the removal of "myth" from the Scriptures, insisting that humanity today would more quickly welcome a Gospel message devoid of the myths that Modernity views as scientifically implausible. This work shows that as younger generations have increasingly accepted Postmodern thought, they are looking for a Gospel message which features God's prominent action in the world. By its very nature, Pentecostalism has been well suited to present this message. Our increasing acceptance of Evangelical hermeneutics, however, may serve to limit our ability to present properly the key doctrines and practices of early Pentecostalism to future generations.

Although many Pentecostals are aware of the need for the movement to address Postmodern thought within their hermeneutical methodology, few have proposed a truly Pentecostal hermeneutic, which is inclusive of Postmodern thought. Kenneth J. Archer, a Church of God in Christ theologian, has done so, and chapter 6 examined his contribution to the current debate. Archer proposes a new Pentecostal hermeneutical strategy, which promotes a tridactic negotiation between the Spirit, the Scriptures, and the Pentecostal community. Archer's work is highlighted as an example of the manner in which Pentecostals must continue to explore new approaches to Scriptural interpretation, which are true to our roots and enable us to speak relevantly to current generations.

Chapter 7 concluded this work by first examining the role of the Holy Spirit in hermeneutics. The work of a variety of scholars was surveyed as I attempted to understand more completely the process by which the Spirit illuminates Scripture for believers. Four options were considered as I explored whether Pentecostal hermeneutical concerns should be wedded to Postmodern thought, thus creating a distinctively Pentecostal hermeneutic. Further, I explored the debate concerning whether Pentecostals have a hermeneutical advantage over non-Pentecostals via their attitudes towards personal experience. Though with notable exceptions, a number of Pentecostal scholars feel that Pentecostalism has an edge hermeneutically, particularly in those passages of Scripture which speak of experiences of the Holy Spirit common to many Pentecostals.

CONTRIBUTIONS OF THIS WORK

Though acknowledging Kenneth Archer's insightful distinction between Postmodern and *Paramodern*, this work demonstrates that in three key areas—the role of experience, the role of community, and the rejection of the hegemony of reason—early Pentecostal thinking and practice clearly resembled current Postmodern thought. Early Pentecostals would have never considered themselves Postmodern (as is currently defined), but their early thinking, as evidenced in both their writing and approach to Scripture, demonstrates remarkable consistencies with Postmodern thought, particularly in the three areas delineated above.

Second, I have demonstrated the tendency of post-1960s Pentecostalism to accept an increasingly Modern approach to hermeneutics via its participation in Evangelical hermeneutical principles. Through my survey of the debate between Gordon Fee and his Pentecostal colleagues, this work demonstrates that Fee's Pentecostal detractors met his challenge of Pentecostal distinctive doctrines via the historical-grammatical methods of Evangelicalism with similar methods. For the most part, the Pentecostal scholars who responded to Fee's challenge did so by using similar hermeneutical methods as Fee. None of the responses to Fee included the suggestion that distinctive Pentecostal theology could not be supported by accepted Evangelical hermeneutical methods; neither did any suggest a distinctive Pentecostal hermeneutic as the way forward from the challenge presented by Fee.

This work makes the significant observation that in terms of connecting with younger generations Pentecostalism is not well served by our indiscriminate acceptance of Evangelical hermeneutics. The preservation of early Pentecostal belief and practice is necessary to reach today's Postmodern youth with the Gospel of Christ, as understood and practiced by Pentecostals. This cannot be fully achieved by the wholesale embracing of the historical-grammatical method. For Pentecostalism to continue its tremendous growth in Western countries as it is now witnessing in other areas of the world, it must not fail to present the transcendent God of the Scriptures to a world open to experiencing the supernatural activity of a caring Creator.

Through the work of Kenneth Archer, I have observed that there are viable options for Pentecostals wishing to employ a hermeneutic that considers both the world of the text and the reader. Though Pentecostalism has become increasingly drawn to Evangelical hermeneutics, some Pentecostal scholars remain convinced of the need for a distinctive Pentecostal hermeneutic, and are endeavoring to provide the same.

Finally, this work argues that Pentecostals must not view themselves as the uneducated cousins of Evangelicals, having nothing to bring to the hermeneutical table. Rather, Pentecostalism must recognize the unique contributions it has to offer in terms of an experiential component to hermeneutics. Pentecostals have always believed that Scripture is as concerned with orthopraxy as it is with orthodoxy; verifying scriptural teaching through the lived experience of believers may not only be advisable, but necessary for a proper interpretation of the Bible.

IMPLICATIONS OF THIS WORK
AND AREAS OF NEEDED RESEARCH

This work presents concerns relative to Pentecostalism's acceptance of Evangelical hermeneutics, and the resultant consequences in terms of our ability to connect with youth influenced by Postmodern thought. While Postmodernity has undoubtedly made a significant impact on the minds of youth throughout North America and Western Europe, the same cannot be assumed for other areas of the world. Further study would assess whether Pentecostalism has been significantly impacted by Modernity in other parts of the world; whether Postmodernity has made substantial inroads into the thinking of non-Western youth; and whether the hermeneutics of Pentecostals in the non-Western world have also become increasingly Modern. Depending on the answers to the above questions, it could be ascertained whether Pentecostalism must be wary of incorporating Modern hermeneutics into Pentecostal hermeneutics in the non-Western world.

While I argue that Pentecostals have much to contribute to Evangelical hermeneutics relative to experiential verification, further work may be done on the specific format of this contribution. Though the proposals of Kenneth Archer and others have taken steps to ensure that Pentecostal hermeneutical concerns regarding the work of the Holy Spirit and the role of community have been beneficial, more research is necessary to consider the experiential component of Pentecostal hermeneutics, as well.

Additional research is needed to determine specific areas of diversity between those considered Generation X and the Millennials. As time progresses, differences in these two groups will become more apparent, particularly as the younger generation grows into adulthood and exhibits characteristics either convergent or incongruous with GenX.

Finally, one may consider the extent to which Pentecostalism has been complicit in spreading the Postmodern mindset. Given that there are now almost 600 million Pentecostals worldwide, each of whom holds to several philosophical suppositions considered viable by most Postmodern thinkers, it is axiomatic that with one-tenth of the world's population exhibiting thought and practice characteristic of the Postmodern mindset, Pentecostalism itself may well be responsible in part for the spread of Postmodernity. Further study could confirm the role Pentecostalism may have had, and may be having, in the rise of Postmodern thought.

Bibliography

Adam, A. K. A., ed. *Postmodern Interpretations of The Bible: A Reader.* St. Louis, MO: Chalice Press, 2001.

Adams, Daniel J. "Toward a Theological Understanding of Postmodernism." No pages. Online: http://www.crosscurrents.org/adams.htm.

Ahn, Yongnan Jeon. "Various Debates in the Contemporary Pentecostal Hermeneutics." *The Spirit & Church* 2.1 (2000) 19–52.

Aichele, George, et al. *The Postmodern Bible: The Bible and Culture Collective.* New Haven: Yale University Press, 1995.

Aker, Ben C. "Some Reflections on Pentecostal Hermeneutics." *Paraclete* 19.2 (1985) 18–20.

Allen, Diogenes. *Christian Belief in a Postmodern World: The Full Wealth of Conviction.* Louisville: Westminster/John Knox Press, 1989.

Allison, David B., ed. *New Nietzsche: Contemporary Styles of Interpretation.* Cambridge, MA: The MIT Press, 1985 [1977].

Anderson, Allan. "The Hermeneutical Processes of Pentecostal-type African Initiated Churches in South Africa." *Missionalia* 24.2 (1996) 171–85.

———. *An Introduction to Pentecostalism: Global Charismatic Christianity.* Cambridge, UK: Cambridge University Press, 2004.

Anderson, Gordon L. "Pentecostal Hermeneutics." In *Drinking From Our Own Wells: Defining a Pentecostal-Charismatic Spirituality.* Collected Paper presented to the Society for Pentecostal Studies, Springfield, MO, 12–14 November, 1992, vol. 2.

———. "Pentecostal Hermeneutics—Part I." *Paraclete* 28.1 (1994) 1–11.

———. "Pentecostal Hermeneutics—Part 2." *Paraclete* 28.2 (1994) 13–22.

Anderson, Robert Mapes. *Vision of the Disinherited: The Making of American Pentecostalism.* Peabody, MA: Hendrickson, 1990 [1979].

Anderson, Walter Truett. *Reality Isn't What It Used to Be: Theatrical Politics, Ready-to-Wear Religion, Global Myths, Primitive Chic, and Other Wonders of the Postmodern World.* San Francisco: HarperSanFrancisco, 1990.

Archer, Kenneth J. "Early Pentecostal Biblical Interpretation." *Journal of Pentecostal Theology* 18 (2001) 32–70.

———. *A Pentecostal Hermeneutic for the Twenty-First Century: Spirit, Scripture and Community.* Journal of Pentecostal Theology Supplement Series 28. London: T&T Clark International, 2004.

———. "Pentecostal Hermeneutics: Retrospect and Prospect." *Journal of Pentecostal Theology* 8 (1996) 63–81.

———. "Pentecostal Story as the Hermeneutical Filter." Collected paper presented to the Society for Pentecostal Studies, Tulsa, OK, 8–10 March, 2001.

Arrington, French L. *The Acts of the Apostles.* Peabody, MA: Hendrickson, 1988.

——. "The Use of the Bible by Pentecostals." *Pneuma* 16.1 (1994) 101–7.

Atkinson, William. "Pentecostal Responses to Dunn's *Baptism in the Holy Spirit*: Luke–Acts." *Journal of Pentecostal Theology* 6 (1995) 87–131.

Autry, Arden C. "Dimensions of Hermeneutics in Pentecostal Focus." *Journal of Pentecostal Theology* 3 (1993) 29–50.

Badcock, Gary D. *Light of Truth and Fire of Love: A Theology of the Holy Spirit*. Grand Rapids: Eerdmans, 1997.

Baker, Robert O. "Pentecostal Bible Reading: Toward a Model of Reading for the Formation of Christian Affections." *Journal of Pentecostal Theology* 7 (1995) 34–48.

Ballard, P. "Practical Theology as an Academic Discipline." *Theology* XCVIII (1995) 112–22.

Banks, Robert. *Reenvisioning Theological Education: Exploring a Missional Alternative to Current Models*. Grand Rapids: Eerdmans, 1999.

Barna, George. *Baby Busters: The Disillusioned Generation*. Chicago: Northfield Publishing, 1994.

——. *The Barna Report: What Americans Believe: An Annual Survey of Values and Religious Views in the United States*. Ventura, CA: Regal, 1991.

——. *Real Teens: A Contemporary Snapshot of Youth Culture*. Ventura, CA: Regal, 2001.

Barrett, D. B., and T. M. Johnston. "Global Statistics." In *The New International Dictionary of Pentecostal and Charismatic Movements*. Revised and expanded edition, edited by Stanley M. Burgess and Eduard M.Van der Maas. Grand Rapids: Zondervan, 2002.

Barth, Marcus. "Introduction to Demythologizing." *The Journal of Religion* 37.3 (1957) 148.

Bartholomew, Craig. *After Pentecost: Language and Biblical Interpretation*. Scripture and Hermeneutics Series, vol. 2. Grand Rapids: Zondervan, 2001.

——, et al., ed. *"Behind" the Text: History and Biblical Interpretation*. Scripture and Hermeneutics Series, vol. 4. Grand Rapids: Zondervan, 2003.

——, et al., ed. *Renewing Biblical Interpretation*. Scripture and Hermeneutics Series, vol. 1. Grand Rapids: Zondervan, 2000.

Bartleman, Frank (ed., John G. Myers). *Another Wave of Revival*. Springdale, PA: Whitaker House, 1982 [1962].

——. *Azusa Street: The Roots of Modern-day Pentecost*. Plainfield, NJ: Logos International, 1980 [1925].

Beaudoin, Tom. *Virtual Faith: The Irreverent Spiritual Quest of Generation X*. San Francisco: Jossey-Bass, 1998.

Becker, Matthias. "A Tenet under Examination: Reflections on the Pentecostal Hermeneutical Approach." *The Journal of the European Pentecostal Theological Association* 24 (2004) 30–48.

Bedard, Robert L. "Emerging Models of Ministerial Training for the Pentecostal Assemblies of Canada." Th.D. diss., University of South Africa, 2007.

Berkhof, Louis. *Principles of Biblical Interpretation*. Grand Rapids: Baker, 1950.

Bibby, Reginald W. *Canada's Teens: Today, Yesterday, and Tomorrow*. Toronto: Stoddart, 2001.

——. *Restless Churches: How Canada's Churches Can Contribute to the Emerging Religious Renaissance*. Ottawa, ON: Novalis, 2004.

——. *Restless Gods: The Renaissance of Religion in Canada*. Toronto: Novalis, 2002.

——, and Donald C. Posterski. *Teen Trends: A Nation in Motion*. Abridged edition. Toronto: Stoddart, 2000 [1992].

———, with Sarah Russell and Ron Rolheiser. *The Emerging Millennials: How Canada's Newest Generation is Responding to Change and Choice*. Lethbridge, AB: Project Canada Books, 2009.

Bloch-Hoell, Nils. *The Pentecostal Movement: Its Origin, Development, and Distinctive Character*. New York: Humanities Press, 1964.

Blumhofer, Edith L. *Restoring the Faith: The Assemblies of God, Pentecostalism, and American Culture*. Urbana: University of Illinois Press, 1993.

———, and Randall Balmer, ed. *Modern Christian Revivals*. Urbana and Chicago: University of Illinois Press, 1993.

———, et al., ed. *Pentecostal Currents in American Protestantism*. Urbana and Chicago: University of Illinois Press, 1999.

Borlase, Craig. *William Seymour: A Biography*. Lake Mary, FL: Charisma House, 2006.

Briggs, Richard. *Reading the Bible Wisely*. Grand Rapids: Baker, 2003.

Brooks, John P. *The Divine Church*. Columbia, MO: Herald, 1981.

Brown, Jeannine K. *Scripture as Communication: Introducing Biblical Hermeneutics*. Grand Rapids: Baker, 2007.

Brown, Paul E. *The Holy Spirit and the Bible: The Spirit's Interpreting Role in Relation to Biblical Hermeneutics*. Fearn, Ross-shire, Scotland: Christian Focus Publications, 2002.

Browning, Don. "Methods and Foundation for Pastoral Studies in the University." In *Pastoral Studies in the University Setting: Perspectives, Methods, and Praxis*, edited by Adrian M. Visscher. Ottawa: University of Ottawa Press, 1990.

———. "The Revival of Practical Theology." *The Christian Century* 1–8 February, 1984, 84.

Brubaker, Malcolm. "Postmodernism and Pentecostals: A Case Study of Evangelical Hermeneutics." *Evangelical Journal* 15.1 (Spring 1997) 33–45.

Bruce, F. F. *The Book of the Acts*. The New International Commentary on the New Testament. Revised edition. Grand Rapids: Eerdmans, 1988 [1954].

———. *The Canon of Scripture*. Downers Grove: InterVarsity, 1988.

———. "Interpretation of the Bible." In *Evangelical Dictionary of Theology*. Edited by Walter A. Elwell. Grand Rapids: Baker, 1984.

Brumback, Carl. *What Meaneth This? A Pentecostal Answer to a Pentecostal Question*. Springfield, MO: Gospel Publishing House, 1947.

Bruner, Frederick Dale. *A Theology of the Holy Spirit: The Pentecostal Experience and the New Testament Witness*. London: Hodder & Stoughton, 1970.

Bultmann, Rudolf. *The History of the Synoptic Tradition*. Translated by John Marsh. Oxford: Basil Blackwell, 1963.

———. "Is Exegesis Without Presuppositions Possible?" In *Existence and Faith: Shorter Writings of Rudolf Bultmann*. Selected, translated, and introduced by Schubert M. Ogden. Cleveland: Meridian Books, 1960.

———. *Jesus and the Word*. Translated by Louise Pettibone Smith and Erminie Huntress Lantero. New York: Charles Scribner's Sons, 1958.

———. *Jesus Christ and Mythology*. New York: Charles Scribner's Sons, 1958.

———. *New Testament and Mythology and Other Basic Writings*. Selected, edited, and translated by Schubert M. Ogden. Philadelphia: Fortress Press, 1984.

———. *Theology of the New Testament*. 2 vols. Translated by Kendrick Grobel. New York: Charles Scribner's Sons, 1951 and 1955.

Bundy, D. D. "Gee, Donald." In *The New International Dictionary of Pentecostal and Charismatic Movements*.

Byrd, Joseph. "Paul Ricoeur's Hermeneutical Theory and Pentecostal Proclamation." *Pneuma* 15.2 (1993) 203–14.

Calvin, John. *Institutes of the Christian Religion.* Vol. I. Edited by John T. MacNeil. Philadelphia: Westminster Press, 1960.

Caputo, John. *The Prayers and Tears of Jacques Derrida: Religion Without Religion.* The Indiana Series in the Philosophy of Religion. Bloomington and Indianapolis: Indiana University Press, 1997.

Cargal, Timothy B. "Beyond the Fundamentalist-Modernist Controversy: Pentecostals and Hermeneutics in a Postmodern Age." *Pneuma* 15.2 (1993) 163–87.

Carroll, Coleen. *The New Faithful: Why Young Adults Are Embracing Christian Orthodoxy.* Chicago: Loyola Press, 2002.

Carson, D.A. *The Gagging Of God: Christianity Confronts Pluralism.* Grand Rapids: Zondervan, 1996.

Cartledge, Mark J. "Empirical Theology: Towards an Evangelical-Charismatic Hermeneutic." *Journal of Pentecostal Theology* 9 (1996) 115–26.

Chan, Simon. *Pentecostal Theology and the Christian Spiritual Tradition.* Journal of Pentecostal Theology Supplement Series 21. Sheffield: Sheffield Academic Press, 2000.

Clark, Mathew S. "Pentecostal Hermeneutics: The Challenge of Relating to (Post)-Modern Literary Theory." *The Spirit & Church* 2.1 (2000) 67–93.

———, et al. *What is Distinctive About Pentecostal Theology?* Pretoria: University of South Africa, 1989.

Clayton, Philip. *Transforming Christian Theology For Church and Society.* Minneapolis: Fortress, 2010.

Cobb, Jr., John B. "Constructive Postmodernism." No pages. Online: http://www .religiononline.org/showarticle.asp?title=2220.

———. *Reclaiming the Church: Where the Mainline Church Went Wrong and What to Do About It.* Louisville, KY: Westminster John Knox, 1997.

Cohen, Michael Lee. *The Twenty-Something American Dream: A Cross-Country Quest for a Generation.* New York: Dutton, 1993.

Copley, Albert S. In *The Way of Faith and Neglected Themes.* Columbia, SC: The Way of Faith, 23 July, 1908.

Corley, Bruce, et al., ed. *Biblical Hermeneutics: A Comprehensive Introduction to Interpreting Scripture.* Second edition. Nashville: Broadman & Holman, 2002.

Couch, Mal, ed. *An Introduction to Classical Evangelical Hermeneutics: A Guide to the History and Practice of Biblical Interpretation.* Grand Rapids: Kregel, 2000.

Coupland, Douglas. *Generation X: Tales for an Accelerated Culture.* New York: St. Martin's, 1991.

Cowan, M. "Introduction to Practical Theology." No pages. Online: http://www.loyno .edu/~mcowan/PracticalTheology.html.

Cox, Harvey. *Fire From Heaven: The Rise of Pentecostal Spirituality and the Reshaping of Religion in the Twenty-First Century.* Cambridge, MA: De Capo Press, 2001.

Craddock, Fred B. *Preaching.* Nashville: Abingdon Press, 1985.

Cross, Terry L., and Emerson B. Powery, ed. *The Spirit and the Mind: Essays in Informed Pentecostalism.* Lanham, MD: University Press of America, 2000.

Crossan, John Dominic. *In Fragments: The Aphorisms of Jesus.* San Francisco: Harper & Row, 1983.

———. *In Parables: The Challenge of the Historical Jesus.* New York: Harper & Row, 1973.

Curry, S. S. *Vocal And Literary Interpretation Of The Bible*. New York: Macmillan, 1907.

Curtis, Byron G. "Charismata as Hermeneutical Help? 'Private Spirits' in Catholic-Protestant Debate (1588–1650) and in 'The Westminster Confession of Faith.'" Paper presented to the Evangelical Theological Society, Lisle, IL, 17–19 November, 1994.

Damboriene, Prudencio. *Tongues as of Fire: Pentecostalism in Contemporary Christianity*. Washington: Corpus Books, 1969.

Danto, Arthur Coleman. *Nietzsche as Philosopher*. Columbia Classics in Philosophy. Expanded edition. New York: Columbia University Press, 2005.

Davis, Richard B. "Can There Be an 'Orthodox' Postmodern Theology?" *Journal of the Evangelical Theology Society* 45.1 (2002) 111–23.

Dayton, Donald W. "The Holy Spirit and Christian Expansion in the Twentieth Century." *Missiology* 164 (1988) 397–407.

———. "The Limits of Evangelicalism: The Pentecostal Tradition." In *The Varieties of American Evangelicalism*, edited by Donald W. Dayton and Robert K. Johnston. Downers Grove: InterVarsity, 1991.

———. *Theological Roots of Pentecostalism*. Grand Rapids: Francis Asbury Press, 1987.

Deleuze, Gilles. *Nietzsche and Philosophy*. New York: Columbia University Press, 2006 [1962].

Dempster, Murray W., et al., ed. *The Globalization of Pentecostalism: A Religion Made to Travel*. Irvine, CA: Regnum Books, 1999.

DePaul, Michael R., ed. *Resurrecting Old-Fashioned Foundationalism*. Lanham, MD: Rowman & Littlefield., 2001.

Derrida, Jacques. *Acts of Religion*. Edited by Gil Anidjar. New York: Routledge, 2002.

———. *A Derrida Reader: Between the Blinds*. Edited by Peggy Kamuf. New York: Columbia University Press, 1991.

———. "Force of Law: The Mystical Foundations of Authority." In *Deconstruction and the Possibility of Justice*, edited by Drucilla Cornell, et al. New York: Routledge, 1992.

———. *The Gift of Death*. Translated by David Wills. Chicago: University of Chicago Press, 1996 [1995].

———. *Margins of Philosophy*. Translated by Alan Bass. Chicago: University of Chicago Press, 1982.

———. *Of Grammatology*. Translated by Gayatri Chakravorty Spivak. Baltimore: The Johns Hopkins University Press, 1976 [1974].

———. *Of Spirit: Heidegger and the Question*. Translated by Geoffrey Bennington and Rachel Bowlby. Chicago: University of Chicago Press, 1989.

Dieter, Melvin E. "The Wesleyan/Holiness and Pentecostal Movements: Commonalities, Confrontation, and Dialogue." *Pneuma* 12.1 (1990) 4–13.

Dingemans, G. D. J. "Practical Theology in the Academy: A Contemporary Overview." *The Journal of Religion* 76.1 (1996) 82–96.

Dockery, David S, "The Challenge of Postmodernism." In *The Challenge of Postmodernism: An Evangelical Engagement*. Second edition. Grand Rapids: Baker, 2001 [1995].

Dodd, C. H. *The Parables of the Kingdom*. New York, Charles Scribner's, 1961.

Dunn, James D. G. *Baptism in the Holy Spirit: A Re-examination of the New Testament Teaching on the Gift of the Spirit in Relation to Pentecostalism Today*. Philadelphia: The Westminster Press, 1970.

———. "Baptism in the Spirit: A Response to Pentecostal Scholarship on Luke-Acts." *Journal of Pentecostal Theology* 3 (1993) 3–27.

———. *The Living Word*. Philadelphia: Fortress Press, 1987.

——. *Unity and Diversity in the New Testament: An Inquiry into the Character of Earliest Christianity.* Harrisburg, PA: Trinity Press International, 1991 [1977].

Durasoff, Steve. *Bright Wind of the Spirit: Pentecostalism Today.* Plainfield, NJ: Logos International, 1972.

Eco, Umberto. *Interpretation and Overinterpretation.* Edited by Stefan Collini. Cambridge: Cambridge University Press, 1992.

——, et al. *Postscript to the Name of the Rose.* Translated by William Weaver. New York: Harcourt Brace Jovanovich, 1989 [1984].

Eddy, Paul Rhodes, and Gregory A. Boyd. *The Jesus Legend: A Case for the Historical Reliability of the Synoptic Jesus Tradition.* Grand Rapids: Baker, 2007.

Egger, Wilhelm. *How to Read The New Testament: An Introduction to Linguistic and Historical-Critical Methodology.* Edited by Hendrikus Boers. Translated by Peter Heinegg. Peabody, MA: Hendrickson, 1996.

Elbert, Paul. "Possible Literary Links Between Luke–Acts and Pauline Letters Regarding Spirit–Language." In *The Intertextuality of the Epistles: Explorations of Theory and Practice,* edited by Thomas L. Brodie, et al. New Testaments Monographs 16. Sheffield: Sheffield Phoenix Press, 2006.

——. "Toward a Pentecostal Hermeneutic: Observations on Archer's Progressive Proposal." *Asian Journal of Pentecostal Studies* 9:2 (2006) 320–8.

Ellington, Scott A. "History, Story, and Testimony: Locating Truth in a Pentecostal Hermeneutic." *Pneuma* 23.2 (2001) 245–64.

——. "Pentecostalism and the Authority of Scripture." *Journal of Pentecostal Theology* 9 (1996) 16–38.

Erickson, Millard J. *Evangelical Interpretation: Perspectives on Hermeneutical Issues.* Grand Rapids: Baker, 1993.

——. *The Postmodern World: Discerning the Times and the Spirit of Our Age.* Wheaton: Crossway Books, 2002.

——. *Truth or Consequences: The Promise and Perils of Postmodernism.* Downers Grove: InterVarsity, 2001.

Ervin, Howard M. *Conversion-Initiation and the Baptism in the Holy Spirit: An Engaging Critique of James D.G. Dunn's "Baptism in the Holy Spirit."* Peabody, MA: Hendrickson, 1984.

——. "Hermeneutics: A Pentecostal Option." *Pneuma* 3.2 (1981) 11–25.

Espinosa, Gastón. "Ordinary Prophet: William J. Seymour and the Azusa Street Revival." In *The Azusa Street Revival and Its Legacy,* edited by Harold D. Hunter and Cecil M. Robeck Jr. Cleveland, TN: Pathway Press, 2006.

Evans, Craig A. *Fabricating Jesus: How Modern Scholars Distort the Gospel.* Downers Grove: InterVarsity, 2006.

Ewart, Frank J. *The Phenomenon of Pentecost.* Revised edition. Hazelwood, MO: Word Aflame Press, 1975.

Farley, Edward. "Interpreting Situations: An Inquiry into the Nature of Practical Theology." In *The Blackwell Reader in Pastoral and Practical Theology,* edited by James Woodward and Stephen Pattison. Malden, MA: Blackwell, 2000.

——. *Theologia: The Fragmentation and Unity of Theological Education.* Philadelphia, PA: Fortress, 1983.

Faupel, William D. *The Everlasting Gospel: The Significance of Eschatology in the Development of Pentecostal Thought.* Journal of Pentecostal Theology Supplement Series 10. Sheffield: Sheffield Academic Press, 1996.

Fee, Gordon D. *The First Epistle to the Corinthians*. The New International Commentary on the New Testament. Edited by Gordon D. Fee. Grand Rapids: Eerdmans, 1987.

———. *God's Empowering Presence: The Holy Spirit in the Letters of Paul*. Peabody: MA: Hendrickson, 1994.

———. *Gospel and Spirit: Issues in New Testament Hermeneutics*. Peabody, MA: Hendrickson, 1991.

———. Interview by author. 5 December 1997 (telephone) and 27 January 1998 (email).

———. *New Testament Exegesis: A Handbook for Students and Pastors*. Revised edition. Louisville, KY: Westminster John Knox Press, 1993.

———. "Response to Roger Stronstad's 'The Biblical Precedent for Historical Precedent.' " *Paraclete* 27.3 (1993) 11–4.

———. "Tongues–Least of the Gifts? Some Exegetical Observations on 1 Corinthians 12–14." *Pneuma* 2.2 (1980) 3–14.

———. *To What End Exegesis? Essays Textual, Exegetical, and Theological*. Grand Rapids: Eerdmans, 2001.

———. "Why Pentecostals Read their Bibles Poorly–and Some Suggested Cures." *The Journal of the European Pentecostal Theological Association* 24 (2004) 4–15.

———, and Douglas Stuart. *How to Read the Bible for all Its Worth: A Guide to Understanding the Bible*. Second and third editions. Grand Rapids: Zondervan, 1993, 2004.

Finger, T. "Modernity, Postmodernity–What in the World Are They?" *Transformation* 10.4 (1993) 20–6.

Foucault, Michel. *The Archaeology of Knowledge and the Discourse on Language*. Translated by A.M. Sheridan Smith. London: Tavistock Press, 1972.

———. "The Minimalist Self." In *Politics, Philosophy, Culture: Interviews and Other Writings, 1977–1984*, edited by Lawrence D. Kritzman. New York: Routledge, 1988.

———. *The Order of Things: An Archaeology of the Human Sciences*. Translated by A.M. Sheridan Smith. New York: Random House–Pantheon, 1971.

———. "Truth and Power." In *Power/Knowledge: Selected Interviews and Other Writings, 1972–1977*, edited by Colin Gordon. New York: Pantheon Books, 1980.

———. *The Use of Pleasure*. Vol. 2 of *History of Sexuality*. Translated by Robert Hurley. New York: Pantheon Books, 1985.

Funk, Robert Walter, and The Jesus Seminar. *The Acts of Jesus: The Search for the Authentic Deeds of Jesus*. San Francisco: HarperSanFrancisco, 1998.

———, et al. *The Five Gospels: The Search for the Authentic Words of Jesus: New Translation and Commentary*. Santa Costa, CA: Polebridge Press, 1993.

———, and The Jesus Seminar. *The Gospel of Jesus, According to the Jesus Seminar*. Santa Costa CA: Polebridge Press, 1999.

———. *Language, Hermeneutic, and Word of God: The Problem of Language in the New Testament and Contemporary Theology*. New York: Harper & Row, 1966.

———. "The Watershed of the American Biblical Tradition: The Chicago School, First Phase, 1892–1920." *Journal of Biblical Literature* 95.1 (1976) 4–22.

Gadamer, Hans–Georg. *Truth and Method*. New York: Continuum, 2004 [1975].

Gasque, W. Ward. *A History of the Interpretation of the Acts of the Apostles*. Peabody, MA: Hendrickson, 1989 [1975].

Gee, Donald. *God's Grace and Power for Today*. Springfield, MO: Gospel Publishing House, 1936.

———. *A New Discovery* (formerly, *Pentecost*). Springfield, MO: Gospel Publishing House, 1932.

——. *Pentecostal Experience: The Writings of Donald Gee.* Edited by David A. Womack. Springfield, MO: Gospel Publishing House, 1993.

Gitlin, Todd. "The Postmodern Predicament." *The Wilson Quarterly* 13 (1989) 67–76.

Goff, Jr., James R. *Fields White Unto Harvest: Charles F. Parham and the Missionary Origins of Pentecostalism.* Fayetteville, AK: University of Arkansas Press, 1988.

——. "Parham, Charles Fox." In *The New International Dictionary of Pentecostal and Charismatic Movements.*

Gohr, G. W. "Pearlman, Myer." In *The New International Dictionary of Pentecostal and Charismatic Movements.*

Goldingay, John. *Models for Interpretation of Scripture.* Grand Rapids: Eerdmans, 1995.

Goldsworthy, Graeme. *Gospel-Centered Hermeneutics: Foundations and Principles of Evangelical Biblical Interpretation.* Downers Grove: InterVarsity, 2006.

Green, Joel B. and Max Turner, ed. *Between Two Horizons: Spanning New Testament Studies and Systematic Theology.* Grand Rapids: Eerdmans, 2000.

Gregersen, Niels Henrik. "What Theology Might Learn (and Not Learn) from Evolutionary Psychology: A Postfoundationalist Theologian in Conversation with Pascal Boyer." In *The Evolution of Rationality: Interdisciplinary Essays in Honor of J. Wentzel Van Huyssteen*, edited by F. LeRon Shults. Grand Rapids: Eerdmans, 2006.

Grenz, Stanley J. *A Primer on Postmodernism.* Grand Rapids: Eerdmans, 1996.

——, and John R. Franke. *Beyond Foundationalism: Shaping Theology in a Postmodern Context.* Louisville, KY: Westminster John Knox, 2001.

Griffin, David Ray, et al. *Varieties of Postmodern Theology.* SUNY Series in Constructive Postmodern Thought. Albany, NY: State University of New York Press, 1989.

Grigg, Viv. "The Spirit of Christ and the Postmodern City: Transformative Revival Among Auckland's Evangelicals and Pentecostals." Ph.D. diss., University of Auckland, 2005.

Groome, Thomas H. "Theology on Our Feet: A Revisionist Pedagogy for Healing the Gap Between Academia and Ecclesia." In *Formation and Reflection: The Promise of Practical Theology*, edited by Lewis S. Mudge and James N. Poling. Minneapolis: Fortress Press, 1987.

Guinness, Os. *Fit Bodies, Fat Minds: Why Evangelicals Don't Think and What to do About It.* Grand Rapids: Baker, 1994.

Guthrie, Donald. *New Testament Theology.* Downers Grove: InterVarsity, 1981.

Hampshire, Stuart, ed. *The Age of Reason: The Seventeenth Century Philosophers.* Boston: Houghton Mifflin, 1956.

Harrington, Hannah K., and Rebecca Patten. "Pentecostal Hermeneutics and Postmodern Literary Theory." *Pneuma* 16.1 (1994) 109–14.

Hart, Larry. "Hermeneutics, Theology, and the Holy Spirit." *Perspectives in Religious Studies* 14 (1987) 53–64.

Harvey, David. *The Condition of Postmodernity: An Enquiry Into the Origins of Cultural Change.* Malden, MA: Blackwell Publishing, 1990.

Hawkes, Gerald. "The Relationship Between Theology and Practice in Southern Africa." *Journal of Theology for Southern Africa* 68 (1989) 29–39.

Hays, Richard B. *Echoes of Scripture in the Letters of Paul.* New Haven: Yale University Press, 1993 [1989].

Heidegger, Martin. *Being and Time.* Malden, MA: Blackwell Publishing, 1962.

Heitink, Gerben. *Practical Theology: History, Theory, Action Domains.* Studies in Practical Theology. Grand Rapids: Eerdmans, 1999.

Henry, Carl F. H. "Postmodernism: The New Spectre?" In *The Challenge of Postmodernism: An Evangelical Engagement*.

Heyns, L. M., and H. J. C. Pieterse. *A Primer in Practical Theology*. Pretoria: Gnosis, 1990.

Himmelfarb, Gertrude. *The Roads to Modernity: The British, French, and American Enlightenments*. Colchester, UK: Vintage Publishing, 2005.

Hirch, Jr., E. D. *Validity in Interpretation*. New Haven: Yale University Press, 1967.

Hocken, P. D. "Charismatic Movement." In *The New International Dictionary of Pentecostal and Charismatic Movements*.

———. "A Charismatic View of The Distinctiveness of Pentecostalism." In *Pentecostalism in Context: Essays in Honor of William W. Menzies*, ed. Wonsuk Ma and Robert R. Menzies. Journal of Pentecostal Theology Supplement Series 11. Sheffield: Sheffield Academic Press, 1997.

Hoekema, Anthony A. *Holy Spirit Baptism*. Grand Rapids: Eerdmans, 1972.

Hofstadter, Richard. *Anti-intellectualism in American Life*. New York: Alfred A. Knopf, 1963.

Hollenweger, Walter J. "After Twenty Years' Research on Pentecostalism." *Theology* 87 (1984): 403–12.

———. "The Black Roots of Pentecostalism." In *Pentecostals After a Century: Global Perspectives on a Movement in Transition*, edited by Allan H. Anderson and Walter J. Hollenweger. Journal of Pentecostal Theology Supplement Series 15. Sheffield: Sheffield Academic Press, 1999.

———. "Charisma and Oikoumene: The Pentecostal Contribution to the Church Universal." *One in Christ* 7 (1971) 324–43.

———. "The Contribution of Critical Exegesis to Pentecostal Hermeneutics." *The Spirit & Church* 2:1 (2000) 7–18.

———. *Pentecostalism: Origins and Developments Worldwide*. Peabody, MA: Hendrickson, 1997.

———. *The Pentecostals*. Translated by R.A. Wilson. Third edition. Peabody, MA: Hendrickson, 1988 [1972].

Holman, Charles L. "A Response to Roger Stronstad's 'The Biblical Precedent for Historical Precedent.'" *Paraclete* 27.4 (1993) 11–4.

Howe, Neil and William Strauss, *Millennials Rising: The Next Great Generation*. New York: Vintage Books, 2000.

———, et al. *13th Gen: Abort, Retry, Ignore, Fail?* New York: Vintage, 1993.

Hudson, Neil. "British Pentecostalism's Past Development and Future Challenges." No pages. Online: http://salfordelimchurch.org/heritage.php.

Hunter, Harold D. *Spirit-Baptism: A Pentecostal Alternative*. Lanham, MD: University Press of America, 1983.

———, and Cecil M. Robeck, Jr., ed. *The Azusa Street Revival and Its Legacy*. Cleveland, TN: Pathway Press, 2006.

Hyatt, Eddie, ed. *Fire on the Earth: Eyewitness Reports from the Azusa Street Revival*. Lake Mary, FL: Creation House, 2006.

Israel, Richard D, et al., "Pentecostals and Hermeneutics: Texts, Rituals and Community." *Pneuma* 15:2 (1993): 137–61.

Jacobsen, Douglas. *Thinking in the Spirit: Theologies of the Early Pentecostal Movement*. Bloomington, IN: Indiana University Press, 2003.

Jaichandran, Rebecca, and B.C. Madhav. "Pentecostal Spirituality in a Postmodern World." *Asian Journal of Pentecostal Studies* 6.1 (2003) 39–61.

Johns, Jackie David. "Pentecostalism and the Postmodern Worldview." *Journal of Pentecostal Theology* 7 (1995) 73–96.

———. "Yielding to the Spirit: The Dynamics of a Pentecostal Model of Praxis." In *The Globalization of Pentecostalism: A Religion Made to Travel.*

Johnson, Luke Timothy. *The Acts of the Apostles.* Sacra Pagina Series, vol.5. Edited by David J. Harrington. Collegeville, MN.: The Liturgical Press, 1992.

———. *The Real Jesus: The Misguided Quest for the Historical Jesus and the Truth of the Traditional Gospels.* San Francisco: HarperSanFrancisco, 1996.

Johnson, Roger A. *Rudolf Bultmann: Interpreting Faith for the Modern Era.* The Making of Modern Theology: 19th and 20th Century Texts 2. Ottawa, ON: Collins Liturgical in Canada, 1987.

Johnston, Robert K. "Pentecostalism and Theological Hermeneutics: Evangelical Options." *Pneuma* 6.1 (1984) 51–66.

Jones, Tony. *Postmodern Youth Ministry: Exploring Cultural Shift, Creating Holistic Connections, Cultivating Authentic Community.* Grand Rapids: Zondervan, 2001.

Kaiser, Walter C., and Moisés Silva. *An Introduction to Biblical Hermeneutics: The Search for Meaning.* Grand Rapids: Zondervan, 1994.

Kant, Immanuel. *Critique of Pure Reason.* New York: Prometheus Books, 1998.

Kärkkäinen, Veli-Matti. "Pentecostal Hermeneutics in the Making: On the Way from Fundamentalism to Postmodernism." *Journal of the European Theological Association* 18 (1998) 76–115.

———. *Pneumatology: The Holy Spirit in Ecumenical, International, and Contextual Perspective.* Grand Rapids: Baker, 2002.

Käsemann, Ernst. "The Problem of the Historical Jesus." In *Essays on New Testament Themes.* Translated by W. J. Montague. Studies in Biblical Theology, vol. 41. London: SCM Press, 1964.

Kay, James F. "Theological Table-Talk: Myth or Narrative?" *Theology Today* 48 (1991) 326–32.

Kay, William K. "Donald Gee: An Important Voice of the Pentecostal Movement." *Journal of Pentecostal Theology* 16.1 (2007) 133–53.

Kea, Perry V. "The Road to the Jesus Seminar." No pages. Online: http://www.westarinstitute.org/Periodicals/4R_Articles/roadtojs.html.

Kegley, Charles W., ed. *The Theology of Rudolf Bultmann.* New York: Harper & Row, 1966.

King, Joseph H. *From Passover to Pentecost.* Senath, MO: F.E. Short, 1914.

Klein, William W., et al. *Introduction to Biblical Interpretation.* Revised and expanded edition. Nashville: Thomas Nelson, 2004 [1993].

Klooster, Fred H. "The Role of the Holy Spirit in the Hermeneutic Process: The Relationship of the Spirit's Illumination to Biblical Interpretation." In *Hermeneutics, Inerrancy and the Bible,* edited by Earl D. Radmacher and Robert D. Preus. Grand Rapids: Zondervan, 1984.

Krodel, Gerhard. *Acts.* Augsburg Commentary on the New Testament. Minneapolis: Augsburg, 1986.

LaBerge, Agnes N. O. *What God Hath Wrought.* The Higher Christian Life Series. New York: Garland, 1985.

Ladd, George Eldon. *The New Testament and Criticism.* Grand Rapids: Eerdmans, 1967.

———. *A Theology of the New Testament*. Revised edition. Grand Rapids: Eerdmans, 1993 [1974].

Land, Steven J. *Pentecostal Spirituality: A Passion for the Kingdom*. Journal of Pentecostal Theology Supplement Series 1. Sheffield: Sheffield Academic Press, 1993.

Larkin, William J., Jr. *Culture and Biblical Hermeneutics: Interpreting and Applying the Authoritative Word in a Relativistic Age*. Grand Rapids: Baker, 1988.

Lawler, Peter Augustine, "Conservative Postmodernism, Postmodern Conservatism." *The Intercollegiate Review*. Fall 2002. 16–25. Online: http://www.mmisi.org/ir/38_01 /lawler.pdf.

Lawrence, Bennett F. *The Apostolic Faith Restored*. St. Louis, MO: Gospel Publishing House, 1916.

Lentricchia, Frank. *After the New Criticism*. Chicago: University of Chicago Press, 1980.

Letson, Harry. "Pentecostalism as a Paradigm Shift: A Response to Hans Küng's Paradigmatic Model." *Journal of the European Theological Association* 27 (2007) 104–17.

Lewis, Paul W. "Towards a Pentecostal Epistemology: The Role of Experience in Pentecostal Hermeneutics." *The Spirit & Church* 2.1 (2000): 95–125.

Livingston, James C. *Modern Christian Thought: The Enlightenment and the Nineteenth Century*. Vol. 1. Englewood Cliffs, NJ: Prentice-Hall, 1996.

Loewen, Jacob A. *The Bible in Cross-Cultural Perspective*. Pasadena, CA: William Carey Library, 2000.

Luther, Martin. *What Luther Says: An Anthology*. Compiler, Ewald M. Plass. St. Louis, MO: Concordia, 1959.

Lyotard, Jean-François. *The Postmodern Condition: A Report on Knowledge*. Translated by Geoff Bennington and Brian Massumi. Theory and History of Literature, vol. 10. Minneapolis: University of Minnesota Press, 1984.

Macchia, Frank D. "The Spirit and the Text: Recent Trends in Pentecostal Hermeneutics." *The Spirit & Church* 2.1 (2000) 53–65.

MacDonald, William G. "Pentecostal Theology: A Classical Viewpoint." In *Perspectives on the New Pentecostalism*, edited by Russell P. Spittler. Grand Rapids: Baker, 1976.

MacIntyre, Alasdair. *After Virtue: A Study in Moral Theory*. Second edition. Notre Dame, Indiana: University of Notre Dame Press, 1984 [1981].

Mackay, Hugh. "One for all and all for one: it's a tribal thing." *The Sydney Morning* Herald, 13 July 2002. No pages. Online: http://www.smh.com.au/articles/2002/07/12/1026185109842 .html.

Macquarrie, John. *Twentieth Century Religious Thought*. Philadelphia: Trinity Press International, 1988.

Maddox, Randy L. "Practical Theology: A Discipline in Search of a Definition." *Perspectives in Religious Studies* 18 (1991) 159–69.

Madison, Gary B. *The Hermeneutics of Postmodernity: Figures and Themes*. Studies in Phenomenology and Existential Philosophy. Bloomington: Indiana University Press, 1990.

Manala, Matsobane J. "The Church's Ministry to the Sick in a Black South African Context." Th.D. diss., University of South Africa, 2006.

Marsden, George M. *Fundamentalism and American Culture: The Shaping of Twentieth-Century Evangelicalism: 1870–1925*. New York: Oxford University Press, 1980.

Marshall, I. Howard. *Acts*. Tyndale New Testament Commentaries. Grand Rapids: Eerdmans, 1980.

——. *Luke: Historian and Theologian.* New Testament Profiles. Downers Grove: InterVarsity, 1998 [1970].

——, and David Peterson, ed. *Witness to the Gospel: The Theology of Acts.* Grand Rapids, Eerdmans, 1998).

Martin, Francis. "Spirit and Flesh in the Doing of Theology." *Journal of Pentecostal Theology* 18 (2001) 5–31.

Martin, Larry E. *The Life and Ministry of William J. Seymour.* The Complete Azusa Street Library. Vol. 1. Joplin, MO: Christian Life Books, 1999.

——. *The Topeka Outpouring of 1901.* Revised and expanded edition. Joplin, MO: Christian Life Books, 2000.

May, Robert J. "The Role of the Holy Spirit in Biblical Hermeneutics." No pages. Online: http://www.biblicalstudies.org.uk/th_spirit.html.

Mayhue, Richard. *How to Interpret The Bible For Yourself.* Chicago: Moody Press, 1986.

McCartney, Dan, and Charles Clayton. *Let The Reader Understand: A Guide To Interpreting And Applying The Bible.* Wheaton: Victor Books, 1994.

McClung, Grant, ed. *Azusa Street and Beyond.* Plainfield, NJ: Bridge Publishing, 1986.

McDonald, Lee M. *The Biblical Canon: Its Origin, Transmission, and Authority.* Peabody, MA: Hendrickson, 2007.

McGee, Gary B., ed. *Initial Evidence: Historical and Biblical Perspectives on the Pentecostal Doctrine of Spirit Baptism.* Peabody, MA: Hendrickson, 1991.

McKay, John. "When the Veil is Taken Away: The Impact of Prophetic Experience on Biblical Interpretation." *Journal of Pentecostal Theology* 5 (1994) 17–40.

McKim, Donald K. "Foundationalism," "Logical Positivism," and "Relativism." In *Westminster Dictionary of Theological Terms.* Louisville, KY: Westminster John Knox, 1996.

McLaren, Brian D. *More Ready Than You Realize: Evangelism as Dance in the Postmodern Matrix.* Grand Rapids: Zondervan, 2002.

McLean, Mark D. "Toward a Pentecostal Hermeneutic." *Pneuma* 6.2 (1984) 35–56.

McQuilkin, Robert, and Bradford Mullen. "The Impact of Postmodern Thinking on Evangelical Hermeneutics." *Journal of the Evangelical Theological Society* 40.1 (1997) 69–82.

McQuillian, Jeff. *The Literacy Crisis: False Claims, Real Solutions.* Portsmouth, NH: Heinemann, 1998.

Menzies, Robert P. *The Development of Early Christian Pneumatology with Special Reference to Luke–Acts.* Journal for the Study of the New Testament Supplement Series 54. Sheffield: JSOT Press, 1991.

——. "The Distinctive Character of Luke's Pneumatology." *Paraclete* 25.4 (1991) 17–30.

——. *Empowered for Witness: The Spirit in Luke-Acts.* Journal of Pentecostal Theology Supplement Series 6. Sheffield: Sheffield Academic Press, 1994.

——. "Evidential Tongues: An Essay on Theological Method." *Asian Journal of Pentecostal Studies* 1.2 (1998) 111–23.

——. "Jumping off the Postmodern Bandwagon." *Pneuma* 16.1 (1994) 115–20.

——. "Luke and the Spirit: A Reply to James Dunn." *Journal of Pentecostal Theology* 4 (1994) 115–38.

Menzies, William W. "The Methodology of Pentecostal Theology: An Essay on Hermeneutics." In *Essays on Apostolic Themes: Studies in Honor of Howard M. Ervin Presented to him by Colleagues and Friends on his Sixty-Fifth Birthday*, edited by Paul Elbert. Peabody, MA: Hendrickson, 1985.

——, and Stanley M. Horton. *Bible Doctrines: A Pentecostal Perspective.* Springfield, MO: Gospel Publishing House, 1993.

Michaels, J. Ramsey. "Evidences of the Spirit, or the Spirit as Evidence? Some Non-Pentecostal Reflections." In *Initial Evidence: Historical and Biblical Perspectives on the Pentecostal Doctrine of Spirit Baptism.*

Mickelsen, A. B. *Interpreting the Bible.* Grand Rapids: Eerdmans, 1963.

Middleton, J. Richard., and Brian J. Walsh. *Truth is Stranger than it Used to Be: Biblical Faith in a Postmodern Age.* Downers Grove: InterVarsity, 1995.

Miller, James. *The Passion of Michel Foucault.* New York: Simon and Schuster, 1993.

Mohler, Jr., R. Albert. "The Integrity of the Evangelical Tradition and the Challenge of the Postmodern Paradigm." In *The Challenge of Postmodernism: An Evangelical Engagement.*

Msomi, Vivian. "Recent Trends in Practical Theology." No pages. Online: http://www .ukzn.ac.za/sorat/theology/bct/msomi.htm.

Mueller, Walt. *Engaging the Soul of Youth Culture: Bridging Teen Worldviews and Christian Truth.* Downers Grove: InterVarsity, 2006.

Murphy, Nancey, and James W. McClendon Jr., "Distinguishing Modern and Postmodern Theologies." *Modern Theology* 5.3 (1989): 191–214.

Myers, Kenneth A. *All God's Children and Blue Suede Shoes: Christians and Popular Culture.* Wheaton: Crossway Books, 1989.

Myland, D. Wesley. *The Latter Rain Covenant and Pentecostal Power with Testimony of Healings and Baptism.* Chicago: Evangel Publishing House, 1910.

Nañez, Rick. *Full Gospel, Fractured Minds: A Call to Use God's Gift of the Intellect?* Grand Rapids: Zondervan, 2005.

Nichol, John T. *Pentecostalism.* New York: Harper & Row, 1966.

Nietzsche, Friedrich. *The Antichrist.* Amherst, NY: Prometheus, 2000.

——. *The Will to Power.* Edited by Walter Kaufmann. Translated by Walter Kaufmann and R.J. Hollingdale. New York: Random House, 1967.

Noel, Bradley Truman. "Gordon Fee and the Challenge to Pentecostal Hermeneutics: Thirty Years Later." *Pneuma* 26.1 (2004) 60–80.

——. "Gordon Fee's Contribution to Contemporary Pentecostalism's Theology of Baptism in the Holy Spirit." M.A. thesis, Acadia University, 1998.

Noll, Mark A. *Between Faith and Criticism: Evangelicals, Scholarship, and the Bible in America.* Second edition. Grand Rapids: Baker, 1991 [1986].

——. *A History of Christianity in the United States and Canada.* Grand Rapids: Eerdmans, 1992.

——. *The Scandal of the Evangelical Mind.* Grand Rapids: Eerdmans, 1994.

"O Come All Ye Faithful," *The Economist.* 1 November, 2007. No pages. Online: http: //latinamericanliberals.blogspot.com/2008/01/o-come-all-ye-faithful.html.

Oden, Thomas C. *After Modernity. . .What? Agenda for Theology.* Grand Rapids: Zondervan, 1990.

——. *Two Worlds: Notes on the Death of Modernity in America and Russia.* Downers Grove: InterVarsity, 1992.

Ogden, Schubert M. "Bultmann's Project of Demythologization and the Problem of Theology and Philosophy." *The Journal of Religion* 37.156 (1957) 150–73.

Osbourne, Grant R. *The Hermeneutical Spiral: A Comprehensive Introduction to Biblical Interpretation.* Downers Grove: InterVarsity, 1991.

Overholt, David L. and James Penner. *Soul Searching the Millennial Generation: Strategies for Youth Workers*. Toronto: Stoddart, 2002.

Owens, Robert R. *The Azusa Street Revival: Its Roots and Its Message*. Longwood, FL: Xulon Press, 2005.

Packer, James I. "Infallible Scripture and the Role of Hermeneutics." In *Scripture and Truth*, edited by D.A. Carson and J.D. Woodbridge. Grand Rapids: Zondervan, 1983.

———. *Knowing God*. Downers Grove: InterVarsity, 1993.

Parham, Charles Fox. *The Everlasting Gospel*. Baxter Springs, KS: Apostolic Faith Bible College, n.d. [1911].

———. *Kol Kare Bomidbar: A Voice Crying in the Wilderness*. Baxter Springs, KS: Apostolic Faith Bible College, n.d. [1944].

Parham, Sarah A. "Earnestly Contend for the Faith Once Delivered to the Saints. Jude 3." In *Selected Sermons of the Late Charles F. Parham, Sarah E. Parham: Co-Founders of the Original Apostolic Faith Movement*. Compiled by Robert L. Parham. Baxter Springs, KS: Apostolic Faith Bible College, 1941.

———. *The Life of Charles F. Parham: Founder of the Apostolic Faith Movement*. Joplin, MO: Hunter Publishing Company, 1969 [1930].

Pearlman, Myer. *Knowing the Doctrines of the Bible*. Springfield MO: Gospel Publishing House, 1937.

Pearson, Birger A. "The Gospel According to the Jesus Seminar." No pages. Online: http://www.veritas-ucsb.org//library/pearson/seminar/home.html.

"Pentecostals: Christianity Reborn." *Economist* 2006 (#8509) 84–6. Online: http://www.economist.com/world/displaystory.cfm?story_id=E1_RQDTNDG.

Percesepe, Gary John. "The Unbearable Lightness of Being Postmodern." *Christian Scholar's Review* 20 (1990) 118–35.

Perkins, J. "Practical theology: What Will it Become?" *The Christian Century*, 1–8 February (1984) 116.

Perrin, Norman. *The Kingdom of God in the Teaching of Jesus*. Philadelphia: Westminster, 1963.

———. *The Promise of Bultmann: The Promise of Theology*. Philadelphia: J.B. Lippincott, 1969.

———. *Rediscovering the Teaching of Jesus*. New York: Harper & Row, 1967.

Petersen, Douglas. "The Kingdom of God and the Hermeneutical Circle: Pentecostal Praxis in the Third World." In *Called and Empowered: Global Mission in Pentecostal Perspective*.

Phillips, Alfred. *Lawyer's Language: How and Why Legal Language is Difficult*. London: Routledge, 2003.

Pierard, Richard V. "Evangelicalism." In *Evangelical Dictionary of Theology*.

Pierson, Arthur T. "The Coming of the Lord: The Doctrinal Center of the Bible." In *Addresses on the Second Coming of the Lord: Delivered at the Prophetic Conference, Allegheny, PA, December 3–6, 1895*. Pittsburgh, PA, 1895.

Pieterse, Hennie. "The empirical approach in practical theology: a discussion with J.A. van der Ven." *Religion & Theology* 1.1 (1994) 77–83.

Pinnock, Clark H. "The Role of the Spirit in Interpretation." *Journal of the Evangelical Theological Society* 36.4 (1993) 491–7.

———. "The Work of the Holy Spirit in Hermeneutics." *Journal of Pentecostal Theology* 2 (1993) 3–23.

———, and Grant R. Osborne. "A Truce Proposal for the Tongues Controversy." *Christianity Today* 16 (October 8, 1971) 6–9.

Plüss, Jean-Daniel. "Azusa and Other Myths: The Long and Winding Road from Experience to Stated Belief and Back Again." *Pneuma* 15:2 (1993) 189–201.

Poirier, John C. & B. Scott Lewis. "Pentecostal and Postmodernist Hermeneutics: A Critique of Three Conceits." *Journal of Pentecostal Theology* 15.1 (2006) 3–21.

Poling, James N., and Donald E. Miller. *Foundations for a Practical Theology of Ministry.* Nashville: Abingdon, 1985.

Poloma, Margaret M. *The Assemblies of God at the Crossroads: Charisma and Institutional Dilemmas.* Knoxville, TN: University of Tennessee Press, 1989.

———. "The Spirit Bade Me Go: Pentecostalism and Global Religion." Paper presented to the Association for the Sociology of Religion, Washington, DC: 11–13 August, 2000.

Pomerville, Paul A. *The Third Force in Missions: A Pentecostal Contribution to Contemporary Mission Theology.* Peabody, MA: Hendrickson, 1985.

Powers, Janet Everts. " 'Your Daughters Shall Prophesy': Pentecostal Hermeneutics and the Empowerment of Women." In *The Globalization of Pentecostalism: A Religion Made to Travel.*

Rabinow, Paul, ed. *The Foucault Reader.* New York: Pantheon Books, 1984.

Ramm, Bernard. *Protestant Biblical Interpretation: A Textbook of Hermeneutics.* Third revised edition. Grand Rapids: Baker, 1993 [1956].

———. *The Witness of the Spirit: An Essay on the Contemporary Relevance of the Internal Witness of the Holy Spirit.* Grand Rapids: Eerdmans, 1959.

Raschke, Carl. *The Next Reformation: Why Evangelicals Must Embrace Postmodernity.* Grand Rapids: Baker, 2004.

Reed, David A. "Origins and Development of the Theology of Oneness Pentecostalism in the United States." Ph.D. diss., Boston University, 1978.

Ricoeur, Paul. *Interpretation Theory: Discourse and the Surplus of Meaning.* Fort Worth, TX: Texas Christian University Press, 1976.

Riss, Richard M., *A Survey of 20th-Century Revival Movements in North America.* Peabody, MA: Hendrickson, 1988.

Robeck, Jr., Cecil M. *The Azusa Street Mission and Revival: The Birth of the Global Pentecostal Movement.* Nashville, TN: Thomas Nelson, 2006.

———. "Seymour, William Joseph." In *The Dictionary of Pentecostal and Charismatic Movements.*

Robinson, E. B. "Myland, D.W." In *The New International Dictionary of Pentecostal and Charismatic Movements.*

Rorty, Richard. *Essays on Heidegger and Others.* Cambridge, UK: Cambridge University Press, 1991.

———. *Objectivity, Relativism, and Truth.* Cambridge, UK: Cambridge University Press, 1991.

———. *Philosophy and the Mirror of Nature.* Princeton: Princeton University Press, 1980 [1979].

———. "Pragmaticism." In *The Consequences of Pragmatism.* Minneapolis: University of Minnesota Press, 1982.

Said, Edward W. "Michael Foucault, 1926–1984." In *After Foucault: Humanistic Knowledge, Postmodern Challenges,* edited by Jonathan Arac. New Brunswick, NJ: Rutgers University Press, 1988.

Schaeffer, Francis A. *The Church at the End of the 20th Century.* Wheaton: Crossway Books, 1994 [1970].

Schweitzer, Albert. *The Quest of the Historical Jesus: a Critical Study of its Progress from Reimarus to Wrede.* Translated by William Montgomery. Mineola, NY: Dover Publications, 2005 [1910].

Schweitzer, Friedrich, and Johannes A. van der Van, ed. "An empirical approach in practical theology." In *Practical Theology–International Perspectives.* Frankfurt: Peter Lang, 1999).

Schweizer, Eduard. "Pneuma." In *Theological Dictionary of the New Testament.* Vol 6, edited by Gerhard Kittle and Gerhard Friedrich. Translated by Geoffrey W. Bromiley. Grand Rapids: Eerdmans, 1968.

Scofield, C.I. *A Mighty Wind: Plain Papers on the Doctrine of the Holy Spirit.* Grand Rapids: Baker, 1973 [1899].

Seymour, William J. "Christ's Messages to the Church." In *The Apostolic Faith* 1.11 (January 1908) 3. Los Angeles: The Apostolic Faith Mission.

———. *The Doctrines and Discipline of the Azusa Street Apostolic Faith Mission of Los Angeles, Cal. with Scripture Readings.* Los Angeles: William J. Seymour, 1915.

———, ed. *The Apostolic Faith.* Los Angeles: The Apostolic Faith Mission.

———, ed. *The Words that Changed the World: The Azusa Street Sermons.* The Complete Azusa Street Library 5. Joplin, MO: Christian Life Books, 1999.

Shaull, Richard, and Waldo Cesar, *Pentecostalism and the Future of Christian Churches: Promises, Limitations, Challenges.* Grand Rapids: Eerdmans, 2000.

Shelton, James B. *Mighty in Word and Deed: The Role of the Holy Spirit in Luke-Acts.* Peabody, MA: Hendrickson, 1991.

Shepherd, Nick. "Postmodern Responses to Being Church." No pages. Online: http://www.yehright.com/files/postmodern.pdf.

Sheppard, Gerald T. "Biblical Interpretation After Gadamer." *Pneuma* 16.1 (1994) 121–41.

———. "Pentecostals and the Hermeneutics of Dispensationalism: The Anatomy of an Uneasy Relationship." *Pneuma* 6.2 (1984) 5–33.

———. "Pentecostals, Globalization, and Postmodern Hermeneutics: Implications for the Politics of Scriptural Interpretation." In *The Globalization of Pentecostalism: A Religion Made to Travel.*

Shults, F. LeRon, ed. *The Evolution of Rationality: Interdisciplinary Essays in Honor of J. Wentzel van Huyssteen.* Grand Rapids: Eerdmans, 2006.

Shumway, C. W. "A Study of 'The Gift of Tongues.' " A.B. thesis, University of Southern California, 1914.

Silva, Moisés, ed. *Foundations of Contemporary Interpretation.* Grand Rapids: Zondervan, 1996.

Simpson, A.B. "What is meant by the Latter Rain?" *Christian and Missionary Alliance.* (19 October 1907) 38.

Smith, James K. A. "The Closing of the Book: Pentecostals, Evangelicals, and the Sacred Writings." *Journal of Pentecostal Theology* 11 (1997) 49–71.

Spittler, Russell P. "Are Pentecostals and Charismatics Fundamentalists? A Review of American Uses of these Categories." In *Charismatic Christianity as a Global Culture,* edited by Karla O. Poewe. Columbia, SC: The University of South Carolina Press, 1994.

———. "Scripture and Theological Enterprise: View from a Big Canoe." In *The Use of the Bible in Theology/Evangelical Options,* edited by Robert K. Johnston. Atlanta: John Knox Press, 1985.

———. "Theological Style Among Pentecostals and Charismatics." In *Doing Theology in Today's World*, edited by John D. Woodbridge and Thomas Edward McComiskey. Grand Rapids: Zondervan, 1991.

Stark, Rodney and William Sims Bainbridge. *The Future of Religion: Secularization, Revival, and Cult Formation.* Berkeley: University of California Press, 1986.

"Statement of Fundamental Truths." *Minutes of the Thirty-Fifth General Council of the Assemblies of God.* Miami Beach, FL: 12–16 August, 1973.

Stephenson, Peter. "Christian Mission in a Postmodern World." Online http://www .postmission.com (accessed 13 November, 2006).

Stott, John R. W. *The Baptism and Fullness of the Holy Spirit.* Downers Grove: InterVarsity, 1964.

———. *The Message of Acts: The Spirit, the Church and the World.* The Bible Speaks Today. Downers Grove: InterVarsity, 1990.

Stout, Harry S. "Theological Commitment and American Religious History." *Theological Education* (Spring, 1989) 44–59.

Stronstad, Roger. "The Biblical Precedent for Historical Precedent." *Paraclete* 27.3 (1993) 1–10.

———. *The Charismatic Theology of St. Luke.* Peabody, MA: Hendrickson, 1984.

———. "The Hermeneutics of Lucan Historiography." *Paraclete* 22.4 (1988) 5–17.

———. "The Holy Spirit in Luke–Acts." *Paraclete* 23.1 (1989) 8–13.

———. "The Holy Spirit in Luke–Acts: A Synthesis of Luke's Pneumatology." *Paraclete* 23.2 (1989) 18–26.

———. "Pentecostal Experience and Hermeneutics." *Paraclete* 26.1 (1992) 14–30.

———. Review of *Gospel and Spirit: Issues in New Testament Hermeneutics*, by Gordon D. Fee. *Pneuma* 15.2 (1993) 215–22.

———. *Spirit, Scripture and Theology: A Pentecostal Perspective.* Baguio City, Philippines: APTS Press, 1995.

———. "Trends in Pentecostal Hermeneutics." *Paraclete* 22.3 (1988) 1–12.

Susanto, Johanes L. "A Practical Theological Investigation of the Divine Healing Ministries of Smith Wigglesworth and John G. Lake: A Continuationist Reformed Perspective." Th.D. diss., University of South Africa, 2007.

Swartley, Willard M. *Slavery, Sabbath, War and Women: Case Issues in Biblical Interpretation.* Scottsdale, PA: Herald Press, 1983.

Sweet, Leonard, ed. *The Church in Emerging Culture: Five Perspectives.* Grand Rapids: Zondervan, 2003.

———. *Post-modern Pilgrims: First Century Passion for the 21st Century World.* Nashville: Broadman & Holman, 2000.

Synan, Vinson. "Cashwell, G. B." In *The New International Dictionary of Pentecostal and Charismatic Movements.*

———. *The Holiness-Pentecostal Movement in the United States.* Grand Rapids: Eerdmans, 1971.

———. "Pentecostalism." In *Evangelical Dictionary of Theology.*

———. "Taylor, G. F." In *The New International Dictionary of Pentecostal and Charismatic Movements.*

Tannehill, Robert C. *The Sword of His Mouth.* Philadelphia: Fortress Press, 1975.

Tarr, Jr., Delbert H. "Transcendence, Immanence, and the Emerging Pentecostal Academy." In *Pentecostalism in Context.*

Taylor, Charles. *Sources of the Self: The Making of the Modern Identity.* Cambridge: Cambridge University Press, 1989.

Taylor, George F. *The Spirit and the Bride: A Scriptural Presentation of the Operations, Manifestations, Gifts and Fruit of the Holy Spirit in His Relation to the Bride with Special Reference to the "Latter Rain" Revival.* Dunn, NC: George F. Taylor, 1907.

Thiselton, Anthony C. *New Horizons in Hermeneutics: The Theory and Practice of Transforming Bible Reading.* Grand Rapids: Zondervan, 1992.

———. *The Two Horizons.* Exeter: The Paternoster Press, 1980.

———. *The Two Horizons: New Testament Hermeneutics and Philosophical Description.* Grand Rapids: Eerdmans, 1980.

Thistlethwaite, Lilian. "The Wonderful History of the Latter Rain." In *Selected Sermons of the Late Charles F. Parham, Sarah E. Parham: Co-Founders of the Original Apostolic Faith Movement.*

Thomas, John Christopher. "Women, Pentecostals and the Bible: An Experiment in Pentecostal Hermeneutics." *Journal of Pentecostal Theology* 5 (1994) 41–56.

Thomas, Robert L. *Evangelical Hermeneutics: The New Versus the Old.* Grand Rapids: Kregel, 2002.

Tomlinson, A. J. *The Last Great Conflict.* Cleveland, TN: Press of Walter R. Rodgers, 1913.

Twenge, Jean M. *Generation Me: Why Today's Young Americans Are More Confident, Assertive, Entitled–and More Miserable Than Ever Before.* New York: Free Press, 2006.

Tyson, Paul. "Contemporary Australian Youth Spiritualities and Evangelical Youth Ministry." Online: www.ea.org.au/content/documents/pdf%20files/Tyson%20-%20 Youth%20Spirituality%20Spectrum.pdf.

Valdez, Sr., A.C. *Fire on Azusa Street: An Eyewitness Account.* Costa Mesa, CA: Gift Publications, 1980.

van der Ven, Johannes A. "Practical Theology: From Applied to Empirical Theology." *Journal of Empirical Theology* 1 (1998) 7–28.

Van Gelder, Craig. "Postmodernism as an Emerging Worldview." *Calvin Theological Journal* 26 (1991) 412–6.

Vanhoozer, Kevin J. *Is There a Meaning in This Text? The Bible, the Reader, and the Morality of Literary Knowledge.* Grand Rapids: Zondervan, 1998.

———, ed. *The Cambridge Companion to Postmodern Theology.* Cambridge: Cambridge University Press, 2003.

———, et al., ed. *Hermeneutics at the Crossroads.* Indiana Series in the Philosophy of Religion. Bloomington, IA: Indiana University Press, 2006.

Van Wyk, A.G "From 'applied theology' to 'practical theology.' " *Andrews University Seminary Studies.* 33 (1995) 85–101.

Veith, Jr., Gene Edward. *Postmodern Times: A Christian Guide to Contemporary Thought and Culture.* Wheaton: Crossway Books, 1994.

Via, Dan Otto. *The Parables; Their Literary and Existential Dimension.* Philadelphia, Fortress Press, 1967.

Vickers, Jason E. Review of *A Pentecostal Hermeneutic for the Twenty-First Century,* by Kenneth J. Archer. *Pneuma* 28.2 (2006) 384–6.

Volf, Miroslav, and William Katerberg, eds. *The Future of Hope: Christian Tradition Amid Modernity and Postmodernity.* Grand Rapids: Eerdmans, 2004.

Wacker, Grant. "The Functions of Faith in Primitive Pentecostalism." *Harvard Theological Review* 77 (1984) 353–75.

———. *Heaven Below: Early Pentecostals and American Culture.* Cambridge, MA: Harvard University Press, 2001.

Wallace, Stan. "The Real Issue: Discerning and Defining the Essentials of Postmodernism." No pages. Online : http://www.leaderu.com/real/ri9802/wallace.html.

Waltke, Bruce K. "Exegesis and the Spiritual Life: Theology as Spiritual Formation." *Crux* 30.3 (1994) 28–35.

Warrington, Keith, ed. *Pentecostal Perspectives.* Carlisle, UK: Paternoster Press, 1998.

Webber, Robert E. *Ancient-Future Faith: Rethinking Evangelicalism for a Postmodern World.* Grand Rapids: Baker, 1999.

———. *The Younger Evangelicals: Facing the Challenges of the New World.* Grand Rapids: Baker, 2002.

West, Charles C. *Power, Truth, and Community in Modern Culture.* Christian Mission and Modern Culture. Harrisburg, PA: Trinity Press International, 1999.

"What is Process Thought?" The Centre for Process Studies. No pages. Online: http://www.ctr4process.org/about/process/.

Wiebe, Phillip H. "The Pentecostal Initial Evidence Doctrine." *Journal of the Evangelical Theological Society* 27 (1984) 465–72.

Wilder, Amos Niven. *The Language of the Gospel: Early Christian Rhetoric.* New York: Harper & Row, 1964.

Wilkins, Michael J., and J.P. Moreland, eds. *Jesus Under Fire: Modern Scholarship Reinvents the Historical Jesus.* Grand Rapids: Zondervan, 1995.

Wilkinson, Loren. "Hermeneutics and the Postmodern Reaction Against 'Truth.' " In *The Act of Bible Reading: A Multidisciplinary Approach to Biblical Interpretation,* edited by Elmer Dyck. Downers Grove: InterVarsity, 1996.

Williams, Stephen N. *The Shadow of the Antichrist: Nietzsche's Critique of Christianity.* Grand Rapids: Baker, 2006.

Wilson, D. J. "Brumback, Carl." In *The New International Dictionary of Pentecostal and Charismatic Movements.*

Winquest, C. "Re-visioning Ministry: Postmodern Reflections by Charles E. Winquest." Online: http://www.religion-online.org/showchapter. asp?title=586&C=850 (accessed 25 August, 2006).

Witherington III, Ben. *The Jesus Quest: The Third Search for the Jew of Nazareth.* New expanded edition. Downers Grove: InterVarsity, 1997.

Wolfaardt, J. A., et al., eds. *Introduction to Practical Theology.* Study Guide for PTA200-W. Pretoria: University of South Africa, 1992.

Wolterstorff, Nicholas. *Reason Within the Bounds of Religion.* Second edition. Grand Rapids: Eerdmans, 1984 [1976].

Woodmorappe, John. "The Jesus Seminar Reeks with Rationalism in its most Primitive Form." No pages. Online: http://www.rae.org/jseminar.html.

Wright, N. T. *Jesus and the Victory of God.* Christian Origins and the Question of God. Vol. 2. Minneapolis: Augsburg Fortress, 1997.

Yong, Amos. "Pentecostalism and the Academy." *Theology Today* 64 (2007) 244–50.

———. *Spirit-Word-Community: Theological Hermeneutics in Trinitarian Perspective.* Eugene, OR: Wipf & Stock, 2002.

Zuck, Roy B., ed. *Rightly Divided: Readings in Biblical Hermeneutics.* Grand Rapids: Kregel, 1996.

———. "The Role of the Spirit in Hermeneutics." *Bibliotheca Sacra* 141 (1984) 120–9.